Get the eBook FREE!

(PDF, ePub, Kindle, and liveBook all included)

We believe that once you buy a book from us, you should be able to read it in any format we have available. To get electronic versions of this book at no additional cost to you, purchase and then register this book at the Manning website.

Go to https://www.manning.com/freebook and follow the instructions to complete your pBook registration.

That's it!
Thanks from Manning!

RxJava for
Android Developers

RxJava for
Android Developers

Timo Tuominen

MANNING
SHELTER ISLAND

For online information and ordering of this and other Manning books, please visit
www.manning.com. The publisher offers discounts on this book when ordered in
quantity. For more information, please contact

> Special Sales Department
> Manning Publications Co.
> 20 Baldwin Road, PO Box 761
> Shelter Island, NY 11964
> Email: orders@manning.com

Manning Publications Co.	Development editor: Christina Taylor
20 Baldwin Road	Technical development editor: Alain Couiniot
Shelter Island, NY 11964	Review editor: Ivan Martinovic
	Production editor: Lori Weidert
	Copy editor: Sharon Wilkey
	Proofreader: Elizabeth Martin
	Technical proofreader: Cody Sand
	Typesetter: Dennis Dallinik
	Cover designer: Marija Tudor

ISBN: 9781617293368
Printed in the United States of America
1 2 3 4 5 6 7 8 9 10 – SP – 24 23 22 21 20 19

contents

PART 3: ADVANCED RXJAVA ARCHITECTURES

11 Advanced architectures: Chat client 1

12 Advanced architectures: Chat client 2

preface

Funnily enough, my story of reactive programming started on one of the less-reactive platforms: Adobe Flash. Macromedia, before its acquisition by Adobe, built a sleek framework called Flex (later called Apache Flex). In Flex, one of the main concepts was the setData function of every rendering component. The setData function was intended to receive a data object that fully contained the *information* that the component was tasked to *present*. Having spent my younger years writing crafty DirectX C++ code, this was a beautiful separation of concerns, though I never quite fully figured out how the data was intended to be transformed between its original source and what the component expected to receive.

Fast-forward around six years and a few platforms, and I was starting a project with Samsung. On the way, during my time at the company Futurice, I tried to apply what I'd learned from Flex in different contexts with varying results—but ended up with more conceptual questions than answers.

This time, the task was to create a real-time sports application on Android with a range of data sources in different forms and delays. We'd often receive *partial data* that would be used to update, say, the match score only. It seemed like a nontrivial system to build with the standard tools. As the classic story goes, my colleague Juha Ristolainen had read a blog post about the new tool that could help: RxJava. I thought I'd give it a go.

I have to admit, learning and applying RxJava to my problem domain of data processing was one of the two most profound experiences I've had learning a new technology. Ironically, the first one was when I picked up my first programming book on Java 20 years ago. Seeing what RxJava enabled was much like finding the one missing piece of the puzzle over and over again, to the point where I didn't even realize I'd been missing them.

Four years later, it turned out RxJava was not quite as simple to use as it was conceptually powerful. Having chosen my fight, my colleague Olli Jokinen and I spent numerous nights trying to meet deadlines with an unexplored technology. This was the time when RxJava 1 was still in beta. Eventually, we ironed out the issues from our code, and the codebase ended up as one of the most brilliant ones I've had the pleasure to work with.

What you have in your hands is the book based on thousands of hours of writing Android apps with RxJava. This is the book I wish I had when I started.

acknowledgments

I would like to thank my father and my late mother for getting me my first computer and giving their unquestionable support in anything I have ever aspired to do; my neighbor Jari Nummela for letting me read his computer magazines; my cousin Eero Salminen for downloading the Java Development Kit and burning it on a CD; and my local library at Ulvila for satisfying my desire to learn more about programming patterns.

Regarding my professional career, I wish to wholeheartedly thank software agency Futurice and everyone there I have had the pleasure to work with: Mikko Viikari and Lenita Syrjänen for hiring me; Hannu Nevanlinna for encouraging my technical explorations; Michael Samarin for teaching me to be more precise with my time; Mikko Vihonen and Harri Kauhanen for being my first guides in the enterprise environment; Sampo Hämäläinen and Lauri Eloranta for dragging me along on their business ventures; and Tuomas Syrjänen for being a good enough CEO to put a picture of me on the wall.

My most sincere gratitude to the entire Samsung Kick team: Clement Courdeau for driving the whole thing; Olli Jokinen for being there for the whole ride; Antti Poikela and Pawel Polanski for stretching the limits of RxJava; Juha Ristolainen for choosing RxJava; Lauri Larjo, Lauri Eloranta, and Sampo Hämäläinen for somehow managing it all; Ikhoon Chon and Hongkyu Park for keeping the backend together; Iiro Isotalo, Mark Schlussnuss, and Chris Houghton for making kick-ass designs; and everyone in the Kick Android team for their unfaltering support: Aniello Del Sorbo, Guillaume Valverde, Johan Paul, Johnny Cullan, Jose Martinez, Lauri Larjo, Susanne Husebø, and Sunghyun Park. Additionally, special thanks to Guillaume Valverde for creating our first RxJava training together.

Lastly, I would like to thank Kuba Misiorny and Antti Poikela for reviewing early versions of the book as well as the amazing people at Manning without whom this book wouldn't have happened at all. Special thanks to Bert Bates for teaching me how to write books, Christina Taylor for having the patience to deal with us, and each of the following reviewers for their hard work and attention to detail: Alain Couniot, Anderson Silva, Barry Kern, Burk Hufnagel, Cody Sand, David Paccoud, Fabrizio Cucci, Jaume Valls, Kariem Ali, Kent R. Spillner, Mark Elston, Michele Mauro, Nick McGinness, Robert Walsh, Steven Oxley, Ursin Stauss, and William E. Wheeler.

about this book

RxJava for Android is the book I wish I had when I started using the reactive paradigms on Android. RxJava is an incredibly powerful tool, and you will learn how to use it in a way that creates robust and sustainable code. You will understand the change of mental models compared to more traditional ways of programming and what that brings you.

who should read this book

Reactive programming has become a tool that is used at least in some part of almost every Android application—and if not RxJava, then another reactive library. It is helpful for every Android developer to have a little deeper knowledge of reactive programming in case they encounter it.

You should have basic experience with the Android platform to get most out of this book, though you could also learn the basics of the platform from the samples as you go. Just keep in mind that with RxJava, you would do some things differently than on the vanilla Android, which is the whole point of this book!

how this book is organized: a roadmap

You'll find this book divided into three parts. Part 1 introduces RxJava and lets you become familiar with the basics of using it on the Android platform.

- Chapter 1 shows a quick win for RxJava in asynchronous event handling with the debounce operator.
- Chapter 2 explores using RxJava for the basic networking needs of an Android app.
- Chapter 3 outlines the difference between events and changing state and introduces data processing chains.
- Chapter 4 shows you how to build a Flickr client by combining what you have learned so far.
- Chapter 5 dives into custom observables and how to do efficient multithreading with RxJava by building a fully functioning file explorer app.

Part 2 is focused around view models and how to use them to refine your data streams.

- Chapter 6 expands the file explorer app and improves the architecture by separating part of the business logic into a view model.
- Chapter 7 further develops the file explorer app to add a model as the single source of data.
- Chapter 8 explains the connection between a view and a view model with an example app of tic-tac-toe.
- Chapter 9 adds a persisting model to the tic-tac-toe app.
- Chapter 10 shows how you can unit test RxJava code and to add a few tests to the tic-tac-toe app as an illustration.

Part 3 takes a deep dive to more advanced examples of how RxJava can be used to architect your application.

- Chapter 11 uses WebSockets with RxJava to build a live chat client app.
- Chapter 12 adds a model to the chat client app to load existing messages and support messages that have not yet gone out.
- Chapter 13 uses RxJava to create dynamic animations that promptly react to user interaction.
- Chapter 14 finishes the book with an app that uses open source map tiles to create a draggable and zoomable map fully in RxJava.

about the code

This book contains many examples of source code in line with normal text. The source code is formatted in a `fixed-width font like this` to separate it from ordinary text.

In many cases, the original source code has been reformatted; we've added line breaks and reworked indentation to accommodate the available page space in the book. Additionally, comments in the source code have often been removed from the listings when the code is described in the text. Code annotations accompany many of the listings, highlighting important concepts.

All of the chapters of this book have full Android code examples online. The examples range from simple demos to more rounded apps.

The code for this book is available for download from the Manning website at https://www .manning.com/books/rxjava-for-android-developers and from GitHub at https://github .com/tehmou/RxJava-for-Android-Developers.

liveBook discussion forum

Purchase of *RxJava for Android Developers* includes free access to a private web forum run by Manning Publications where you can make comments about the book, ask technical questions, and receive help from the author and from other users. To access the forum, go to https://livebook.manning.com/#!/book/rx-java-for-android-developers/discussion. You can also learn more about Manning's forums and the rules of conduct at https://livebook .manning.com/#!/discussion.

Manning's commitment to our readers is to provide a venue where a meaningful dialogue between individual readers and between readers and the author can take place. It is not a commitment to any specific amount of participation on the part of the author, whose contribution to the forum remains voluntary (and unpaid). We suggest you try asking the author some challenging questions lest his interest stray! The forum and the archives of previous discussions will be accessible from the publisher's website as long as the book is in print.

about the author

Timo Tuominen has used FRP and RxJava extensively as an architect of a major Android project for Samsung while working with Futurice. As a consultant, he has developed dozens of agile projects on almost all relevant platforms—and a number of dead ones—nowadays bringing FRP to wherever he can.

about the cover illustration

Jefferys

The figure on the cover of *RxJava for Android Developers* is captioned "Habit of an Arabian Woman in 1581." The illustration is taken from Thomas Jefferys' *A Collection of the Dresses of Different Nations, Ancient and Modern* (four volumes), London, published between 1757 and 1772. The title page states that these are hand-colored copperplate engravings, heightened with gum arabic.

Thomas Jefferys (1719–1771) was called "Geographer to King George III." He was an English cartographer who was the leading map supplier of his day. He engraved and printed maps for government and other official bodies and produced a wide range of commercial maps and atlases, especially of North America. His work as a mapmaker sparked an interest in local dress customs of the lands he surveyed and mapped, which are brilliantly displayed in this collection. Fascination with faraway lands and travel for pleasure were relatively new phenomena in the late 18th century, and collections such as this one were popular, introducing both the tourist as well as the armchair traveler to the inhabitants of other countries.

The diversity of the drawings in Jefferys' volumes speaks vividly of the uniqueness and individuality of the world's nations some 200 years ago. Dress codes have changed since then, and the diversity by region and country, so rich at the time, has faded away. It's now often hard to tell the inhabitants of one continent from another. Perhaps, trying to view it optimistically, we've traded a cultural and visual diversity for a more varied personal life—or a more varied and interesting intellectual and technical life.

At a time when it's difficult to tell one computer book from another, Manning celebrates the inventiveness and initiative of the computer business with book covers based on the rich diversity of regional life of two centuries ago, brought back to life by Jeffreys' pictures.

<h1>Core reactive programming | part 1</h1>

In this part

This book begins with getting you comfortable using your new tools—RxJava and a couple of libraries to support it.

The first chapter starts with a concrete example that will give you quick wins with the reactive style of programming.

Chapter 2 explores the typical case of handling network requests with RxJava and Retrofit. You'll start to see the different mental models of the way data is processed, as in chapter 3 you'll explore a credit card example with data processing chains. In chapter 4, you'll construct a fully functioning Flickr client against an existing public API.

In the last chapter of the first part, chapter 5, you'll work with an Android file browser. The code from this chapter will serve as the starting point for the second part of this book.

 Life is 10% what happens to you and 90% how you react to it.

—Charles R. Swindoll

Introduction to reactive programming | 1

In this chapter

- What to expect from this book

- How to use this book

- Why RxJava 2 for Android?

- Deep dive in to RxJava 2 on Android

Perhaps you picked up this book because...

1   **Everyone's using RxJava and you have no idea why.**

It's hard to name a large company that would do native Android and not use a reactive programming library such as RxJava 2. In this book you'lll focus on *why* it's hot and *what you can do with it.*

{ You may also have heard of functional reactive programming (FRP), which is indeed related to Rx. You'll learn about both concepts in this book. }

2   **You've used RxJava on Android and want to learn more.**

It's common these days to see snippets of RxJava code that solve a particular asynchronous problem. But a whole world lies behind what sometimes looks like a simple utility.

{ The programming syntax used in Rx can seem like the entire point, but it's just a nice add-on. This book will teach you how to think in Rx. }

3   **You've used RxJava and hate it with a passion.**

In the wrong hands, RxJava can make traditional spaghetti code even worse. With any power comes responsibility. You'll learn where to use RxJava and where not.

{ You'll learn to design applications in a sensible and extensible way. You can be reassured there's a way to maintain your Rx code. }

Whatever your reason, I want you to...

- Learn through extensive illustrations and examples
- Understand a new way of seeing how applications work
- Figure out where to fit Rx in your day-to-day programming

Don't read this book if...

You're new to programming.

Rx is still a new paradigm, and it isn't always smooth sailing. Hopefully in the future this will change, and everyone will start their programming journey with Rx.

or

"I just need to get it done."

The learning curve of reactive programming is a little steeper than usual. Cutting corners isn't as easy as in the more traditional ways of writing applications. This is fundamentally double-edged, but you'll need a curious mind and a healthy dose of patience.

but

Continue reading if you want to learn how to properly make a delayed auto search field in five lines.

This is the example code you'll learn to make in the first chapter. I don't expect you to be able follow just yet, but take it as a preview of how powerful RxJava can be.

```
RxTextView.textChanges(textInput)
    .filter(text -> text.length() >= 3)
    .debounce(150, TimeUnit.MILLISECONDS)
    .observeOn(AndroidSchedulers.mainThread())
    .subscribe(this::updateSearchResults);
```

You'll spend the first chapter constructing this piece of code.

The user writes values, and 150 ms after he writes the last letter, you trigger a search.

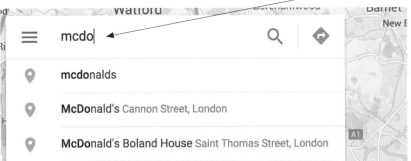

OOP, Rx, FP, and FRP

RxJava is in the club of reactive programming libraries (http://reactivex .io/). They all start with *Rx*, so sometimes they're together called *Rx programming*. To get an idea of where this sits, let's recap the popular paradigms.

OOP, object-oriented programming

The idea of OOP is that everything is an object, a thing, and can interact with other objects. Typically, an object encapsulates its state and allows outside actors to modify it through its member functions.

FP, functional programming

Functional programming is an old programming style that focuses on an almost mathematical precision in describing the program. It turns out that although the mental model of FP seems more complex than OOP, it seems to scale better when the complexity of the state needed increases.

FRP, functional reactive programming

The concept of FRP was introduced 1997, but it has become popular only in recent years. It's a bit like an extension on top of FP, enabling an app to be built to *react* to input in a seamless way. FRP does this by declaring relationships between values.

Rx, reactive programming

Reactive programming, sometimes called *Rx* for *Reactive Extensions*, is an umbrella term for all paradigms that use a data flow to construct the application. RxJava is our tool of choice to implement the data flow in practice. The previous term, FRP, can also be considered reactive programming, but not always the other way around.

What about the Facebook React library?

React is the name of a Facebook UI library made on top of HTML5. Although the concept of programming with React is similar to ours, it isn't considered reactive in the way we define it.

Benefits of Rx

Rx, including RxJava, isn't a typical technology that's made to replace another inferior technology. Rx is more of a way to enable visualizing data flow rather than a mechanical solution—and that's what we're going for in this book.

We'll spend a lot of time covering the basics, but at the core, RxJava implements a publish-subscribe pattern. An observable (the publisher) sends a value, and a subscriber consumes it. But the trick is, *you can modify the values on the way.*

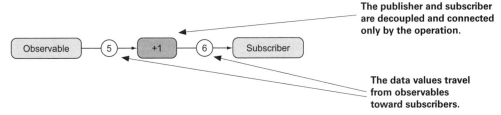

The publisher and subscriber are decoupled and connected only by the operation.

The data values travel from observables toward subscribers.

Handling of asynchronous operations

Asynchronous programming is almost always listed as the first benefit of Rx, and it certainly is a major one. The traditional ways of programming make the handling of background operations a special case, which is often a tricky one.

In Rx, on the other hand, every operation is *potentially asynchronous.* Asynchronous operations aren't special cases but are handled naturally as though nothing unusual happened. It's the synchronous execution that's the exception.

You're able to do this because the operations are decoupled—the next one doesn't know when the previous one is supposed to complete.

You could replace the addition of 1 in the previous picture with an arbitrary operation that can take as long as necessary and return a type that's suitable for your needs.

You'll learn how to do all of this in a bit!

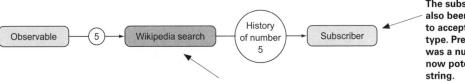

The subscriber has also been changed to accept a different type. Previously, it was a number and now potentially a string.

The operation can be changed to be an asynchronous one; for instance, happening over the network.

What you code is what you get

In Rx, you get what you ask for—and nothing else! The way Rx is written is inherently incremental. To understand what this means, have a look at how software development usually happens.

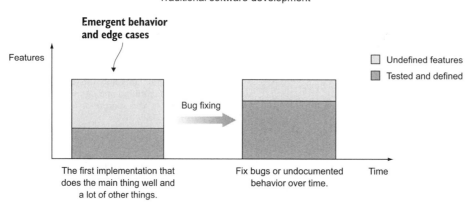

In short, you write an initial bunch of code that works most of the time on most people's machines. In this image, the darker color is what you really needed, and the lighter area represents numerous corner cases and error conditions.

The gray code

You can have automated testing and quality assurance in place to mitigate the impact of the gray functionality (the lighter area in the preceding figure), but it's still there. It's the part of code that works, but we're not quite sure *how exactly*.

This isn't because of bad or lazy developers, but because the tools aren't that precise.

> But all features are defined in the code, no?
>
> In this context, by *features* I mean functionality that can be fine-grained. Scenarios such as a server failing to respond or the user clicking a button rapidly several times are seldom explicitly defined before a bug report comes in.
>
> In the long run, in projects that require high-quality standards, a significant amount of time typically goes into fixing issues that are caused by potentially obscure edge cases.

Reactive programming development

In reactive programming, you typically have fewer "free" features and start having to ask questions early on like, "What happens if the second server response doesn't match the first one?"

If you didn't think of a scenario, it'll be obvious when writing the code, *not when the user stumbles upon it.*

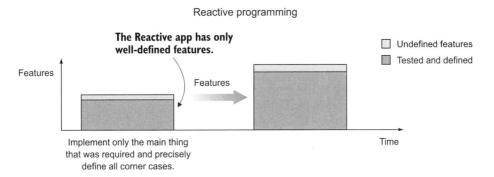

It seems that at first you get less bang for the buck, but over time you'll see less impact from growing scale and technical debt. Reactive programming is less impacted by scale and complexity than traditional ways. This isn't a magic solution, though, but *a result of having to deal with the scale and complexity* instead of sweeping it under the carpet.

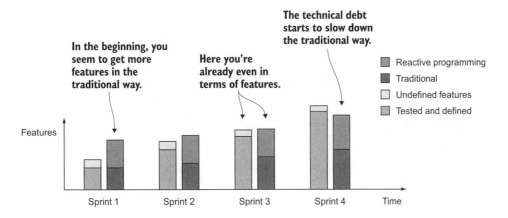

The reactive landscape

This book focuses on Android and RxJava, but that's not all there is to Rx programming. Here's a quick overview of what's out there.

Mobile development

Rx started with Windows Phone, but Android and iOS have been catching up. The biggest problem used to be the lack of resources online, but the situation has much improved.

Android

RxJava is the de facto reactive library to use on Android, though other options have started popping up. Google published an internal one called Agera, and several others exist, such as Sodium.

On Android, the challenge stems from the strictly defined ways of constructing the apps from platform components, such as activities and fragments, though working within this limitation has still yielded good results.

iOS

The way iOS apps are traditionally structured didn't lend well to reactive programming, but nowadays there are well-known ways to get around it. ReactiveCocoa used to be the only serious reactive library on iOS, but its syntax is quite different from the more recent solutions. RxSwift, on the other hand, is more similar to RxJava and is gaining popularity.

Windows Phone

Even if Windows Phone is becoming less frequently used as a mobile platform, it gets a special mention as the best supported mobile platform when it comes to Rx. In fact, Rx is a standard part of it. The Reactive Extensions of C# is considered to be the first implemention of the modern Rx.

Web and HTML5

JavaScript and the web have become one of the most innovative grounds for reactive programming. The biggest benefit of the web is that the browser isn't opinionated about how you should go about constructing a UI, and therefore it's possible to create completely custom approaches.

We won't cover the whole scene of the web here, because it would be difficult to be objective. There are many amazing frameworks and libraries to check out, each providing a different point of view as to what Rx is and what it should be (or whether it should be Rx at all, but that's another discussion).

The same principles covered in this book also apply to the web.

Backend systems and Rx

The best known backend system written partly with reactive programming is the Netflix streaming system. It seems, however, that most services can be made using standard technologies, so there hasn't been a high demand for Rx as such.

On the other hand, functional programming has become increasingly popular, especially in heavy-duty systems. Languages such as Haskell and Go have found their way into the realities of many programmers.

Although this book is more about UI programming and not the specialized functional languages, similarities exist in the mental models.

What do you need to know before you start?

With a suitable library, Rx concepts can be applied to almost any platform and language. But we need to pick one, and we pick Java as our language and Android as the platform. RxJava 2 is our Rx library (normally referred to as just *RxJava*). If you're curious about the reasons, we'll get to them in a bit.

This isn't a book about learning Android development, though, so we won't go into too many details there. If you're completely new to Android, I recommend that you refer to the appendix for a quick dive into Android development.

In terms of basic programming skills, I do expect you to have some.

I expect you to...

- Have a basic understanding of UI development and the challenges it usually poses.

- Be able to read Java code, including lambdas, which were introduced in Java 8. (I provide a small introduction if you're unfamiliar with them.)

You don't need to...

- Be an expert in reactive or object-oriented programming patterns.

- Have previous experience in functional programming (though it can be of use for understanding the concepts).

- Know Git, but it helps going through the example code online.

Java 8 Streams

Although we'll make extensive use of Java 8 lambdas, we don't cover other features that were introduced. Specifically, Java 8 Streams aren't related to any streams we may or may not be talking about in this book.

About this book

This book is divided into three parts. Part 1 is about getting a basic understanding of the RxJava library and what it can do. You'll dive into the different roles it can have in an application on a lower level.

Part 2 focuses on reactive architectures—it's more about how you can organize your code to be robust and maintainable. Part 2 contains the core concepts of serious reactive programming.

The third part contains a few larger example projects that use the skills you've acquired. You can use these projects as learning references for how reactive programming scales for real-life projects.

Online code examples

You can find most of the code featured in the book online at the Manning website at https://www.manning.com/books/rxjava-for-android-developers and from GitHub at https://github.com/tehmou/RxJava-for-Android-Developers.

Coffee breaks

Whenever you see a coffee cup, it means it's time for a small exercise. Get your cup and see how you can apply what you've learned.

Most coffee breaks have the coding starting point defined online, as well as solutions.

To follow the chapter, you don't have to do the exercises, but I recommend you at least go through the given solutions.

> ### What are the gray boxes?
>
> These gray boxes usually answer questions you might already be thinking about. I use them to clarify misunderstandings as well to provide extra information that might be slightly off-topic.

RxJava 2 and Android

As mentioned, in this book you'll use RxJava. It's part of the "ReactiveX" family, which has a more or less standardized syntax. RxJava itself was originally a port of Reactive Extensions on Java, made by the development team at Netflix.

RxJava has found its way through backend programming to UI applications built with Java—including Android. For the teaching purposes of this book, I've chosen Java on Android for the examples. There are a few reasons for this, described next:

Why Java?

- Java is a common language that almost everyone has come across at some point in their developer life.

- Java is strongly and explicitly typed, which makes following the data-type conversions easier.

- Some purely functional languages are already close to functional reactive programming and thus more suitable. But they're still in the minority, especially in UI programming.

Why RxJava?

- Rx, or Reactive Extensions, has proven to be usable in production on a large scale. It's a safe pick for solving real-life problems.

- If you learn the Rx syntax in one language, applying your knowledge to almost any other one won't be difficult. There's hardly a language or platform on which Rx hasn't been ported.

RxJava 1 or 2?

This book uses RxJava version 2.x. This version includes a few major changes in the API. Most notably, `null` values are no longer permitted, there are a few new observable types, and the way subscriptions are internally managed has changed. You should be able to follow the principles of the book even if you're working with RxJava 1, though.

Setting up the Android environment

You can develop Android on Windows, Mac, or Linux. Any modern computer works, though iOS/Android tablet devices or Chromebooks aren't supported for development.

Google Android Studio

All our development happens on Android Studio. Download the installer from https://developer.android.com/studio/ and follow instructions. Android Studio comes with the Android SDK, though it might ask to install additional parts.

Git

You can download the examples from the online repositories at https://github.com/tehmou/RxJava-for-Android-Developers, though I encourage you to use Git for managing your own coding as well. But using Git isn't a requirement, and we don't cover its use in this book. If you're new to Git, I recommend using resources online to become familiar with it.

RxJava 2 dependencies

Android Studio comes with everything set up except for the RxJava 2 library. All of our example code has it included, but if you're starting a new project, you can add it to the app/build.gradle file:

app/build.gradle

```
dependencies {
    ...

    // RxJava
    compile 'io.reactivex.rxjava2:rxjava:2.1.7'
    compile 'io.reactivex.rxjava2:rxandroid:2.0.1'

    // RxBinding wrappers for UI
    compile 'com.jakewharton.rxbinding2:rxbinding:2.0.0'
```

Remember, you can find most of the code featured in the book online at https://github.com/tehmou/RxJava-for-Android-Developers.

Java 8 lambdas

Even if you're familiar with Java, you might still not be familiar with lambdas. They're an added feature that you can start using with a bit of configuration:

app/build.gradle

```
defaultConfig {
  ...

  compileOptions {
    sourceCompatibility JavaVersion.VERSION_1_8
    targetCompatibility JavaVersion.VERSION_1_8
  }

  ...
```

This is the part you need to add to the configuration.

Do you need to do this configuration every time?

For new projects, yes, though all our example projects already have these settings turned on.

What is a lambda function?

In short, a *lambda* is an unnamed inline function. If you take a `sum` function as an example, you can see what this means:

```
int sum(int x, int y) {
  return x + y;
}
```

This is just a standard Java function (a method). If you write the same in a lambda form, you can leave out the types altogether:

```
(x, y) -> {
  return x + y;
}
```

The types are *inferred* from what's given as the input and what's expected as the output.

The anatomy of a lambda function

Just like a normal function, a *lambda function* declares the parameters it can take as well as the function body with a possible return value.

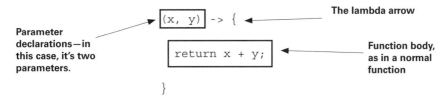

If the lambda is just one `return` statement, it can be written even more concisely:

```
(x, y) -> x + y
```

This is *exactly the same* as the form you saw before, including the return value. But if you want more than one statement, you need to use a code block. *The preceding example is a short notation for simple lambdas.*

What's it good for?

What's the point, then? For instance, if you want to define an event handler function, you can do it in a shorter way:

```
setOnClickListener(event -> { ... });
```

This saves you from the hassle of needing to define a separate named method just for the click.

You can also save function references into variables. The `sum` function you had is a function that takes two parameters and returns an integer. It can be saved as a BiFunction (*Bi* for *two*).

After BiFunction come Function3 and Function4.

```
BiFunction<Integer, Integer, Integer> sum = (x, y) -> x + y;
```

If this looks unfamiliar, don't worry. We'll always go through the code to make sure it's all clear.

Deep dive into Rx: Live search

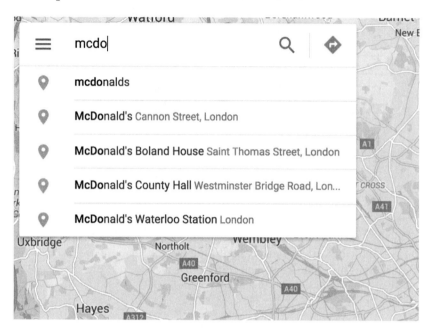

Screenshot of Google Maps web application doing a search (not our app)

To get a quick and dirty idea of what Rx is capable of, let's look at an example: a live search based on user input in a text field. The user starts typing in the text field, and Google helpfully shows suggestions without requiring the user to press a search button.

You want to trigger a search through a network API and show results based on the text the user has written so far. But you want to do so only when the user has typed a minimum of three characters and has momentarily paused typing.

Conditions for triggering search:

1 **Ignore input shorter than three characters.**

2 **Perform a search only when the user hasn't been typing for 150 ms.**

Project setup

You won't build a full maps client here, so you'll use a simple project that has a dummy implementation. You can find the starting point of it in the online code examples.

A quick implementation

Your first task is to establish a basic connection between the editable text input and the list that renders the search results. If you assume that you have an `updateSearchResults` function already in place, the flow goes from the text change to the updated list in the UI.

Text change → **Check text is long enough** → **Call function updateSearchResults** → **Request update...** → **Update the UI**

If you first get started without RxJava, you can set a listener to the `EditText` component. On Android, this is done with `editText.setOnChangeListener`. It allows you to declare a function that's executed whenever the text changes (the user is typing). You'll use our nifty lambdas here for brevity:

```
editText.setOnChangeListener(text -> {
    if (text.length() >= 3) {
      updateSearchResults(text);
    }
});
```

Everything in the middle is executed after each change in the EditText.

Here you have a handler that checks that the length of the input is more than three characters. If not, the handler ignores the change event.

Filtering text changes based on time

The code in the event handler executes immediately, or in other words, synchronously. But the second condition of waiting for 150 ms before executing the search is dependent on *time passed after it was called*. How do you deal with passing time? Threads?

This is where things get tricky: to build such a system is no small feat with traditional Java. Fortunately, handling time-based events is one of the technical problems Rx is good at.

Text input as an emitter of data

To get to the Rx implementation, you'll first take a step back and reshape the way you view the problem. You have two sides: the text input that *emits* text values, and a function that you call with those values to make something happen.

> ### How can data be "emitted"?
>
> In this case, when the text input changes, it sends an event to all its listeners, informing them of the state change. From the point of view of an individual listener, the text input just produced a new value of type `String`, and you should do something with it.
>
> This may sound a little strange, but it's the first step toward the thinking that enables you to use Rx.

The `updateSearchResults` function is the consumer of the data. The function does something with the data every time a new value arrives.

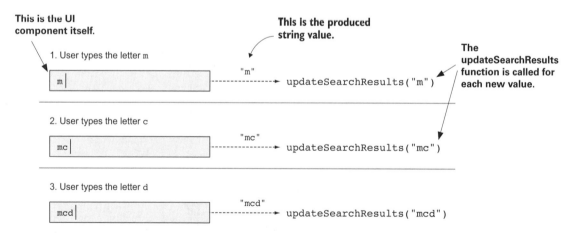

In the code you had before, the text input would give the new string value `text` to the event listener, which in turn would give it to the `updateSearchResults` function.

Because the user isn't typing at infinite speed, these values would arrive at different times. This is how typing into a text input works—*whether or not you're using RxJava.*

The publish-subscribe pattern

As mentioned, at the core of RxJava is a pattern in which you have event sources and functions that listen to them. An example is an `EditText` emitting (publishing) its new value whenever it changes. You'll see next how to write this the RxJava way, but remember that in reality you'll still always have an `onChange` listener attached to the `EditText`.

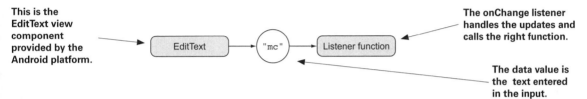

This is the EditText view component provided by the Android platform.

The onChange listener handles the updates and calls the right function.

The data value is the text entered in the input.

In Rx terminology, the `EditText` *publishes* or *emits* an update, and the listener functions are *subscribed* to it. This makes the listener functions *subscribers*.

Notice that the code still uses the same `EditText` and a change listener; you're simply interpreting it in a different way.

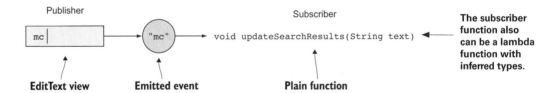

Publisher

Subscriber

The subscriber function also can be a lambda function with inferred types.

EditText view   **Emitted event**   **Plain function**

Should you emit the whole value or just the change?

If you think about it from the point of view of the *change* event, couldn't you emit just the newest character and not the whole string?

You could indeed, but that would leave the subscriber a big responsibility of aggregating the full string over time. In reactive programming, you usually want to emit the *entire data value* to the subscriber.

Text input as an observable

Now you know that an `EditText` can be considered an emitter of string values over time. A producer like this in Rx terminology is called an *observable*—supposedly because the values it emits can be observed.

Converting the UI view into observables

You'll now use the RxBindings library to create a proper `Observable` out of the `EditText`. What you want to do is wrap the text input into an observable—essentially hiding the implementation and making it a pure producer of data.

The counterpart of an observable is the subscriber, and it can be a function, as you saw.

```
Observable<String> textObservable =
    RxTextView.textChanges(textInput);
```
Create an observable based on the text input change events.

```
textObservable
    .subscribe(this::updateSearchResults);
```
Establish a connection between the observable and the subscriber.

You can still use the same diagrams as before. `updateSearchResults` is called as before, though without the minimum limit of three characters (we'll get to that).

This column now represents the observable itself.

Here's the subscription mechanism provided by the library.

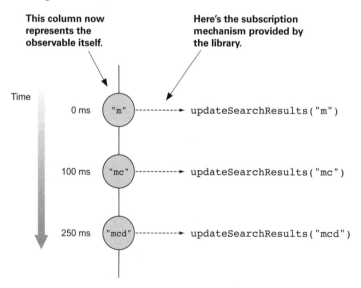

Time

0 ms	`"m"`	┄┄┄➤ `updateSearchResults("m")`
100 ms	`"mc"`	┄┄┄➤ `updateSearchResults("mc")`
250 ms	`"mcd"`	┄┄┄➤ `updateSearchResults("mcd")`

Filtering observables

Now that you have everything set up, you can start with real Rx. Everything you'll do is based on the kind of publisher-subscriber pattern I described. There are emitters of data and subscribers: what happens between the two is the Rx logic.

Most of this book is really about what goes between the observable and the subscriber.

With the decoupling of observables and subscribers, you've created a convenient arrangement for your logic. *The subscriber doesn't know where the data comes from and when, or how many times.*

You can manipulate the data as it's *on the way* to the subscriber. For instance, you can disqualify data items based on certain conditions, such as whether the string is at least three characters long.

At the beginning of the book, you were adding +1 to all values. You can also block any values from propagating altogether.

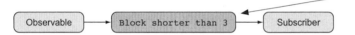

Technically, you create a *new* observable based on the original one, but one in which the strings that are too short are missing.

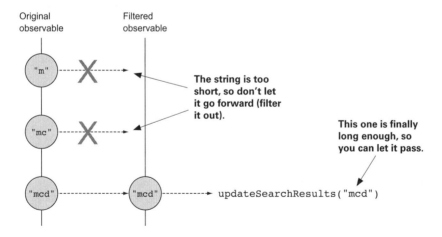

The result for now will be the same as with the `if` clause you had in the quick implementation. On the next page you can find the code.

The filter operator

Conveniently, RxJava, like most Rx libraries, has a method to perform filtering. It works by calling `.filter` on an observable and giving it a filter function that validates the values *one by one*. ◀───────

The filter function is called for each item in the stream, with the item as the argument. The function then evaluates the item and either lets it pass (returns `true`), or filters it out (returns `false`). The filtered values will disappear and never reach the subscriber (in our case, the `updateSearchResults` function).

To refresh your memory, here's the initial implementation from a few pages back:

```
textInput.setOnChangeListener(text -> {
    if (text.length() >= 3) {
        updateSearchResults(text);
    }
});
```

Now you can write the same in RxJava, using the `RxTextView` utility to convert the `TextView` into an observable first. Notice that this code calls `updateSearchResults`, just like the preceding code:

```
RxTextView.textChanges(textInput)
    .filter(text -> text.length() >= 3) ◀────────
    .subscribe(this::updateSearchResults);
```

Done! Great! It works ... the same as before. Why the effort, you might ask? That brings us to our next topic.

Time decoupling of observables and subscribers

You've finally reached the point where Rx gets interesting and incredibly helpful. You'll see how to deal with the second condition of filtering items based on the point in time when they were emitted.

The preceding code is already based on data items emitted by the `TextView` observable and data items received by the listener function, the subscriber. With the filter function, you already saw that *these aren't necessarily the same data items*. The subscriber doesn't know what to expect, so you can delete some of them on the way.

A less obvious aspect is that because a subscriber doesn't know anything about where the data comes from, *a data item doesn't need to arrive at the same time it was sent.*

The filter function is called for each passing value. You have to be careful not to save state outside the function.

The filter operator sits between the TextView and the listener function, wrapped into the RxJava way of doing it.

The subscriber is just a function. It can be called at any time a new data item is available.

Bending time

It turns out that with an Rx library, you can easily manipulate time relationships of data emitted and data consumed. You could, for instance, delay all data items by 50 ms. In our example, that would mean that the search queries are always made 50 ms later.

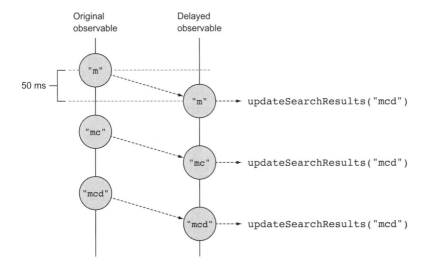

For instance, the first marble could be described as follows:

1 The user types an m in the text input.

2 The text input observable emits the string m into the stream.

3 Because of the delay operation, the Rx system makes the marble wait for 50 ms.

4 After 50 ms have passed, the marble can continue its journey and in this case end up being consumed by the updateSearchResults function.

The code in RxJava is simple to write with the tools in the library. You tell your Rx system to delay all data items emitted from the source by 50 ms, effectively creating a new observable that's a bit late.

```
RxTextView.textChanges(textInput)
    .delay(50, TimeUnit.MILLISECONDS)
    .subscribe(this::updateSearchResults);
```

This is the operator that delays everything it gets its hands on.

> ### Can you use a delay with a negative number?
>
> In case you had your hopes up, unfortunately the delay operator doesn't work with negative values, and thus can't receive data items from the future. There have been theories about time travel, and currently it's deemed possible, but only if another end of a portal is set up in the future "first." It seems this hasn't yet happened.

Bending time to your benefit

Delaying everything isn't usually desired behavior. But the seed of the solution is in there. Let's look at our second condition again, the one about not triggering the update too often:

Perform a search only when the user hasn't been typing for 150 ms.

Because emitting an item to the subscriber triggers the search, this condition seems to imply that you indeed have to send the last item with a 150ms delay—*but only if no other item was emitted during the time the item was waiting.*

If you received another item right after, that would mean the user is still typing, and you want to let them finish.

The bus stop

Effectively, what you have is a bus stop. The bus will leave only after everyone is on the bus and the driver has managed to close the doors. As long as someone is still coming in, the doors can't close and the departure won't happen.

The time you have between the latest person stepping in and the doors closing is 150ms. As long as the user hasn't stopped typing for long enough, the `updateSearchResults` bus has to wait.

Debounce: The bus stop operator

In this section, we're going to cut the explanation short and get
to the more precise details of operators later. Fortunately, what I
described on the preceding page is a reasonably common problem in
reactive programming, and an operator already exists for it. It's called
debounce:

> Debounce: only emit an item from an Observable if a particular timespan has
> passed without it emitting another item.
>
> —ReactiveX Wiki

This may sound a bit abstract, but that's how the wiki is written. Often
seeing an example of *what you can do* with the operator makes its use
clearer. But there might be more than one use for each, which is why
the wiki is kept on a high level.

In our case, we already have an example, so let's next see how it works
from the user's point of view:

1 The user starts typing "m" in the search box.

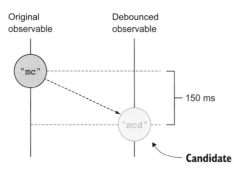

Original observable

Debounced observable

150 ms

Candidate

The user presses the M
key, and you receive the
item in your observable.
The debounce puts
the m in the store as a
potential candidate, but
waits for 150ms before
confirming that the
string indeed should be
allowed to go forward.

2 The user types "c" immediately afterward.

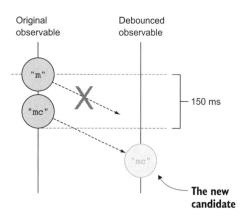

The user continues typing before 150 ms have passed, which makes the previous candidate invalid! Instead, the debounce stores mc as the new candidate and *resets the 150 ms timer.*

Notice that here the observable always emits the full text in the field. This is how the RxBindings library works.

3 The user stops typing.

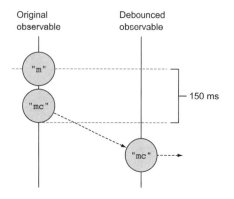

Finally, the user stops typing long enough for the 150 ms timer to trigger. You can now send out the candidate you had—this time, mc.

Subsequent items won't affect this string anymore, as it's already out there.

The code

When you apply the debounce to the previous code, you get the final solution:

```
RxTextView.textChanges(textInput)
    .filter(text -> text.length() >= 3)
    .debounce(150, TimeUnit.MILLISECONDS)
    .subscribe(this::updateSearchResults);
```

This really does fulfill the conditions originally imposed on you: the code filters out searches fewer than three characters and waits until the user hasn't typed for 150 ms before sending a search request.

The entire picture looks like this:

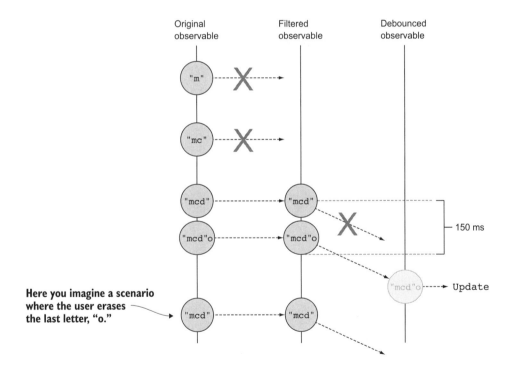

Putting your code into Android

So far you've seen code without specifying where to exactly put it in your traditional Android application. Skip this section if you aren't interested in the details. We have a couple of requirements for how the code you've written needs to be run inside an Android application:

1. The code is run after the UI is created.

2. The code is run only once.

Seemingly, the most obvious place appears to be either the onCreate activity or the onViewCreated fragment. Either will do—in this case, you'll use an activity, because this UI isn't complex:

```
public class MainActivity extends AppCompatActivity {
    @Override
    protected void onCreate(Bundle savedInstanceState) {
        super.onCreate(savedInstanceState);
        setContentView(R.layout.activity_main);

        final EditText textInput =
            (EditText) findViewById(R.id.text_input);

        RxTextView.textChanges(textInput)
            .filter(text -> text.length() >= 3)
            .debounce(150, TimeUnit.MILLISECONDS)
            .observeOn(AndroidSchedulers.mainThread())
            .subscribe(this::updateSearchResults);
    }

    private void updateSearchResults(String search) {
        ...
    }
}
```

You've added a thread change in the middle, because you need to be sure that any operations that manipulate the UI are executed on the main thread. In this case, *the debounce operator will automatically switch the thread to a background one* in order to not block the execution while you wait for more input. Most operators don't switch the thread, but ones that are delayed do.

Later chapters cover thread changes more extensively, but usually it's enough to call .observeOn(AndroidSchedulers.mainThread()) just before doing a UI operation in the next step (or subscriber). This call changes the thread for anything *downstream*, meaning the steps that come after it are in the thread it defined.

Coffee break

Make your own application now! Use the coffee break base in the online examples, or follow the instructions in the appendix to set up your dependencies.

Try to use other kinds of input components that the RxBinding library has. They all start with Rx, for instance:

- `RxCompoundButton.checkedChanges`

- `RxRadioGroup.checkedChanges`

These two return a Boolean instead of a string.

```
RxCompoundButton.checkedChanges(compoundButton)
    .subscribe(isChecked -> {
        myLabel.setText(
            isChecked ? "box checked!" : ":("
        );
    });
```

This is a special case in which you aren't obliged to use observeOn. You know that the observable here is on the main thread because it originates from the UI.

When looking at the functions `RxTextView` offers, you can also see ones that don't return observables. These are functions that you can invoke on a `TextView`, such as the following:

```
Action1<CharSequence> text(TextView).
```

You can use them instead of the lambda syntax, if you want to. Which one you prefer is up to you, but we'll continue using lambdas for brevity.

Exercise

Make an `EditText` and a `TextView`. Have the `TextView` say, "Text too long" after user has typed more than seven characters. You can see the solution in the online code examples.

Principles of reactive programming

You've now seen a bit of reactive programming in action. This is just the tip of the iceberg, but you can start to see the pattern here already:

- *A program is seen as a data processing system—something goes in, and something comes out.* The data might come out as a text change or an animation on screen.

- *Data processing is done with small functions that take an input and produce an output (or an effect, such as debounce).* An Rx library is the glue between these functions, giving the data from the previous function to the next.

- *Every function is considered asynchronous.* Running a function takes time. It might be just a millisecond or two, but there's no such thing as "instant." You therefore declare only what should happen after a function has been executed, but you don't hang around waiting for it.

The application becomes a big pipeline of different points of inputs and outputs. What happens in between is the isolated Rx logic. It models the way you can calculate the output based on your input.

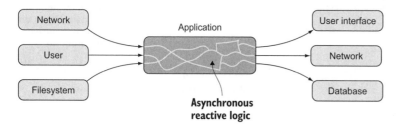

In our example, the input was the user typing into the `EditText`. You wrapped the input into an observable and pushed the generated data into the asynchronous Rx logic. The output in this case was shown in `updateSearchResults`.

Events and marble diagrams

RxJava is good at handling events that occur at certain points in time. So good, in fact, that a new way of representing events has become a standard for it: the marble diagram.

The marble diagram

You already saw time-based diagrams with circles representing pieces of data that appear at certain points in time. The standard, however, is to put the circles horizontally. You also usually omit the data represented by the "marbles."

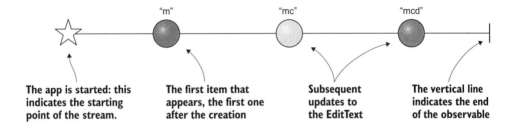

| The app is started: this indicates the starting point of the stream. | The first item that appears, the first one after the creation | Subsequent updates to the EditText | The vertical line indicates the end of the observable |

You'll later see different kinds of diagrams, but marbles are popular with the *event-based problems* that Rx can solve. You'll see many of those in this first part of this book.

Wait, isn't the diagram the wrong way?

If you think about a traditional stack, the item on the right would be the first one to be emitted. But the marble diagram is more of a "historical" representation of *what happened* on a time line. In these kinds of time lines, the time flows from left to right.

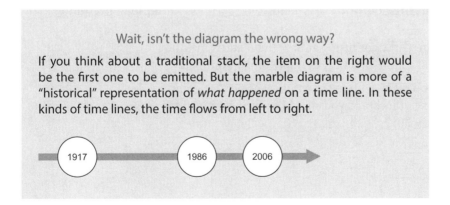

Summary

Wow! That was almost 30 pages to write five lines. You're probably wondering whether it was really necessary. I mean, couldn't we just check Stack Overflow and copy the snippet?

The answer is yes and no. You can check the internet and copy the snippet, *if you know what you're looking for.* Many problems become almost trivial after they're framed in the right way. In our case, it took a while to get to a point where we have a good representation of the input stream.

Learning how to ask the question

In reactive programming, phrasing of the question is sometimes 90% of the work. Often your problem isn't as unique as it first seems, and there might already be an Rx feature that solves it.

This book focuses on presenting the thinking patterns that allow you to formulate your requirements in a way that makes sense.

Often you start by converting the inputs into streams and seeing how they can be combined. Sometimes figuring out how to write the program is about drawing the marble diagrams and checking the Rx wiki for similar ones (reactivex.io).

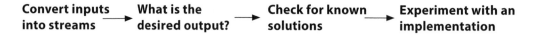

Convert inputs into streams → **What is the desired output?** → **Check for known solutions** → **Experiment with an implementation**

The process may seem a little confusing at first, but it starts making sense after you get a few more practical example under your belt.

You also don't need too many patterns in a typical app. After going through the examples in this book, you should be well equipped for most scenarios in the wild.

Networking with observables | 2

In this chapter

- Implementing the network layer with RxJava

- Taking a deeper look at the RxJava library

- Working with observables and subscribers

- Basic error handling

- Introducing immutability

RxJava and event streams

In the preceding chapter, you briefly saw how to use RxJava and the RxBindings utility to handle events originating in the UI—namely, the text the user has entered in an `EditText`.

In that case, your flow was simple: you'll have some events that come, you'll apply a bit of processing, and then you'll show results.

In this chapter, you'll look at an example that is commonplace: network requests.

RxJava and networking

In the beginning, RxJava looks like a more convenient way of declaring callbacks, but later in the chapter you'll see a couple of cases that can get smelly fast with the traditional ways of implementation.

RxJava is indeed often adopted as a way to alleviate the "callback hell" that results when you need to combine data from multiple APIs. You'll see how this can be elegantly handled with observables.

Libraries for network requests on Android

In this book, you'll use a library called *Retrofit* from Square for networking purposes. It's a reasonably standard one, and has a powerful syntax for declaring interfaces. It's also able to play well with RxJava, which you'll use to your benefit.

You can add the dependence in your Gradle file like this (check the latest version on http://square.github.io/retrofit/):

```
dependencies {
    ...
    compile 'com.squareup.retrofit2:retrofit:2.0.0-beta4'
    ...
}
```

Subscribers

When you want to react to a change in state of one of your observables—a signal of sorts—you'll define a function that's called with that value as an argument. This function is called a *subscriber* or *observer*. In the context of a simple observable, it's very much like a callback function that's called every time you have a new value.

```
numberOfOrangesObservable
  .subscribe(
    numberOfOranges ->
      Log.d("Number of oranges: " + numberOfOranges)
  );
```

The observable from which you want to get updates.

This is the subscriber function. It'll be called on each value the observable emits.

Subscribers are also sometimes called *observers*, though we don't use the term because it's too easy to confuse with the word *observable*.

Subscribers and marbles

You can create a marble diagram in which each marble represents the number of oranges that are in a basket at a given moment. Here you can also see the log commands executed at the times oranges are put into a basket.

```
numberOfOrangeObservable.subscribe(number -> Log.d(number));
```

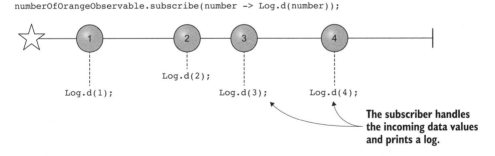

The subscriber handles the incoming data values and prints a log.

From one point of view, an observable is a window to the *future*. You declare what *will happen* to any and all values of this observable.

Decoupling of data sources

The subscriber itself doesn't know where values come from; it's only a simple function. They could come from the UI, network, or even a triggered timer. The subscriber is concerned only with what to do with the value *once it arrives*.

RxJava 2 observable types

One of the biggest changes in RxJava 2 was the introduction of several more observable types and the split between the `Subscriber` and `Observable` classes.

Observable

The `Observable` type is the most used observable that's the default for our purposes. The `Observable` class is what we've been exclusively using so far. It can emit any number of values and then complete or emit an error.

Single

This type is for the following special cases when you expect exactly one value to be emitted. `Single` either emits a value and completes or emits an error. `Single` can't complete without emitting a value. This type is useful for the following:

- Network responses
- Results from complex calculations
- `toList` operator that converts items of an observable into a single list (you'll see this in action later)

Maybe

`Maybe` is like `Single`, but with no guarantee of getting that single value. `Maybe` can either emit an item and complete, or just complete. It can also emit an error.

Completable

`Completeable` doesn't emit anything, but just completes or not. This type may also emit an error. This is basically an "event" that indicates something happened or finished. It could be used to indicate state change, such as when a fragment is destroyed (which can happen only once).

Flowable

In later vesions of RxJava 1, a concept called *back pressure* was introduced to manage situations in which an observable produces too many items for the subscriber to handle. But because this is an unusual scenario in many applications, in RxJava 2 the special back-pressure techniques were moved into a `Flowable` type. In `Flowable`, you're forced to define what happens if the source produces too many items.

For the purposes of Android UIs, `Flowable` is definitely overkill, and in general we don't use it in this book. If you're building an application to do things like processing thousands of messages from an IoT sensor, for instance, you might need flowables to manage the flow, but in most cases we're just fine with the default observable that uses a simplified mechanism that queues all items in a buffer.

Subscribing to and converting different observables

To make things a bit confusing, only the `Flowable` type uses a class called `Subscriber` to listen to the items emitted. The others use `Observer`. This is because of the ReactiveX standard that was developed after RxJava 1 was already implemented—RxJava 2 was retroactively fitted to conform to the standard.

In terms of the terminology used in this book, however, we talk about only observables and subscribers, regardless of the specific class.

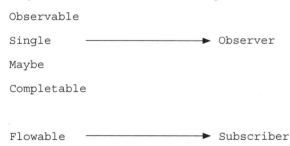

```
Observable

Single            ───────────────►  Observer

Maybe

Completable


Flowable          ───────────────►  Subscriber
```

To convert one of the simple observables to another one is straightforward. For instance, `Single` has the function `toObservable()` that returns an instance of the less-retrictive basic `Observable` class.

What happens when you make a normal network request?

To see where network requests fit in our mental model of observables, you have to take a step back and see what happens in the lifecyle of one. Here are the steps of a typical network request:

1a. Initiate the network request.

To make things simple, you'll call the `retrieveData` function to start the request. This function does everything necessary, including running the request in a background thread.

1b. Pass a callback to the function.

The code doesn't stop while waiting for a response. Instead, you'll put the request in the background and declare a point of reentry after it's finished. The point is also known as a callback. It tells the runback where you wish to continue after the background operation is ready.

With lambda notation, you can define the function like this:

```
retrieveData(this:processData);
```

> Here you again use the lambda notation, assuming "this" is able to handle the processing.

this::processData?

`this:processData` refers to the `processData` of `this`. It doesn't call the method; it just returns a reference to it, to be called at a later time.

2. Wait for a response.

While the request is ongoing, you can continue executing other code and allow users to interact with the application as usual. You probably want to show a spinner somewhere, indicating the process.

3. Receive data in the callback and do stuff.

When everything is ready, your callback will be triggered with the fresh data from the network. Typically, you execute code to display the data you just received.

The `processData` method could, for instance, just log the result:

```
public void processData(String string) {
  Log.d("New data: " + string);
}
```

What happens when you make a network request with an observable?

With RxJava, the network flow will be similar, but you can define `retrieveData` so that it returns an *observable* to which you can later subscribe. Here you can see how the flow on the preceding page can be implemented in RxJava:

1. Create a network observable.

Instead of a function with a callback to start the request, you can split the task into two. The first step is to create an observable and start the request. *At this point, you don't yet know what you're going to do with the result data.*

```
public Observable<String> retrieveData() {
    ...
}
```

2. Subscribe to the network observable.

You now have an observable that will give you the data as soon as it's available. You can subscribe to the observable to set the handling function that replaces the callback you saw on the preceding page.

```
retrieveData()
    .subscribe(this::processData);  ◄───
```

You don't need to declare a callback yet. This function doesn't know what you're going to do with the results.

3. Wait for a response.

4. Receive data in the subscriber and do stuff.

When everything is ready, your callback will be triggered with the fresh data from the network. The subscriber function can be exactly the same as you saw on the preceding page—a function that takes the right type of data as a parameter.

Network request as an observable

Coming back to your marble diagrams, a network request can be depicted as one that has only one marble and a completion.

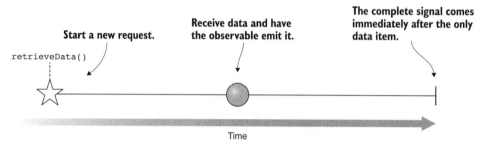

Here the marbles represent data of type `String`, though it's not relevant to this level of abstraction. The star indicates the creation of the observable—in this case, when the request starts.

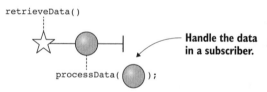

The function you'll use for processing the data is triggered at the point when the data arrives (the marble). The subscriber function is executed then and there.

The `processData` function is likely to be triggered on another thread, so we'll have to remember to specify the thread just before the subscriber. You always specify the thread if you know you need a specific one. You can use the `observeOn` operator to switch all *following* operations and subscribers onto the thread specified:

```
retrieveData()
  .observeOn(AndroidSchedulers.mainThread())
  .subscribe(this::processData);
```

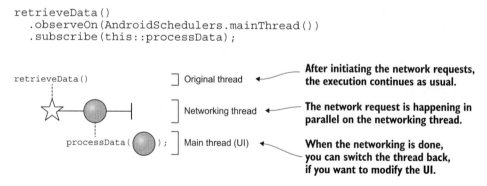

But how does changing the network request into an observable make your life easier? Let's look at an example to find out.

Example: An RSS feed aggregator

To make things more concrete, you'll make a little app that can load multiple RSS feeds and show them in one list, ordered by date. You'll start with two feeds to keep it simple and then expand to have more.

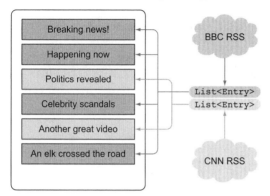

You have two API endpoints but only one list of mixed content. You need to make two calls and combine the results.

For testing, you can use these two feeds (actually we're opting for Atom instead of RSS, but it's the same thing in practice).

```
Google News
https://news.google.com/?output=atom

The Register Software Headlines
http://www.theregister.co.uk/software/headlines.atom
```

These two feeds are of a standard format, and you'll use a parser that's included in our code examples online. This standard XML parser was originally part of Google Examples, though Google has since removed it.

The feed structure

The parser produces a list of items of type `Entry`, which it defines itself.
It looks like this:

```java
public static class Entry {
    public final String id;
    public final String title;
    public final String link;
    public final long updated;

    Entry(String id,
        String title,
        String link,
        long updated) {
      this.id = id;
      this.title = title;
      this.link = link;
      this.updated = updated;
    }

    public String toString () {
      return new Date(updated).toString() + "\n" + title;
    }
}
```

The title of the feed entry. We will show this on the list.

Link to the actual article that the feed contains. This is a URL.

Timestamp that you'll use for sorting.

For convenience, you define a toString method. It'll be used on the lists at first.

For practical purposes you also have a small wrapper that converts the
HTTP responses into observables of type `List<Entry>`. Usually, you
wouldn't need to do this, but XML is a bit of a special case because most
APIs nowadays are JSON. You can see the code in the online examples,
though it's not in the scope of this chapter.

With these utilities, you declare the `Observable<List<Entry>`
`getFeed(String url)` function that takes the feed URL and returns a
list of entries it returns, as soon as the network request is ready.

```
Observable<List<Entry>> getFeed(String url)
```

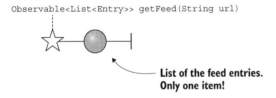

**List of the feed entries.
Only one item!**

Notice that the observable will still be in the networking thread, so
any operations or subscribers will be called in that as well. Normally, it
doesn't matter, but you need to remember to switch back to the main
thread just before making changes to the UI.

Getting the data

To get the data, you need two calls—or rather two observables. For illustration purposes, we'll name them `purple` and `yellow`. The parsing function is omitted here; see the online code examples for details.

```
Observable<List<Entry>> purpleFeedObservable =
    getFeed("https://news.google.com/?output=atom");

Observable<List<Entry>> yellowFeedObservable =
  getFeed(
"http://www.theregister.co.uk/software/headlines.atom");
```

The next thing you want to do is somehow figure out how to combine these two observables into one and draw the list. You're opting to wait for both before showing anything—instead of drawing them as they come.

In addition to the two data retrieval functions, you need someone to use the data and draw the list items. You'll create a function `drawList(List<Entry>)`. Here's the sequence followed to get the data in RxJava:

1. Start requests for both feeds.

2. Wait until the requests are completed.

3. Call drawList with the combined results.

If you draw it in a marble diagram, you can represent the two requests as observables—one for news articles and one for videos.

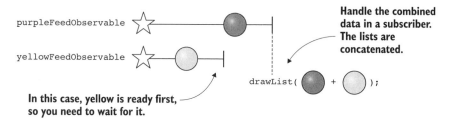

It's starting to look interesting. You now have all the pieces you need: the two observables, which are the input, and the function that consumes the results. That function is the output of the Rx graph.

The combineLatest operator

When you have multiple observables as inputs that need to be aggregated into one, you can use the FRP operator `combineLatest`. More specifically, use it when you need one item from each of the observables.

`combineLatest` is a common operator, and you'll be using it a lot. In our case of using `Pair`, the marble diagram becomes like this.

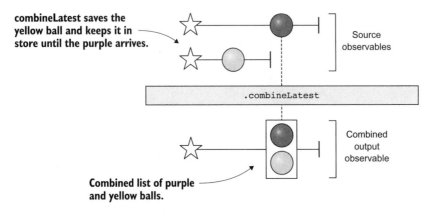

combineLatest saves the yellow ball and keeps it in store until the purple arrives.

Source observables

.combineLatest

Combined output observable

Combined list of purple and yellow balls.

As you can see, here you combine two observables into one that depends on both. You can now treat this as a single observable!

The code is even shorter than the picture, and the only unobvious thing is telling the operator how to combine the two data items. In this case, you have two lists of type `List<Entry>`:

```
Observable<List<Entry>> combinedObservable =
  Observable.combineLatest(
    purpleFeedObservable, yellowFeedObservable,
    (purpleList, yellowList) -> {
      final List<Entry> list = new ArrayList<>();
      list.addAll(purpleList);
      list.addAll(yellowList);
      return list;
    }
  );
```

Our combined observable emits data values of type List<Entry>.

This is the combine function that tells combineLatest how to merge the values from the source observables.

The Rx code so far

As before, you can put everything into `MainActivity` for now. The only addition here is the part where you subscribe to `combinedObservable` and eventually draw the list.

The drawing is one-off right now, as you create a new list adapter based on the new data. You'll make more elegant solutions later, but for this it's good enough for now.

```
public class MainActivity extends Activity {
    private static final String TAG =
        MainActivity.class.getSimpleName();

    @Override
    protected void onCreate(Bundle savedInstanceState) {
        super.onCreate(savedInstanceState);
        setContentView(R.layout.activity_main);

        Observable<List<Entry>> purpleFeedObservable =
                FeedObservable.getFeed(
                    "https://news.google.com/?output=atom");

        Observable<List<Entry>> yellowFeedObservable =
                FeedObservable.getFeed(
                    "http://www.theregister.co.uk/software/
                        headlines.atom");

        Observable<List<Entry>> combinedObservable =
                Observable.combineLatest(
                    purpleFeedObservable, yellowFeedObservable,
                    (purpleList, yellowList) -> {
                        final List<Entry> list = new ArrayList<>();
                        list.addAll(purpleList);
                        list.addAll(yellowList);
                        return list;
                    }
                );

        combinedObservable
                .observeOn(AndroidSchedulers.mainThread())
                .subscribe(this::drawList);
    }

    private void drawList(List<Entry> listItems) {
        final ListView list = (ListView) findViewById(R.id.list);
        final ArrayAdapter<Entry> itemsAdapter =
                new ArrayAdapter<>(this,
                    android.R.layout.simple_list_item_1,
                        listItems);
        list.setAdapter(itemsAdapter);
    }
}
```

The beginning of the Rx logic you already saw, but here it's in the Activity context.

In this version, the feeds are retrieved only once and there's no update. You might add one later!

Switch the thread to the main thread and pass the aggregated list to the drawing function.

Create a new ArrayAdapter and populate the list with your retrieved items.

Coffee break

You saw how to combine two observables, or streams, into one. This is one of the most important ways of manipulating your input into output.

Whenever you see that you have more inputs than outputs, you probably need to combine them at some point. `combineLatest` is the most straightforward way to do this.

Exercise

Experiment by using `combineLatest` with the user inputs you used in the first chapter. Create a text field that shows the combination of the contents of two editable text fields. You can use the same `RxTextView.textChanges` that we used before.

The solution

The solution this time doesn't require much code, but the key is to identify the input and output. Here we'll assume that you have two input fields, `editText1` and `editText2`, and one `TextView` for output, called `outputTextView`.

```
Observable<String> input1 =
  RxTextView.textChanges(editText1);
Observable<String> input2 =
  RxTextView.textChanges(editText2);

Observable<String> combinedString =
  Observable.combineLatest(input1, input2,
    (a, b) -> a + " " + b
);

combinedString.subscribe(outputTextView::setText);
```

The combine function looks abstract, but all it does is concatenate the two strings into one with a space in between.

Asynchronous data processing chains

I'll now properly introduce the concept of a *processing chain*—or a pipeline, if you will—that can take the inputs in one end and transform the data into the final product. The chain is essentially many operations, put one after another.

A processing chain is a bit like a string of dominoes where, at each step, the incoming piece of data triggers the next operation.

Dominoes aren't a bad mental model because they also support slightly more interesting configurations. For instance, here's one input that our system reacts to—two bells will chime at different times.

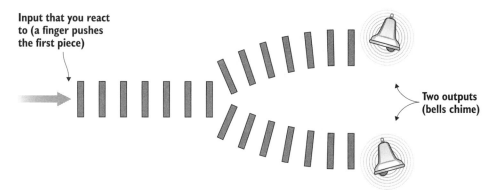

This scenario can be expressed with one event observable that gives its output to two subscribers.

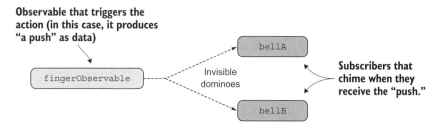

Arrow diagrams vs. marble diagrams

The arrow diagram that you just saw is good when you want to display relationships or indicate where the data goes. On the other hand, marble diagrams are good for showing what happens inside one particular step of the arrow diagram. A marble diagram is like a close inspection of one step in the chain.

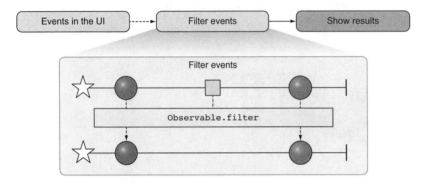

Marbles in arrow diagrams

Depending on the need, you can also depict marbles (data) going through parts of the arrow diagram—the reactive chain. In this case, you're capturing the behavior of the operation *at one point in time*.

The operation in the middle would still filter this marble as it does. This detailed behavior can be read from the marble diagram.

Putting the list in order

Getting back to our example, how does the list look now?

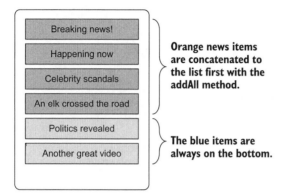

Because you just concatenated the two lists, they aren't sorted by date.

In terms of observables, you already have one that gives us the list. It's our `Observable<List<Item>> listObservable`. What you want to do is apply a sorting algorithm to it before giving it to `drawList`, which is the subscriber in this case.

You could sort it already in the combine function, but one of the principles of Rx is to keep the steps as small as possible—doing one thing at a time. Fortunately, there's a simple way to apply transformations to all values that an observable emits.

We call this the `.map` operator. It applies a function to every single value that an observable emits. It does this as soon as it receives the value, so no thread changes occur. Just be careful because map might block the thread when doing expensive computations.

The map operator

If you take an abstract example of a `.map` that turns circles into squares, it would look like this:

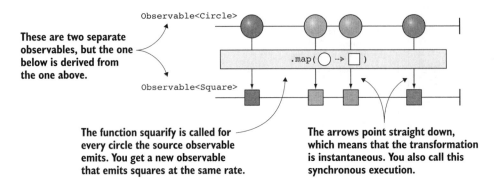

These are two separate observables, but the one below is derived from the one above.

The function squarify is called for every circle the source observable emits. You get a new observable that emits squares at the same rate.

The arrows point straight down, which means that the transformation is instantaneous. You also call this synchronous execution.

Here the function that's applied to all items is of the signature Square `squarify(Circle circle)`. It takes a circle and returns a square. What it exactly does we don't know, but this isn't necessary to know in order to use it.

`.map` is the most common operator you're likely to use, because it's a simple transformation. It takes in one item of data and sends out another one.

The life of an operator

An operator creates a new observable that's based on the old one. It's a little logic circuit that can decide what to do with the incoming items and what to emit. There are no rules of what it has to do in regards to its source, as long as it behaves like a proper observable to the outside.

Using map to sort a list

In this case, you get an unsorted list in and you send out a sorted one.

For sorting, let's add a simple comparable interface to the `Entry` class:

```java
public class Entry implements Comparable<Entry> {

    ...

    @Override
     public int compareTo(@NonNull Entry another) {
        if (this.updated > another.updated) {
            return -1;
        } else if (this.updated < another.updated) {
            return 1;
        }
        return 0;
    }
}
```

You can now make a function that takes in a list and returns another one that's sorted:

```java
List<Entry> sortList(List<Entry> list) {
  List<Entry> sortedList = new ArrayList<>();
  sortedList.addAll(list);
  Collections.sort(sortedList);
  return sortedList;
}
```

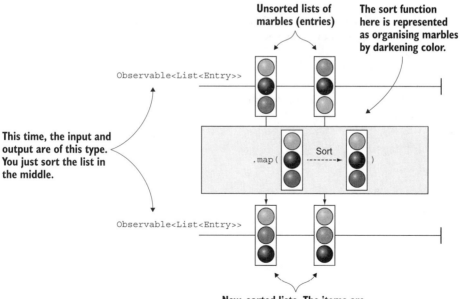

Unsorted lists of marbles (entries)

The sort function here is represented as organising marbles by darkening color.

Observable<List<Entry>>

This time, the input and output are of this type. You just sort the list in the middle.

`.map (` Sort `)`

Observable<List<Entry>>

New, sorted lists. The items are the same, but are contained in an instance of a list.

You might wonder why you create a copy, but this is how it has to be as long as you're in the Rx chain. One instance in, another instance out. On the next page, you'll have a short dive into the concepts of immutability and why you need it in Rx logic.

Keeping that in mind, you can now use the `sortList` function in our code with the `.map` operator:

```
Observable<List<Entry>> sortedListObservable =
  listObservable.map(this::sortList);
```

After you have sorted the observable, you can switch the subscriber to use this one. After all, *the subscriber doesn't need to know where the data comes from.*

```
sortedListObservable
  .observeOn(AndroidSchedulers.mainThread())
  .subscribe(this:drawList);
```

The sorted list is now ready and you can finally see your aggregated news feed! We'll now take a little step aside and discuss related topics that we didn't yet cover.

What is an Rx chain?

When we put many operations one after another, we sometimes call it a *chain* of operations. In Rx, the data always travels through the chains in only one direction.

A synonym to an *Rx chain* is an *Rx pipeline*. Depending on what we're talking about, we might choose the mental model of a pipeline to support our understanding.

Brief introduction to immutability

You probably wondered why you don't simply sort the list and return the same instance. It would be more efficient, right?

```
List<Item> sortList(List<Item> list) {
  List<Item> sortedList = new ArrayList<>();
  sortedList.addAll(list);
  Collections.sort(sortedList);
  return sortedList;
}
```

It's a good question, and not modifying the original array wasn't an accident. Modifying is more efficient than creating a copy and changing it, but we choose not to. You'll see why next.

The short reason is someone else might be using the same value, because an observable can have multiple subscribers. You must be respectful of those and always make a copy if there's a chance of creating a modification.

This is what we call the *immutability* of data. Because you don't know (or care) who else is using the data you receive, you must never ever modify it. Doing so could cause entirely unpredictable behavior.

For instance, let's define two functions that sort in a different way from the function before:

```
List<Item> sortListByTitle(List<Item> list) {
  Collections.sort(list, titleComparator);
  return list;
}

List<Item> sortListByDate(List<Item> list) {
  Collections.sort(list, dateComparator);
  return list;
}
```

Whoops! Modifying the original list given to you is bad!

Now you might use the two badly behaving functions you've just defined to create two separate observables based on the same one. This is completely allowed and, in fact, common.

```
Observable<List<Item>> sortedByTitleObservable =
  listObservable.map(this::sortListByTitle);

Observable<List<Item>> sortedByDateObservable =
  listObservable.map(this::sortListByDate);
```

When a new list arrives, both of these functions would get the same new value simultaneously (theoretically). They wouldn't both try to sort the same instance at the same time. This obviously isn't good!

Chain without immutability

Here's an example of an Rx chain in which you don't use immutability.
It might work if you have only one stream, but you can't assume that.
Modifying data in the stream can produce very strange behavior.

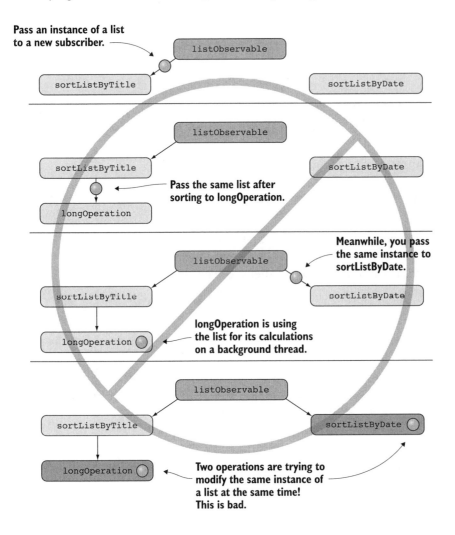

Chain with immutable data

In a proper Rx chain, you always pass new references if you want to modify the data. There are techniques for this, such as builder constructors.

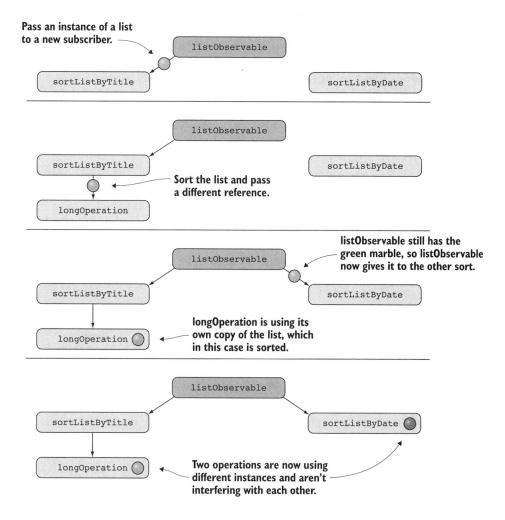

Pass an instance of a list to a new subscriber.

Sort the list and pass a different reference.

listObservable still has the green marble, so listObservable now gives it to the other sort.

longOperation is using its own copy of the list, which in this case is sorted.

Two operations are now using different instances and aren't interfering with each other.

Immutability as a problem solver

Immutability of data might seem like a harsh limitation, and indeed it's sometimes a little inconvenient in a language such as Java. But, you no longer have to guess when a data value might have changed without your noticing—it never will. Every time a change occurs, you'll receive a completely new instance of data.

Isn't it slower to create new objects all the time? you might ask. The answer is yes, it's slightly slower. The performance implication on modern platforms is small, though, because the discarded data values can be garbage collected as soon as a new one comes in. This generally isn't considered a problem on most platforms.

Builders in Java

What do you do if you want to change only one field in a complex class and pass it to the next guy in the FRP chain? The Java answers are builders. They work pretty much like this:

```
Customer increaseCustomerVisitCount(Customer customer) {
    Customer.Builder builder =
        new Customer.Builder(customer);
    builder.setVisitCount(customer.getVisitCount() + 1);
    return builder.build();
}
```

Create a builder based on a Customer instance.

Set the visit count of the builder to visitCount + 1.

Tell the builder to create a new instance based on its values.

The `Builder` class is usually declared as an internal class:

```
public class Customer {
    private final int visitCount;

    private Customer(Builder builder) {
        this.visitCount = builder.visitCount;
    }

    public static class Builder {
        private int visitCount;

        public Builder() { }
        public Builder(Customer customer) {
            this.visitCount = customer.visitCount;
        }

        public Builder setVisitCount(int visitCount) {
            this.visitCount = visitCount;
        }

        public Customer build() {
            return new Customer(this);
        }
    }
}
```

Private constructor: only the Builder is allowed to create instances.

Builder is a mutable "proto-instance" in which everything can be changed. But notice there's no getter.

The build() method always creates a new instance of Customer. The instances are immutable.

Error handling

In addition to completing, observables can finish by emitting an error. This is useful for dealing with unexpected situations—or reasonably expected, such as network errors.

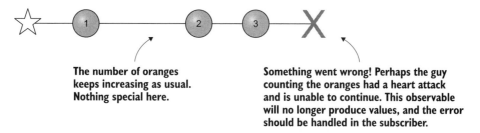

The number of oranges keeps increasing as usual. Nothing special here.

Something went wrong! Perhaps the guy counting the oranges had a heart attack and is unable to continue. This observable will no longer produce values, and the error should be handled in the subscriber.

An error is used to indicate that something unexpected happened and you weren't able to continue the stream.

An error in RxJava won't stop the execution of the program itself, but will produce a *notification* that's of type `error`. You can then deal with the error similarly to the way you would with normal values.

What is a notification?

A *notification* is a message that the observable emits. There are three types of notifications:

- Data value (contains the data itself)
- Completion (no further information)
- Error (contains information about the error)

RxJava processes these notifications independently from each other—so, for instance, an error would end up in the error handler of the subscriber. It's important to understand that an error is just another kind of notification that an observable can emit.

What exactly should be an error is a good question.

In some cases, it doesn't make sense for an observable to emit an error at all. A case like this might occur when the observable is a permanent connection between two parts of an application.

On the other hand, we can use exceptions liberally for situations that are *expected* but which need to be handled in a different way from normal program logic. Network errors are an example of this.

Network errors and handling them

In this case, you can use an error to imply that the request failed for some reason. You can deal with this in a simple way—by logging that something went wrong.

```
combinedObservable
    .subscribe(
        pair -> drawList(pair.first, pair.second),
        error -> Log.e("Error occurred", error)
    );
```

The second parameter of subscribe is a function that's called when an error is emitted

Of course, this isn't a very nice way to handle the errors because it just means you drop the balls on the ground if the network request fails.

The nice thing about Rx is that you can manipulate the streams of asynchronous data in any way you want. In this case, you can use an operator called .retry.

The ReactiveX wiki provides one definition:

The Retry operator responds to an onError notification from the source Observable by not passing that call through to its observers, but instead by resubscribing to the source Observable and giving it another opportunity to complete its sequence without error.

You remember how you subscribed to the network observable in order to get a response? It turns out that subscribing itself starts the request. What retry does is simply try again and cross its fingers that this time you won't see an error.

But because you have two requests, you need to do the retry for both independently:

```
Observable<List<Entry>> combinedObservable =
    Observable.combineLatest(
        purpleFeedObservable.retry(3),
        yellowFeedObservable.retry(3),
        ...
    );
```

You define both of these operations to be retried three times before letting the error fall though.

In real life, the code that creates the retry logic is probably better put into the function that creates the observables, because initialization of the retry logic should happen transparently for all of them.

What to do when a real error comes?

What happens if the retry didn't help? Errors in RxJava work a lot like exceptions in function call stacks in many traditional languages. An error travels directly through the chain to the subscriber, and when the error reaches the subscriber, it aborts the whole chain. After an error is triggered, the stream is over.

This isn't desired behavior in our case, because even if one of the feeds fails to load, that doesn't mean you wouldn't want to show the others. In this case, for now, the most useful option seems to be to ignore the one that errors and at least display what you have.

RxJava provides a simple way to accomplish that: you can declare a policy for returning an empty list in case the feed network observable emits an error. The operator for this is called `onErrorReturn`, and it takes a function that knows how to convert the error into an item of data.

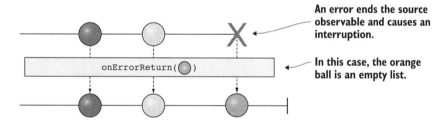

An error ends the source observable and causes an interruption.

In this case, the orange ball is an empty list.

Our network observables emit only marbles or an error, so they're a special case for `onErrorReturn`. It works the same nevertheless.

So where should you insert this? Because you want to show the feeds that didn't error, you have to do it individually for each feed observable. You could handle the error for the combined observable, but then even if one of the feeds failed, you'd see nothing.

The most natural place to insert this is right after the `.retry`. If you did it before the retry, the error would never get to retry. After the number of retries is exceeded, the retry lets the error go through, and you can then catch it.

```
purpleFeedObservable
  .retry(3)
  .onErrorReturn(e -> new ArrayList<>())
```

Again, the place isn't perfect because you'd need to copy it to the yellow one as well, but you'll build more solid network layers later.

Adding more feeds to the client

The `combineLatest` you saw takes only two parameters, so how is it useful when scaling up? Turns out it can take any number of parameters—even a list.

In your case, you happen to have a list of feeds. All of those feeds return a data item of type `List<Entry>`. The `combineLatest` becomes an aggregator for any number of feeds.

A list of feed observables

First you'll need to collect a list of all the feed observables you want. You'll make a list of the URLs and then call the `getFeed` function for each.

```
List<String> feedUrls = Arrays.asList(
    "https://news.google.com/?output=atom",
    "http://www.theregister.co.uk/software/headlines.atom",
    "http://www.linux.com/news/software?format=feed&type=atom"
);

List<Observable<List<Entry>>> observableList =
    new ArrayList<>();

for (String feedUrl : feedUrls) {
    observableList.add(
        getFeed(feedUrl)
            .retry(3)
            .onErrorReturn(e -> new ArrayList<>()));
}
```

Create an observable for each individually. You also add the error handling here.

Next you need to change your combine function to handle a list of lists. Because it's of the generic Object type, you also need to cast it while iterating:

```
Observable<List<Entry>> combinedObservable =
    Observable.combineLatest(observableList,
        (listOfLists) -> {
            final List<Entry> combinedList = new ArrayList<>();
            for (Object list : listOfLists) {
                combinedList.addAll((List<Entry>) list);
            }
            return combinedList;
        }
    );
```

Cast into the right type and add to the combined list.

Now you could, for instance, load the list of URLs from another location or let the user configure it.

combineLatest in detail

Your revised marble diagram still looks similar, but with the difference that you don't mind how many sources there are.

Here the inputs are defined as a list so you don't have to even know how many observables you have when writing the code.

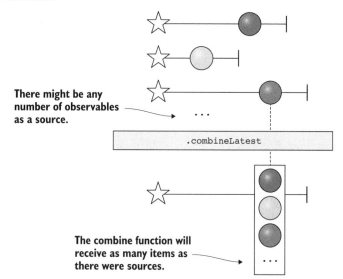

There might be any number of observables as a source.

The combine function will receive as many items as there were sources.

combineLatest with multiple marbles

In this example you've used only source observables that emit a single item (a list of feeds) and then complete. But if you did the previous coffee break exercise, you already got a feeling for how they work with more. Here's our marble diagram expanded to cover the case of more complex sources.

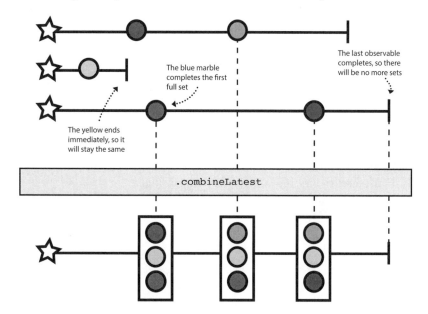

The last observable completes, so there will be no more sets

The blue marble completes the first full set

The yellow ends immediately, so it will stay the same

.combineLatest

Summary

In this chapter, you saw how to combine multiple feeds into one with individual error handling. This is one of the keystones of modeling Rx streams, and here the advantages of a reactive approach and RxJava are starting to show. With immutability, you no longer need synchronized blocks traditionally used in Java, and anything and everything can be asynchronous with ease.

At this point, you should have a reasonable grasp of how observables work and how to work with them. You'll later see how to create custom observables, though usually you'll get them through other sources, such as Rx libraries.

Further developments of the reader

There's still much to do for our news reader app. You can add better error handling (you have only retry and no indication in the UI) or features such as refresh and feed selection.

All of these are more or less straightforward with RxJava, though you have to stop somewhere. You can find an improved version of the app in the code samples, though understanding the code might require you to read a couple more chapters.

If you're feeling ambitious, here are some ideas:

- Show partial results even if all feeds don't give responses.
- Allow opening individual news articles in another activity.
- Show the source of each piece of news by tagging it right after retrieval.

From events to reactive state

The next chapter makes a little conceptual change in what observables can represent. RxJava is focused on *events*, but reactive programming itself is more than managing *state*. You'll see how these two relate.

Building data processing chains | 3

In this chapter

- Understanding the different roles of observables

- Building logical relationships between observables

- Breaking down a complex problem and solving it with the Rx tools you've already learned

Different roles of observables

As you already got a feel for in the preceding chapter, in RxJava the fundamental building blocks are indeed observables. They are technically simple: an observable emits a value whenever it has a new one. It can also complete or throw an error.

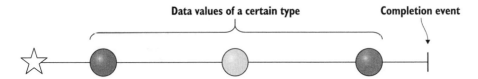

This is how all observables work. How they're used is up to us. Essentially, there are two uses for the `Observable` class: event observables and reactive variables.

Event observables

You saw observables being used as event sources, such as UI clicks or arriving network requests. This is event processing. RxJava is good at event processing.

This is what's typical of an observable that's a plain event source:

- Emitted events are time-based and can be filtered based on the time.
- Events contain little or even no data.
- The clicks observable is a good example of an event observable.

Reactive variables

There's another side to observables. An observable can be used as a reactive variable that tells everyone whenever it changes, as follows:

- Emits its possible previous state immediately to new subscribers
- When _updated, always emits its full state to all subscribers

Let's look at an example of a reactive variable that indicates the number of oranges in a basket.

Number of oranges in a basket

As an example of a reactive variable, imagine a basket of oranges. You'll use an observable to keep track of changes in the number of them.

```
// An observable for how many oranges are in a basket
Observable<Integer> numberOfOrangeObservable = ...;
```

Whenever someone puts more in or takes them out, the observable emits the new value immediately.

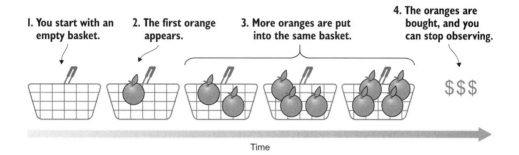

You can make this picture more concise by using an integer number to indicate the number of oranges you have at a given moment. In the marble diagrams that *represent* it, you can see a new marble every time the number of oranges changes.

```
Observable<Integer> numberOfOrangeObservable
```

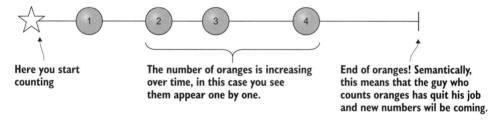

As time passes, you see a different number, and someone could even start taking oranges out of the basket. The observable is a representation of the way the entity changes over time; in this case, the number of oranges in a basket.

Events vs. reactive state

To get a better idea of what I mean when I say observables can either represent a variable or be simple event emitters that fire and forget, let's see an example that has both.

Click event observable

Let's start with an event observable that sends clicks on a particular part of the UI. Notice that the clicks are just events in time; you don't even have the pixel coordinates.

This is an example of a pure event observable. When you don't have any data to transmit, you can use the type `Observable<Object>`.

> ### Event observable
>
> From now on, we'll use the term *event observable* to specifically denote an observable that's used only as an event source. It doesn't represent any kind of state.

The switch button

Events don't have much information except for the time. But you can add logic that does something with the events. You *interpret the events into state*. In this case, you'll take the switch button as an example: clicking it turns it on and off.

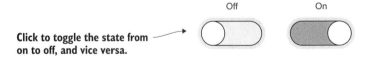

Converting events into state

If you consider the clicks you saw before as happening on the switch button, you can build a layer that interprets the clicks and changes the button state accordingly.

Switch button click event observable

Handle button clicks

Is switch on?

| false | true | false | true |

In a traditional application, the state could be represented as a variable. It could be, for instance, `Boolean isSwitchOn`. But because you're in the reactive world now, instead of the `isSwitchOn` variable, you'd rather use an observable.

Observable as a reactive variable

We'll now take the last step and create an observable of type `Observable<Boolean>` to represent the state indicating whether the switch button is turned on.

Switch button click event observable

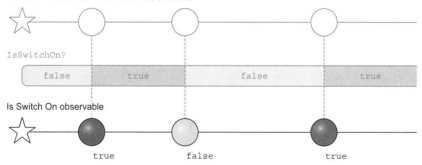

IsSwitchOn?

| false | true | false | true |

Is Switch On observable

true   false   true

Internal state of an observable

What you saw is a true observable: one that emits the full state whenever it changes. What changes is the variable the observable represents, and sometimes it's kept as an internal state of the observable.

The state the observable represents

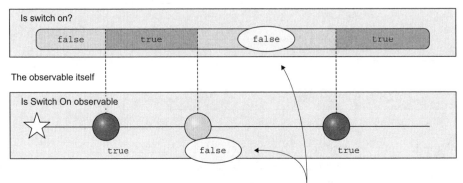

The observable emits the new state as an update whenever it changes.

The biggest difference as compared to the clicks observable is that this one emits the full state (a Boolean value) every time it changes. In case of an event, you didn't even have any data.

> ### Can you see the internal value of an observable?
>
> With some kinds of observables, you can indeed access the internal (latest) value of an observable without subscribing to it. The most notable one is called `BehaviorSubject`, which we'll cover later.
>
> But, in a real reactive application, *there's no need to access the value without subscribing*.

Dualistic nature of observables

With Rx programming, you're sometimes confronted by observables that *could* be either events or states. In these cases, you usually try to get the event processing out of the way as fast as possible and end up with observables that represent state.

When we talk about observables, we usually mean ones that represent state. Observables that don't are referred to as event observables.

Arrow diagrams and different observable types

One last thing is about the difference between events and state updates as you draw your charts.

Here you have the previous scenario depicted in an arrow diagram. It's just a different way of presenting the marble diagram you saw before; but as you can see, it doesn't show the internal logic of what converts into what.

What you do have, though, is an indication of what's an event observable and what's an observable that represents state. The latter is the "normal" one, so I've chosen a solid arrow to depict it.

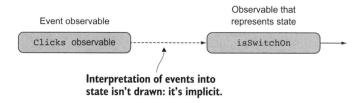

The observables are still of the same type, but what they're emitting represent conceptually different things, hence the indication.

Naming conventions

We don't always pay such close attention to the nature of the observables, but sometimes we choose to add the suffix `EventObservable` to the name of the event observables. It's quite long, but it also encourages us to convert them into state as soon as possible.

```
Observable<Void> clicksEventObservable = ...;
```

If all this sounds confusing, don't worry; often what needs to be done is obvious. When it's not, you can come back to this section and try to understand what's behind the observables.

Example: Credit card validation form

We'll now take a deep dive into dealing with observables that represent state. In this example, there are no event observables at all.

Credit card validator

Often reactive programming boils down to making a precise graph of relationships. To understand what this means in practice, you'll make a credit card validation form. It won't support all card types, though more could be added. I don't advise using this form in production, but it's an interesting case study—and validation certainly is a common problem in UIs.

Credit cards in particular have special validation rules, which we'll go through before starting. The form won't be trivial to implement with Rx, but it's even more difficult without it. So bear with me as we use what you've learned so far to make it happen.

The layout

I created a simple layout with a few text inputs and a button to send the form when everything validates.

There's also a small error text for debugging purposes, to show the list of validation failures, since there might be more than one. Check out the starting point online; it has the boilerplate code included.

How do credit card numbers work?

To establish a common domain vocabulary, let's first see what the different numbers on a credit card are called and understand their function.

creditCardNumber   expirationDate   cvcCode

creditCardNumber

The credit card number is the 16-digit number on your card.

A system is used to indicate the structure of the credit card number, depending on the card type. For instance, a Visa number starts with the number 4 and can have 13, 16, or 19 digits. MasterCard, on the other hand, starts with a 5 and always has 16 digits. You can see a full list on Wikipedia at https://en.wikipedia.org/wiki/Bank_card_number.

In addition to these conditions, all the card numbers have to pass the *Luhn algorithm*, a special check sum function. Fortunately you can find a good implementation online and won't have to write your own.

expirationDate

The expiration date is pretty straightforward. It's the month and year when the card can last be used. It's usually in the form of MM/YY; the month and year are both two digits.

cvcCode

The CVC check code is either three or four digits depending on the card type. With the card types that this example supports, this code is always 3 digits, except for MasterCard, which has a 4-digit CVC.

Validating the numbers in steps

Sounds like a challenge! If you didn't fully read the conditions on the preceding page, don't worry. Here are the steps you need to know when you start building the validation:

1 `creditCardNumber` conforms to one of the card types.

2 `creditCardNumber` passes the check sum function.

3 `cvcCode` is of the right length (depending on the card type).

4 `expirationDate` is properly formatted (MM/YY).

This is how you make sure the values in your text fields match the ones of a real credit card. As you saw in chapter 1, you can use the RxBindings library to make observables based on the text inputs you have. The created observables always emit the whole text they contain whenever it changes.

You don't have to worry about how to implement the algorithms or regular expressions themselves, because there are plenty of resources for those.

Inputs

You have three observables that represent the input of the user:

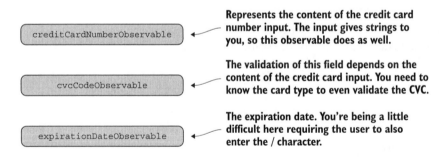

creditCardNumberObservable ← Represents the content of the credit card number input. The input gives strings to you, so this observable does as well.

cvcCodeObservable ← The validation of this field depends on the content of the credit card input. You need to know the card type to even validate the CVC.

expirationDateObservable ← The expiration date. You're being a little difficult here requiring the user to also enter the / character.

Outputs

Ultimately, you have only one goal—to know whether the entire form is valid and you're ready to submit. You define this goal as `isFormValidObservable`.

As soon as everything matches, you can enable the Submit button.

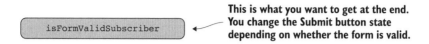

As soon as everything matches, you can enable the Submit button.

**This is what you want to get at the end.
You change the Submit button state
depending on whether the form is valid.**

Solving the equation

In terms of the Rx approach, you've defined the problem: you know what you have, and you know what you want to get out of the pipeline. You can approach it from either way—seeing how to start combining the inputs or what you need to get a satisfying output.

In this case, the latter is more straightforward. You need all fields to be valid, so you start building a *reactive graph* from bottom up. As soon as all the conditions are true, the `isFormValid` output changes to `true`. In RxJava terms, the observable emits the Boolean value `true`.

Here the observables on the bottom indicate whether the field they represent is valid. They're of type `Boolean`. You're missing the middle part of how to deduce whether a given field is valid.

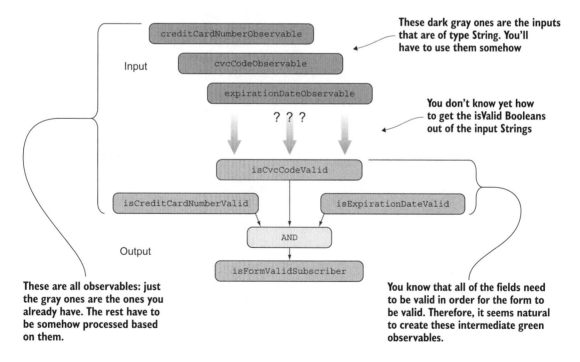

**These dark gray ones are the inputs
that are of type String. You'll
have to use them somehow**

**You don't know yet how
to get the isValid Booleans
out of the input Strings**

**These are all observables: just
the gray ones are the ones you
already have. The rest have to
be somehow processed based
on them.**

**You know that all of the fields need
to be valid in order for the form to
be valid. Therefore, it seems natural
to create these intermediate green
observables.**

First step: Expiration date

You'll start by splitting the problem into smaller pieces. You're now at a point where you need the three green boxes from the preceding page—namely, isCardNumberValid, isCvcCodeValid, and isExpirationDateValid.

Those are the ones that together define whether the entire form is valid. You can deal with the three one-by-one. Let's begin with the seemingly easiest one—the expiration date.

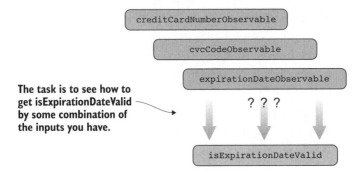

The task is to see how to get isExpirationDateValid by some combination of the inputs you have.

Because you know the pattern, MM/YY, you can validate against that. You'll make a function that takes a string and returns true or false depending on the string. You can use this one for now:

> **The processing functions are best declared static, because their only job is to transform data.**

```
class ValidationUtils {
  static boolean checkExpirationDate(String candidate) {
    return candidate.matches("\d\d\/\d\d");
  }
}
```

> **Checks for the pattern number, number, slash, number, number**

This is the function you'd need anyway, reactive or not.

The idea is that you push all of the values that come from expirationDateObservable to this validation function. This will create a sort of a wrapper that acts as an observable itself.

How do you apply a function on every emitted value of an observable? You already saw it; it's the map function.

You use the `map` function to create the new observable with a transformation. Notice that the type of the new observable is `Observable<Boolean>` instead of `Observable<String>`. You're applying a function that processes a string into a Boolean.

```java
protected void onCreate(Bundle savedInstanceState) {

    ...

    EditText expirationDateInput =
      (EditText) findViewById(R.id.expiration_date_input);

    Observable<String> expirationDateObservable =
      RxTextView.textChanges(expirationDateInput);

    Observable<Boolean> isExpirationDateValid =
      expirationDateObservable
        .map(ValidationUtils::checkExpirationDate);

    ...
```

This fills in the gap in the graph on the previous page. Just as with the dominoes and bells, when you have a new value in `expirationDateObservable`, the value goes to the `checkExpirationDate` function, and is further emitted by the `isExpirationValid` observable.

In the full system, it would continue on its way to the AND operator, as you saw before, but you'll get to that later. One thing at a time.

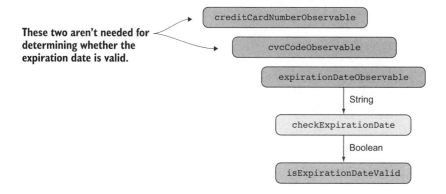

These two aren't needed for determining whether the expiration date is valid.

Credit card number type and checksum

The validation of the credit card number is a little more complex than the expiration date. Here are the conditions we need to fulfill:

1 `creditCardNumber` conforms to one of the card types.

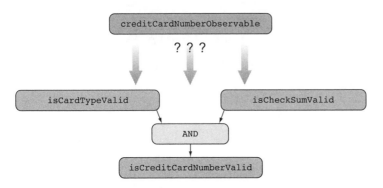

2 `creditCardNumber` passes the check sum function.

Card type

First you need the card type—in order to see whether it matches any of the ones you support. Because you already know the set of possible values, you can create an enumeration. You'll support only types in our example: Visa, MasterCard, and American Express.

The regular expressions for these three can be found online; this isn't a book about writing regular expressions.

```
Pattern regVisa =
  Pattern.compile("^4[0-9]{12}(?:[0-9]{3})?$");
Pattern regMasterCard =
  Pattern.compile("^5[1-5][0-9]{14}$");
Pattern regAmericanExpress =
  Pattern.compile("^3[47][0-9]{13}$");
```

```java
public enum CardType {
    UNKNOWN(-1),
    VISA(3),
    MASTER_CARD(3),
    AMERICA_EXPRESS(4);

    private final int cvcLength;

    CardType(int cvcLength) {
        this.cvcLength = cvcLength;
    }

    public int getCvcLength() {
        return cvcLength;
    }

    public static CardType fromString(String number) {
        if (regVisa
                .matcher(number).matches()) {
            return VISA;
        } else if (regMasterCard
                .matcher(number).matches()) {
            return MASTER_CARD;
        } else if (regAmericanExpress
                .matcher(number).matches()) {
            return AMERICA_EXPRESS;
        }
        return UNKNOWN;
    }

    private static Pattern regVisa =
            Pattern.compile("^4[0-9]{12}(?:[0-9]{3})?$");
    private static Pattern regMasterCard =
            Pattern.compile("^5[1-5][0-9]{14}$");
    private static Pattern regAmericanExpress =
            Pattern.compile("^3[47][0-9]{13}$");
}
```

> You already put here the lengths of the CVC codes because you know you'll need them later.

> The function that can transform a String into a CardType

> The regular expressions you already saw before

If you test this with a couple of example numbers from Google, you can see how it works:

```java
CardType visaType =
    CardType.fromString("4111111111111111");
// visaType == CardType.VISA

CardType masterCardType =
    CardType.fromString("5555555555554444");
// masterCardType == CardType.MASTER_CARD

CardType unknownType =
    CardType.fromString("1234");
// unknownType == CardType.UNKNOWN
```

> An example Visa card number, which always starts with 4

> What comes out of the conversion is an enum type.

> If you can't recognize the type, it's UNKNOWN.

This is what you needed: a function that turns strings into `CardType` enumerations. With this tool, you'll get back to the reactive world.

Checking for a known CardType

Next, you want to see whether the CardType isn't unknown (unknown cards are invalid). You do this by converting the user's text input and checking that it isn't of the enum type UNKNOWN.

```
protected void onCreate(Bundle savedInstanceState) {

    ...

    EditText creditCardNumberInput =
      (EditText) findViewById(R.id.credit_card_number_input);

    Observable<String> creditCardNumberbservable =
      RxTextView.textChanges(creditCardNumberInput);

Observable<CardType> cardTypeObservable =
    creditCardNumberbservable
      .map(CardType::fromString);

Observable<Boolean> isCardTypeValid =
    cardTypeObservable
      .map(cardType -> cardType != CardType.UNKNOWN);

    ...
```

The beginning is boilerplate you already saw.

Here you get the CardType observable from the number that's a String.

Check that the number isn't UNKNOWN. This observable will emit true as soon as a valid number appears.

Calculate check sum

The next condition for the card number is the check sum.

The check sum is calculated by counting the digits of the credit card number in a specific way. Here's the function in case you're curious. It returns true if the number passes, and false if it fails. Think of it as an integrity check for the credit card number.

```
public static boolean checkCardChecksum(int[] digits) {
    int sum = 0;
    int length = digits.length;
    for (int i = 0; i < length; i++) {

        // Get digits in reverse order
        int digit = digits[length - i - 1];

        // Every 2nd number multiply with 2
        if (i % 2 == 1) {
            digit *= 2;
        }
        sum += digit > 9 ? digit - 9 : digit;
    }
    return sum % 10 == 0;
}
```

For this algorithm, the digits need to be read in reverse order.

Multiply every second number by 2.

Sum the digits with a special logic.

Check whether the calculated sum is divisible by 10. If not, return false.

To use the check sum, you first need to convert the string into an array of digits. This is fairly trivial and has nothing to do with Rx, so we won't cover it here; you can check the online examples for the code.

```
. . .
Observable<String> creditCardNumberbservable =
  RxTextView.textChanges(creditCardNumberInput);

Observable<Boolean> isCheckSumValid =
  creditCardNumberbservable
    .map(ValidationUtils::convertFromStringToIntArray)
    .map(ValidationUtils::checkCardCheckSum);

Observable<Boolean> isCreditCardNumberValid =
  ValidationUtils.and(isCardTypeValid, isCheckSumValid);
```

Convert the string into an array of integers.

Apply the check sum functions and return a Boolean.

The big picture of the credit card number input validation

With the check sum in place, the full graph for validating the credit card number is ready.

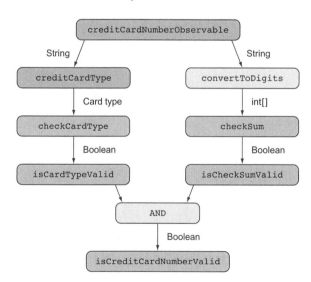

CVC code validation

That's two out of three done! The only input field remaining is the CVC. Bear with me just a bit longer. The validation condition for it is as follows:

1 `cvcCode` is of the right length (depending on the card type).

So you need to know two things: the length and the type of the card. You already have the latter from the previous step, so you can reuse the observable from there.

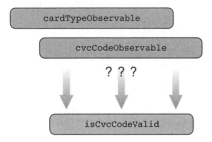

By now you pretty much already know the drill. You transform the `CardType` into the required number of digits in the CVC and compare it with the length of the actual CVC:

```
Observable<Integer> requiredCvcLength =
   cardTypeObservable
      .map(CardType::getCvcLength);

Observable<String> cvcCodebservable =
   RxTextView.textChanges(cvcCodeInput);

Observable<Integer> cvcInputLength =
   cvcCodeObservable
      .map(String::length);


Observable<Boolean> isCvcCodeValid =
   ValidationUtils.equals(
      requiredCvcLength, cvcInputLength);
```

The way this looks in the graph is nothing you haven't seen. The only difference is that you're using the `cardTypeObservable` as a source. It wasn't one of your original sources, but this is one of the cool things about Rx—as soon as you have an observable, you can reuse it for other calculations.

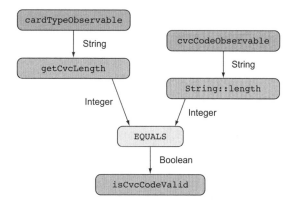

The story behind the AND and EQUALS

In a couple of places now, you've seen AND and EQUALS operators from the validation utils. What are these, and why aren't they part of the RxJava library?

You can see their implementation to understand that they're only short helpers—using our old friend `combineLatest`. You can see that they're simple wrappers for the `combineLatest` combine function.

```
class ValidationUtils {
  public static Observable<Boolean> and(
    Observable<Boolean> a, Observable<Boolean> b) {
      return Observable.combineLatest(a, b,
            (valueA, valueB) -> valueA && valueB);
  }

  public static Observable<Boolean> equals(
    Observable<Object> a, Observable<Object> b) {
      return Observable.combineLatest(a, b,
            (valueA, valueB) -> valueA.equals(valueB));
  }

  // Overloads with more arguments etc.
}
```

The combine function for an operation. It checks that the Booleans match.

The combine function for checking the object equality. In production code, you should probably do null checks too.

Putting it all together

You're now at a point where you have all of the green/shaded blocks from our first picture. You can next write the final lines that connect them and set the Submit button state correctly:

```
...

Observable<Boolean> isFormValidObservable =
  ValidationUtils.and(
    isCreditCardNumberValid,
    isCheckSumValid,
    isCvcCodeValid);

Button submitFormButton =
  (Button) findViewById(R.id.submit_form_button);

isFormValidObservable.
  .observeOn(AndroidSchedulers.mainThread())
  .subscribe(submitFormButton.setEnabled);
```

The form is valid only if these three conditions are fulfilled.

Subscribe with the function that sets the Submit button to enabled, depending on whether the form is valid.

When the code is executed, the runtime goes through your conditions and *constructs a dynamic graph in the memory.* You've declared what should happen when the text in one of the inputs changes, but you don't hang around to wait for it. Instead you leave Post-It notes with instructions for what to do when new data arrives.

Logging in FRP chains

For convenience, you might want to see what's happening during the execution of the program. For this, you can use the simple transparent operator doOnNext. This step in the processing chain is intended to cause side effects, meaning something that's not related to the data processing itself. A side effect could be writing logs. The defined side effect is executed for each passing item of data, and the data remains unchanged.

The doOnNext operator has siblings called doOnError and doOnComplete, for errors and complete notifications, respectively.

```
Observable<Boolean> isFormValidObservable =
  ValidationUtils.and(
    isCreditCardNumberValid
      .doOnNext(value ->
        Log.d(TAG, "isCreditCardNumberValid: " + value),
    isCheckSumValid,
    isCvcCodeValid);
```

You can add these logs anywhere you want in the chains. Here you'd write the value of isCreditCardNumberValid every time it changes.

The full graph

At this point, you can fill the entire gap you originally had.
Notice though, that it isn't Rx "code" as such, but just a logical
description of the way different input affects the output (ultimately,
`isFormValidObservable`). The code is the written description of this
picture.

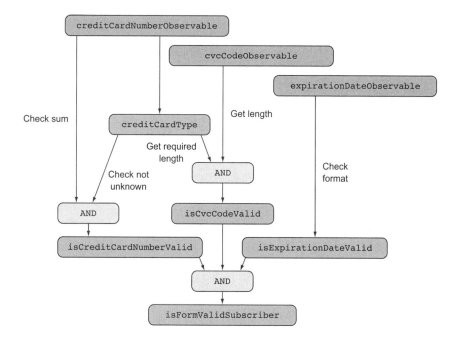

Coffee break

You may have noticed you didn't do the expiry date validation at all. You can now try adding it yourself: use the regular expression of two pairs of digits separated by a slash to create a simple validation:

```
Pattern pattern = Pattern.compile(/^\d\d/\d\d$/);
```

You then need to combine this with the others to determine the full validity of the card.

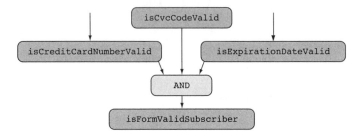

Solution

The bit that creates the observable to represent the validity of the field is a map with this regex:

```
Pattern expirationDatePattern =
  Pattern.compile("^\\d\\d/\\d\\d$");
final Observable<Boolean> isValidExpirationDate =
  creditCardExpirationDate
    .map(text ->
      expirationDatePattern.matcher(text).find());
```

You can find the full solution online.

The abstraction level of reactive programming

Let's take a little step back to explore what Rx is and why we use it.

You might have experienced (or heard of) the old days of programming with Assembler or a similar very low-level language. Those languages are behind all of our programs every day. Even if you run JavaScript in the browser, at the end it goes all the way down to the processor unit and is mostly unreadable to humans.

This brings us to *why* we bother with Rx; after all, it doesn't enable us to do anything that wasn't technically possible before. The key is that programs have become increasingly asynchronous, with many background processes and network requests. The touch screen also provides a whole other way of interacting with the program than a text console.

Rx doesn't allow us to do anything new, but allows us to construct larger and more complex programs that are still *human readable*. There's nothing you can't fundamentally do as pure processor instructions, but that's not practical. Just as in the modern world, the synchronous programming paradigms have come to an end, we need to make room for ways of seeing programs beyond the old, rigid ways of expressing them.

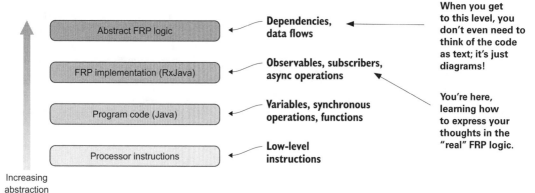

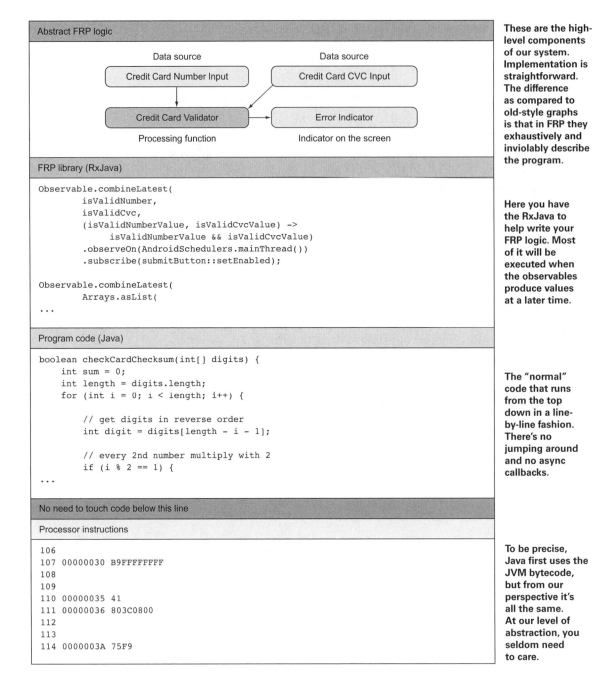

Abstract FRP logic

Data source

Credit Card Number Input

Data source

Credit Card CVC Input

Credit Card Validator

Error Indicator

Processing function

Indicator on the screen

These are the high-level components of our system. Implementation is straightforward. The difference as compared to old-style graphs is that in FRP they exhaustively and inviolably describe the program.

FRP library (RxJava)

```
Observable.combineLatest(
        isValidNumber,
        isValidCvc,
        (isValidNumberValue, isValidCvcValue) ->
                isValidNumberValue && isValidCvcValue)
        .observeOn(AndroidSchedulers.mainThread())
        .subscribe(submitButton::setEnabled);

Observable.combineLatest(
        Arrays.asList(
...
```

Here you have the RxJava to help write your FRP logic. Most of it will be executed when the observables produce values at a later time.

Program code (Java)

```
boolean checkCardChecksum(int[] digits) {
    int sum = 0;
    int length = digits.length;
    for (int i = 0; i < length; i++) {

        // get digits in reverse order
        int digit = digits[length - i - 1];

        // every 2nd number multiply with 2
        if (i % 2 == 1) {
...
```

The "normal" code that runs from the top down in a line-by-line fashion. There's no jumping around and no async callbacks.

No need to touch code below this line

Processor instructions

```
106
107 00000030  B9FFFFFFFF
108
109
110 00000035  41
111 00000036  803C0800
112
113
114 0000003A  75F9
```

To be precise, Java first uses the JVM bytecode, but from our perspective it's all the same. At our level of abstraction, you seldom need to care.

How RxJava works

You've seen how it's possible to describe a reactive graph with lines of code using RxJava. The instructions are executed first and create the dynamic graph in memory. Think of the RxJava code as the building instructions for the reactive logic, which is best described as a directed graph.

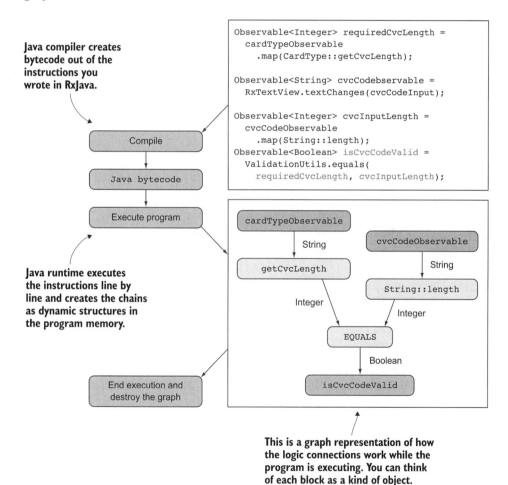

Java compiler creates bytecode out of the instructions you wrote in RxJava.

```
Observable<Integer> requiredCvcLength =
  cardTypeObservable
    .map(CardType::getCvcLength);

Observable<String> cvcCodebservable =
  RxTextView.textChanges(cvcCodeInput);

Observable<Integer> cvcInputLength =
  cvcCodeObservable
    .map(String::length);
Observable<Boolean> isCvcCodeValid =
  ValidationUtils.equals(
    requiredCvcLength, cvcInputLength);
```

Compile

Java bytecode

Execute program

Java runtime executes the instructions line by line and creates the chains as dynamic structures in the program memory.

End execution and destroy the graph

cardTypeObservable

String

getCvcLength

cvcCodeObservable

String

String::length

Integer

Integer

EQUALS

Boolean

isCvcCodeValid

This is a graph representation of how the logic connections work while the program is executing. You can think of each block as a kind of object.

Summary

This chapter was perhaps not as exciting as the previous ones in terms of how much easier or faster you can get things done in Rx. This time, we focused on how to break down the problem at hand and construct an Rx representation of it. *That representation becomes the actual program.*

Benefits of the reactive graph

After the graph is defined as you did, there's little room for strange bugs in which the validation ends up in a state that no one can explain. Each of the processing steps is fully traceable.

If there's nevertheless a problem, there are only two options:

- The implementation of the graph you designed is faulty.
- The graph itself doesn't match the problem you tried to solve.

Usually it's the latter case, which means that you overlooked an aspect or a particular combination of the way you thought the inputs are related to each other. Probably if you hadn't used Rx, this misunderstanding would have lived on and caused issues later.

Form improvements

The form as you made it isn't that usable; it complains about input errors even before the user tries to enter the correct information.

The solution is similar to what you saw, but you have to take into account whether the `EditText` is in focus. If the user is currently typing, you don't want to disturb them. The code for this didn't fit into this chapter, but you can see the solution in the online example.

You might want to get back to the extended example found online later, though, because it uses some techniques you haven't seen yet.

Connecting the user interface with networking | 4

In this chapter

- Using events as a trigger for data retrieval

- Taking a deeper look into how subscriptions work

- Making cascading network requests

Subscriptions explained

In this chapter you'll connect some dots and make data streams that start from the UI, trigger network requests, and end up being displayed to the user. Before you start, though, you'll have a quick look at subscriptions in RxJava programming.

We've talked about subscribing, but not so much about subscriptions. In short, the subscribe function returns a Disposable object that allows us to manage the created relationship between the observable and the subscriber. *Us* in this context is the creator of the logic—the observables and subscribers are just building blocks at our disposal.

To see how the subscription works, you'll explore a real-life example of a newspaper subscription. In this example, an actual newspaper is delivered to the mailbox every morning.

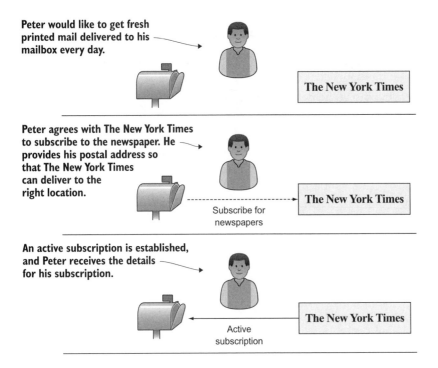

Subscription dynamics

After the subscription has been created, it defines a relationship between the source and the target—or the observable and subscriber. You've seen this before.

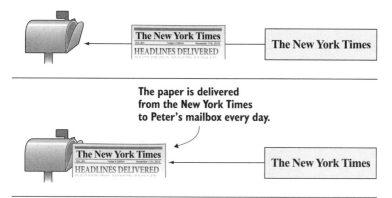

But, in our example isn't Peter the subscriber?

The answer is linguistically yes, but in Rx terms, Peter only establishes the relationship between the mailbox and the newspaper company. He's the one who *defines how the two should interact*.

This may sound a little strange at first. Think about it this way: the mailbox doesn't have any control over what's delivered into it; the same way an Rx subscriber *doesn't know where the data comes from*. It is completely unaware of a subscription.

What is Peter, then? It turns out Peter is the program logic you write: the graph itself. The graph logic contains the instructions that describe how the program should work.

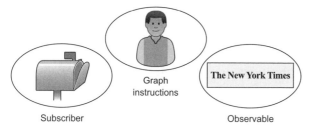

In this case, the logic could be written as follows:

```
newYorkTimesObservable.subscribe(petersMailbox);
```

Terminating subscriptions

There are two conditions for terminating a subscription:

- The observable signals it has completed.
- The `Disposable` object is used to cancel the subscription.

Both conditions are described next.

The observable signals it has completed

Let's say the newspaper subscription Peter purchased was for 12 months and he didn't renew it. After 12 months would *The New York Times* (the observable) one-sidedly consider the subscription completed and stop sending papers?

The mechanism in our Rx world would be akin to a letter of termination. The newspapers stop coming, and as a standard procedure *The New York Times* sends a letter that tells the subscriber that they shouldn't be expecting any more. (At this point in RxJava, the subscription is automatically released.)

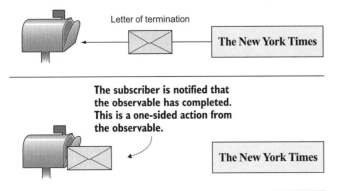

You've seen this behavior before. Our network observables work in this way: after emitting the data retrieved from the network, they send the `onComplete` signal and cut off the subscription.

The Disposable object is used to cancel the subscription

You can save the `Disposable` object created upon subscribing and use it to terminate the subscription. This scenario is less common. Usually, when you would need to forcefully terminate a subscription it's because something happened that made it irrelevant or undesirable.

In our imaginary scenario, you can say Peter has moved to another country and no longer wants to receive the newspaper. He calls the company, gives his subscription information, and asks them to stop sending the paper. The subscription is thus terminated from the initiation of Peter.

In this scenario, the observable never completes and you wouldn't receive the termination letter (the `onComplete` notification).

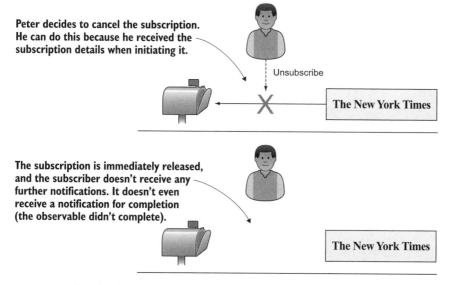

Peter decides to cancel the subscription. He can do this because he received the subscription details when initiating it.

Unsubscribe

The New York Times

The subscription is immediately released, and the subscriber doesn't receive any further notifications. It doesn't even receive a notification for completion (the observable didn't complete).

The New York Times

In terms of code, the whole scenario could look like this:

```
Disposable subscription =
    newYorkTimesObservable.subscribe(petersMailbox);

// Time passes..

// Unsubscribe in case the subscription is still active
if (!subscription.isDisposed()) {
    subscription.dispose();
}
```

Subscribe and save the subscription object.

Use the previously saved subscription reference to cancel it.

This is how all subscriptions work in RxJava. Other Reactive libraries have different ways—some don't even have subscriptions—but in the scope of this book, we'll assume the graphs are always established with subscriptions.

RxJava 2 concepts and subscription management

You already saw that a subscription is of type `Disposable` in RxJava 2. It used to be `Subscription` in RxJava 1, so what changed?

The new subscribe function signature

Because of the standard decided for ReactiveX, the observable subscribe function cannot return anything. But, the `Observer` object has a callback for receiving the `Disposable` object that can be used to terminate the newly created subscription (represented by the `Disposable` object).

```
public interface Observer<T> {
    void onSubscribe(@NonNull Disposable d);
    void onNext(@NonNull T t);
    void onError(@NonNull Throwable e);
    void onComplete();
}
```

The observer is responsible for handling the subscription by receiving the Disposable object.

But wait, this isn't the syntax you've been using. In our code, you just wrote this:

```
Disposable subscription =
    observable.subscribe(observer);
```

???

How can you save the Disposable here when the subscribe function doesn't return anything?

How is this possible? Also, how are you even supposed to get the `Disposable` object out of the observer itself?

Observers and subscribers

To refresh your memory, only the `Flowable` type takes the `Subscribe` class as the subscriber, but we never use it in this book. Observers are subscribers *conceptually*. They are, after all, used as parameters to the subscribe function of the different observable types.

Subscribe function overloads

Long story short, despite the ReactiveX standard, in RxJava everyone was already using the subscription in the way I described before—as something that the `subscribe` function returns. But, the standard dictated you need to have a `subscribe` function that *doesn't return anything*. As a compromise, the `subscribe` function was given several overloads that all return a `Disposable` that represents the subscription.

Ironically this leads us to a situation where we would never use the original `subscribe` method but always one of the overloads.

Basic consumer as a subscriber

The observables all have overloads for simple consumer functions to decide what to do with the emitted values.

The simplest one takes a function for `onNext`:

```
public final Disposable subscribe(
  Consumer<? super T> onNext
)
```

You can also provide functions to handle the `onError` and `onComplete` handlers, in that order.

LambdaObserver

If you want to create an observer as a single object, as opposed to a number of consumers, you can use `LambdaObserver`. It's exactly the same as the original `Observer`, but without the `onSubscribe` function.

Why isn't Disposable called Subscription?

By now you probably think that RxJava 2 terminology is a bit of a mess—and I agree! The last confusion is the creation of the `Disposable` class, because the `Subscription` class name is reserved for an internal implementation of the `Flowable` type. Again, though, we don't use `Flowable` in this book, so from our point of view, the `Disposable` object is the same thing as a subscription. Think of it as a way to dispose of the subscription.

Advanced Rx chains example: Flickr search client

In this chapter, you'll learn how to build a Flickr client that allows you to search for pictures. We'll use the Flickr JSON APIs, which provide the necessary information.

For most usages, the API has a rate limit, so you won't trigger it automatically as you did in the first chapter. In this example you have a distinct Search button that triggers the search.

It's a simple application, though you'll find out that the APIs that Flickr offers don't perfectly match our desired use case. You'll need to combine several APIs to be able to render the list you want—and this is where RxJava comes in handy.

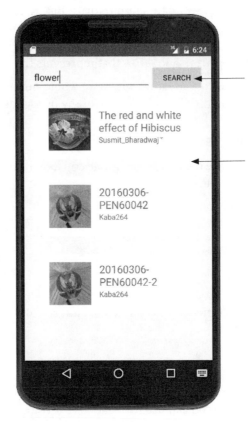

Search field where the user can write a string. Clicking the button initiates a search.

List of search results with thumbnail previews of the found items

API limitations and GraphQL

Lately there have been solutions that remove API limitations. One of the best known ones, GraphQL, allows you to execute a sophisticated query against the backend, removing the need to combine multiple queries in the client.

This is probably the future, but it'll take a while for it to become mainstream. Therefore, I have no doubt you'll find the networking techniques useful at least for the next few years.

Setting up the Flickr client project

Unfortunately, the times of publicly open APIs aren't like they used to be, and Flickr nowadays mandates you have your own free API key to make requests against their backends. Although I'd love to share mine, they limit how much each key can be used, so you'll need to apply for your own.

You can also follow the example without running it yourself, though I recommend your taking the couple of steps to obtain the API key.

Applying for an API key

At the time of writing, you can apply at www.flickr.com/services/apps/create/apply/, where you can choose the non-commercial license to get a free key. You will need to be logged in for this.

The Flickr App Garden

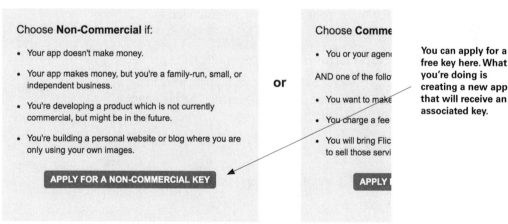

You can write in the description of your app that it's a test app. As long as you are using the API for the purpose of following the examples in this book, the free API is enough for you.

Putting the API in gradle.properties

When the API key has been granted, you can view it in the Apps By You section of the Flickr website. Locate it with your web browser in the App Garden section.

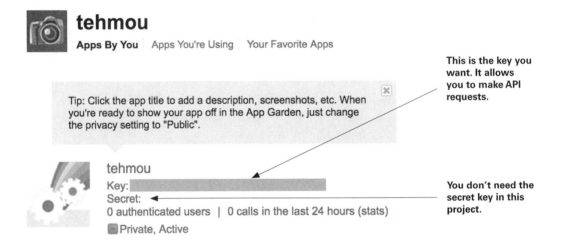

When you have the key, you'll put it in a place on your local machine that won't be committed to the code repository. In general, it isn't advisable to keep any API keys with the code

Gradle properties for local settings

Our example project has been set up in a way that it tries to read a Gradle property called `FlickrAPIKey`. Open or create the file on your computer that contains the *global* Gradle settings:

```
~/.gradle/gradle.properties
```

Then add a line at the end of it, defining the key:

```
FlickrAPIKey=<Your API Key>
```

Put the key you found in the preceding step here. You don't need to use quotation marks. You can try running the finished example to see whether it works: search results and pictures should appear. If you make many requests, you might be temporarily limited.

Overview of the search chain

In this simplified version of a Flickr client, you have only one user
journey, which is a search of public pictures posted on Flickr.

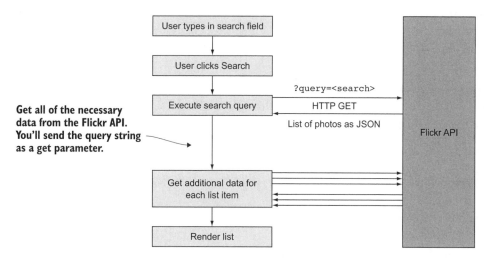

The APIs

You'll use three APIs to get all of the information you need. The first
is the list of all photos, and the two others get details for each picture
individually.

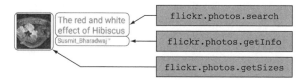

Step 1: A simple hardcoded search

You'll start by seeing how the search API works and test it by calling it on startup. This step 1 will be the longest of them, so bear with me.

You can find the documentation for the Flickr API at www.flickr.com/services/api/, where you'll also find instructions for setting up your API keys to use it. We'll do a search with tags, and the API you want to use is called flickr.photos.search.

Our examples use Retrofit with RxJava adapters, so creating the JSON API client is simple. You can find the details in the online examples. The signature of the API is shown here:

```
Observable<List<SimplePhoto>> searchPhotos(String apiKey,
                                           String search,
                                           int limit);
```

It takes the Flickr API key, your search string, as well as a limit to how many search results you want to see.

You made the client so that it automatically executes the network requests in the network thread. This is done through subscribeOn, which we'll cover in detail in the next chapters. If you try calling the Retrofit API directly from the main thread, you'll get an error.

The data types the search API returns

The search API is made to return minimal information about the photos found, so this is what you're dealing with (in pseudocode):

```
public class SimplePhoto {
    String id;
    String owner;
    String title;
}
```

In the real Java class, these fields are declared as final with only getters to them. This is to enforce immutability.

You have only the photo, the ID of the owner of the photo, and the title of the photo. Of these values, only the title is ultimately displayed to the user. There are a few other properties in the API, but at this time they aren't useful for us.

The API returns a list of photos. Because you use the class SimplePhoto on your side, the type is List<SimplePhoto>. You can just render them into a RecyclerView list for now.

Search and render

The code to render isn't complicated, and you've seen it before. For the record, here it is:

```
protected void onCreate(Bundle savedInstanceState) {
    ...

    searchPhotos(apiKey, "flower", 3)
    .observeOn(AndroidSchedulers.mainThread());
    .subscribe(this::updateList);
```

Switch the execution to the main thread just before updating the UI.

The updateList function handles the list update with the data it receives.

The updateList function does nothing but replace the contents of RecyclerView with the items you just received. You can assume that the search results will change dramatically every time you search, so it isn't necessary to use any smart updating strategies.

```
private void updateList(List<SimplePhoto> photos) {
    // Crudely replace the entire adapter
    PhotoAdapter photoAdapter =
        new PhotoAdapter(this, photos);
    recyclerView.setAdapter(photoAdapter);
}
```

Notice that the updateList function takes the new set of data as a parameter. It acts as the subscriber.

What you have so far

You can now see a basic list of titles in the screen shot on the left.

Notice that the previews and usernames are replaced with a placeholder, because from this API you get only the picture title and ID.

If you're wondering about the strange filenames in this particular search, it looks like someone has uploaded pictures straight from their camera. Most of the time, the titles are less cryptic.

At this point, we can agree that the client isn't yet very useful, though we can already see it coming together.

Making it click

A hardcoded search isn't immersive as a user experience. To get to a usable application as fast as possible, the next step is to add the text field and a search button.

You'll first make the input in the traditional way with event handlers and then streamline it into a proper reactive chain. You'll make heavy use of subscriptions and see how they're managed transparently in the chain.

Using an onClickListener to trigger a search

To make a quick and dirty implementation of the search, you can do this:

```
protected void onCreate(Bundle savedInstanceState) {
   ...

  searchButton.setOnClickListener(e -> {
    String search = searchTextView.getText().toString();
    searchPhotos(apiKey, search, 3)
       .observeOn(AndroidSchedulers.mainThread());
       .subscribe(this::updateList);
  });
```

Standard Android setOnClickListener is used to react to the click. This is what you'd do with Rx too.

Start the search as an observable inside the event handler.

Starting a network request like this isn't particularly elegant, but it works at least in the most common scenario. The problem arises if a search lasts too long and the user makes another one! Ideally, you want to abort any existing searches whenever you start a new one.

Using subscriptions

Whenever you call the subscribe method of an observable, it returns an object of type Subscription. It has two methods:

```
public interface Subscription {
    void unsubscribe();
    boolean isUnsubscribed();
}
```

The first one releases the subscription, and the second one checks whether the subscription has already been released (you don't want to release it twice, because that makes no sense and can cause an error).

Managing subscriptions

Because you have an activity at hand, you can save the last subscription into a field and check for its existence on consecutive button clicks:

```
private Subscription searchSubscription;

protected void onCreate(Bundle savedInstanceState) {
    ...

    searchButton.setOnClickListener(e -> {
        if (searchSubscription != null &&
            !searchSubscription.isUnsubscribed()) {
            // Release the existing subscription before
            // creating a new one
            searchSubscription.unsubscribe();
        }
        String search = searchTextView.getText().toString();
        searchSubscription = searchPhotos(apiKey, search, 3)
            .observeOn(AndroidSchedulers.mainThread());
            .subscribe(this::updateList);
    });
```

A member variable to hold your subscription between consecutive button clicks.

Check whether you already have a live subscription (ongoing search). If so, unsubscribe it (cancel the search).

Save the subscription you get when calling subscribe.

The stream approach

The preceding example code works, but it doesn't expand very well. What if you have multiple sources of UI events? Will you save a subscription for each? Is it even possible if they interfere with each other?

Fortunately, you need to know only that it does get complex, and that there's a simple way to manage *intermediate* subscriptions automatically.

How many subscriptions is reasonable?

The rule of thumb is that you explicitly subscribe only when you want to show the results—and only once during the lifecycle of the Android Activity (or any container for the Rx logic). Usually, if you end up calling `subscribe` in an event handler, something is wrong.

Keeping the subscriptions all in one place makes it much easier for us to react to errors and later to release the subscriptions automatically. Every time you end up needing to save a subscription, ask yourself, "Could I attach this to another chain of subscriptions instead?"

Coffee break

Before diving into a different way of handling
subscriptions, let's look at a couple of utilities:
`SerialDisposable` and `CompositeDisposable`.

SerialDisposable

When you want to replace an existing subscription with a new one
(dispose of the previous one) you can use `SerialDisposable`. It is
much like a manual version of a `switchMap`. It has a `.set(Disposable)`
method that automatically disposes of a previously set subscription.

CompositeDisposable

If you have multiple related subscriptions, you can use a
`CompositeDisposable` to bundle them together and treat them as one
subscription. This is useful, for instance, to dispose of them when the
component that uses them is destroyed.

Exercise in subscription management

This exercise has two parts. You need to create a new application as a
starting point.

1 Create three `TextViews`. Use `Observable.interval` to create an
   observable that emits a number every second. When the user clicks
   a label, that label becomes the active one and shows a changing
   number. Use `SerialDisposable` to make sure only one `TextView` is
   active at a time. (Don't worry that the interval will always start from
   zero when the subscription is reset. In the next chapter you'll see
   how new subscribers might trigger something in the observable.)

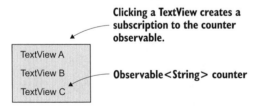

**Clicking a TextView creates a
subscription to the counter
observable.**

Observable<String> counter

2 Change the logic so that every time the user clicks a label, the
   label is activated, but doesn't reset any previous ones. Collect the
   subscriptions into `CompositeDisposable` and add a button to
   release them all at the same time.

Solutions

The exercises this time might have seemed a bit abstract. If you didn't fully understand them, don't worry, the process should be clearer when you see the solutions.

1 The trick here is to first create a `SerialDisposable` and an interval observable *outside* the click subscribers. You can then juggle the active subscription every time one of the `TextViews` is clicked.

```
Observable<Long> obs =
    Observable.interval(1, TimeUnit.SECONDS)
        .map(Long::toString)
        .observeOn(AndroidSchedulers.mainThread());

SerialDisposable s = new SerialDisposable();

RxView.clicks(textViewA).subscribe(ev -> {
    s.set(obs.subscribe(textViewA::setText));
});


RxView.clicks(textViewB).subscribe(ev -> {
    s.set(obs.subscribe(textViewB::setText));
});

...
```

This observable emits a new number every second. It starts from zero for each new subscription because of its implementation details. You'll later learn how to make it keep track of its progress.

2 The solution is similar, but instead of calling `.set` of the `SerialDisposable`, you call `.add` of the `CompositeDisposable`. One detail is that after you release the subscription you have to re-create the whole `CompositeDisposable` (as per its documentation).

```
CompositeDisposable s = new CompositeDisposable();

RxView.clicks(textViewA).subscribe(ev ->
    s.add(obs.subscribe(textViewA::setText))
);


RxView.clicks(textViewB).subscribe(ev ->
    s.add(obs.subscribe(textViewB::setText))
);

...

RxView.clicks(resetButton).subscribe(ev -> {
    // Unsubscribe and recreate the composite
    s.unsubscribe();
    s = new CompositeDisposable();
});
```

The same as before, but using the composite subscription

Here a simple unsubscribe releases all the subscriptions that you've accumulated so far. Normally, you'd either re-create the composite subscription or set it to null.

Implementing the reactive chain

Getting back to the Flickr example, you'll now see how to go fully reactive and eventually hide the manual subscription handling in the click handler. The only subscription that will be left is the one created for rendering the results, and you'll release that one when the activity is destroyed.

You've already seen text fields as data sources, emitting the text as it changes. For a button, this is a bit different, as you're interested in its state changes from down to up—in other words, clicks. No detailed data is of interest here, so the RxBindings library treats clicks as the Observable type (it used to be Void, but null values are no longer allowed).

```
Button searchButton =
    (Button) findViewById(R.id.search_button);
Observable<Object> buttonClickObservable =
    RxView.clicks(searchButton);
```

As a first step, you can use this observable instead of the event handler:

```
buttonClickObservable
    .subscribe(e -> {
        // Handle button click and ignore the e
        ...
    });
```

The subscribe creates a subscription, but at this point you won't manage it.

You can take it a bit further and include the text in the chain too.

```
buttonClickObservable
    .map(e -> searchTextView.getText().toString())
    .subscribe(searchText -> {
        // Handle the text search
        ...

        searchSubscription =
            searchPhotos(apiKey, search, 3)
                .observeOn(AndroidSchedulers.mainThread());
                .subscribe(this::updateList);
    });
```

Map the anonymous event into whatever text was in the field at the time the user clicked.

This is still the same as previously. You have a subscribe inside a subscribe.

The problem with this approach is that the subscriptions aren't connected after they're created: if searchPhotos is ongoing when you click the button again, it'll start a new, overlapping, operation.

The connected data graph

To connect the nested subscriptions into one clean stream, let's take a bird's-eye view of our data chain. It's drawn in the same fashion as the ones in the previous chapter—only this time you also have an asynchronous network API call that might take its time.

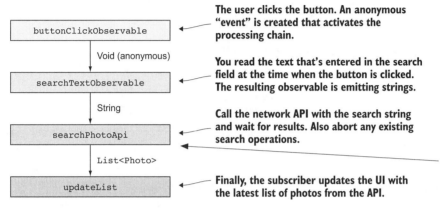

Starting an asynchronous operation in the chain

You've seen some asynchronous operations, such as debounce, that held the values for a given time, but this time you need another one, `switchMap`. It's a little like a map, but it allows you to return a new observable based on an item emitted from the first one. This new observable is then attached to the subscriptions of the original chain.

It sounds a lot harder than it is, so let's see how it looks in its final form and then dig deeper:

```
buttonClickObservable
    .map(e -> searchTextView.getText().toString())
    .switchMap(searchText ->
        searchPhotos(apiKey, searchText, 3))
    .observeOn(AndroidSchedulers.mainThread());
    .subscribe(this::updateList);
```

Only one `subscribe`! The `switchMap` operation does all the subscription handling and unsubscribes existing requests when a new one is created. Based on the button clicks, new `searchText` operations are started and connected automatically to the stream.

How switchMap works

`switchMap` does what you previously did manually. It makes sure that as soon as a new observable appears, you subscribe to it and unsubscribe the possibly previous ongoing one.

The following is an example sequence showing how `switchMap` works in the context of making sequential network requests.

1. The user clicks the Search button, triggering a request to the Flickr API.

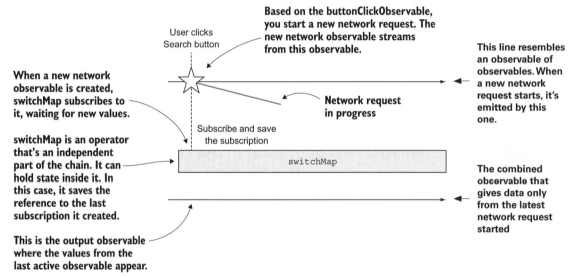

Based on the buttonClickObservable, you start a new network request. The new network observable streams from this observable.

User clicks
Search button

This line resembles an observable of observables. When a new network request starts, it's emitted by this one.

When a new network observable is created, switchMap subscribes to it, waiting for new values.

Network request in progress

Subscribe and save
the subscription

switchMap is an operator that's an independent part of the chain. It can hold state inside it. In this case, it saves the reference to the last subscription it created.

`switchMap`

The combined observable that gives data only from the latest network request started

This is the output observable where the values from the last active observable appear.

Up to this point, you don't see anything you didn't before. You're simply starting a network request (creating an observable to represent it) when the user clicks the button. The button click observable is mapped into an observable that emits network observables.

What's an observable of observables?

An *observable of observables* sounds more complicated than it is. In this case, you have an observable for clicks, and for each click you create a network observable—think of it as a two-dimensional array.

You'll return to this topic later in the chapter, so don't be concerned if the concept sounds complicated. It's more important to understand the desired functionality rather than to immediately understand the concepts that explain it.

2. The user starts a new search before the first one returns from the Flickr API.

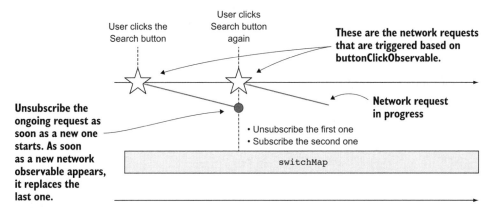

3. The network request finishes without further interruption.

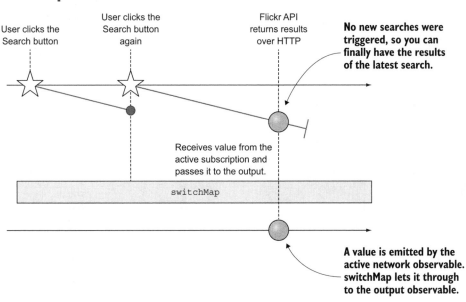

Getting thumbnail information

As you saw before, unfortunately you don't get the thumbnail URL
in the search API directly. For this, you need to go back to the API
documentation and find the proper API. In this case, you can use the
`flickr.photos.getInfo` that we wrap into a `getThumbnailUrl` function.

In a real-life application, you might want to render the list already with
partial information, but in this case you'll wait for all the thumbnails to
arrive before showing anything to the user.

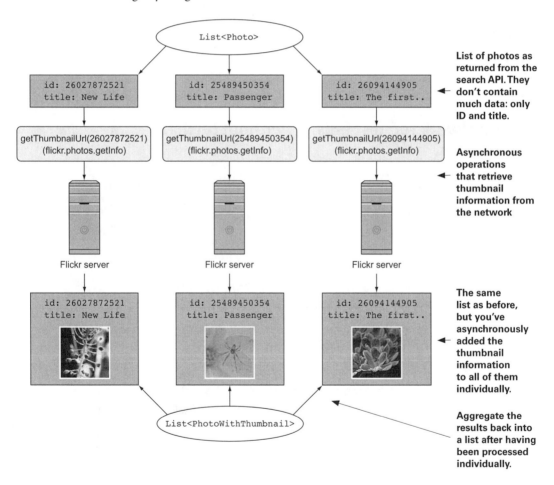

List of photos as
returned from the
search API. They
don't contain
much data: only
ID and title.

Asynchronous
operations
that retrieve
thumbnail
information from
the network

The same
list as before,
but you've
asynchronously
added the
thumbnail
information
to all of them
individually.

Aggregate the
results back into
a list after having
been processed
individually.

The list transform pattern

It's a common problem to apply an asynchronous operation to a list of data. This is also where RxJava shines compared to doing it in OOP style. In general, you need only three steps:

1. Expand the plain list into a single observable that emits all of the data items (of type Photo) on the list individually, one after another.

2. Apply any operations necessary to the "expanded" observable. Each data item gets the same treatment.

3. Collect results back into a list when all of the individual expanded chains have completed.

Step 1: Expand the list into an observable

Every time you get a list of photos from the search API, it comes as one chunk. You want to be able to handle each item on the list individually.

The mechanism to do this is to take the list and make an observable from it that emits those items in the same order. The function to use is called Observable.fromIterable.

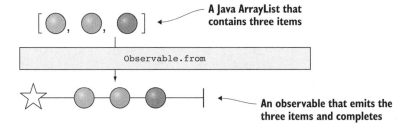

This is a function that converts a simple List type into an observable.

The flatMap operator

To convert a single item into subsequent multiple ones, you need yet
another operator. You want to take an observable that emits a list of
photos and turn it into an observable that emits all those items.

You already saw `switchMap` do something like this, but this time
you aren't interested in the "switching" behavior. `flatMap` works like
`switchMap` but *merges (flattens) all observables that it has started.*
`flatMap` allows for multiple operations to run simultaneously and
outputs everything. If you have experience with `flatMap` from pure
functional languages, try to forget those for the time being.

Let's start with merge, though, because it's related.

Observable.merge

`merge` is a function that takes observables and merges the results into
one:

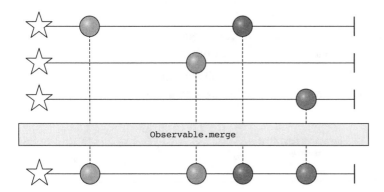

This function takes the source observables either as an iterable list or
an *observable*. This is where things get a little difficult to draw in two
dimensions, but if you think of a "list of lists," it's roughly equivalent to
an "observable of observables." The only difference is the observables
are like asynchronous iterables—the next item comes when it comes.

Observable of observables with merge

To understand an observable of observables better, let's forget the observables for a bit and start with simple lists. You'll still use marbles to depict data items, but everything here is completely traditional.

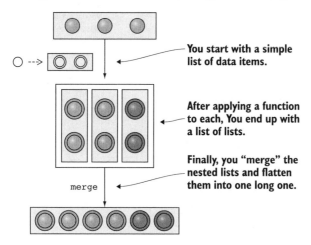

You start with a simple list of data items.

After applying a function to each, You end up with a list of lists.

Finally, you "merge" the nested lists and flatten them into one long one.

merge is the function that collapses the nested structure and returns a simple list again, though this time with the transformed items.

The steps are exactly the same with observables, but the difference is the asynchronous nature of observables. You also don't need to know whether the lists are even finite. As long as you're getting new items, you can push them to the output.

With observables, the most dramatic change to the lists is that the order of the items is no longer guaranteed—the nested observables might emit items at different times. Conceptually, it's still the same, though.

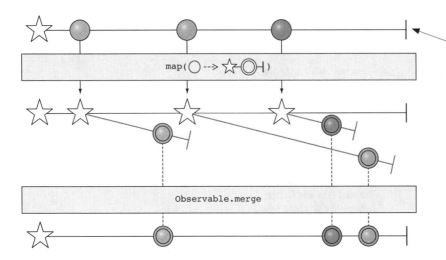

Observable of observables. You start a new observable based on a data value the source emits.

flatMap

The operator you're after is the exact same, but you simplify the syntax by abstracting the map function inside flatMap.

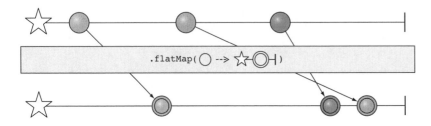

Using flatMap to expand lists

Using flatMap is much easier than describing it. You take an observable and call .flatMap, giving it to the function that will be applied to each item.

The only trick is that the transformation function must take a simple item and return an observable (which will be promptly merged into the resulting observable). The observable that's returned can emit any number of items, which will all be merged into the output. We'll combine it with Observable.fromIterable, which you saw previously.

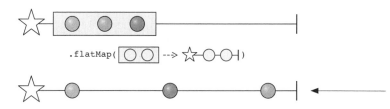

The lengths of the gaps between the marbles are irrelevant; only the order matters, and it's the same as in the original list.The contents of the list are emitted one after another.

How it looks in the code

You'll start from the observable that returns lists of photos and applies a flatMap to expand the list into a stream of singular items:

```
Observable<Photo> photoObservable =
  photoListObservable
    .flatMap(photos -> {
      return Observable.fromIterable(photos);
    })
```

This could be further simplified with a lambda:

```
Observable<Photo> photoObservable =
  photoListObservable
    .flatMap(Observable::from)
```

This code is the same as the preceding illustration.

Later you'll need to tweak the chain a bit, but for now this works for you, and you can see how to process each of the photos individually.

Step 2: Apply operations to each item individually

This part is more or less straightforward. From the previous step, you assume that you'll start with `Photo` and you expect to end up with `Observable<PhotoWithThumbnail>`. The result needs to be an observable because the information is retrieved asynchronously over the network. As before, the observable will emit one data item and complete.

In the following illustration, on the left, you see the different parts of the chain, and on the right the two observables—the top source and bottom output. There's a time shift between them, because the network request takes some time to complete.

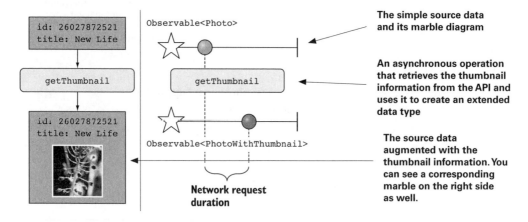

You'll look at the related code after going through the next step. Having seen `flatMap`, though, you can probably imagine how it could be accomplished.

Step 3: Collect results

You've seen how to use `combineLatest` to aggregate data from multiple source observables. You have a similar situation here, and indeed you could use `combineLatest` if you wanted.

But this time you'll structure your chain a little differently, and at the end you can use the `toList` operator to collect the final list.

The Observable.concat + .toList strategy

What you have is a separate observable for each photo. You want to somehow combine them into one observable that emits a list containing the data from all the sources. You'll use `concat` to combine them and `toList` to convert the combined observable into a single emitted list.

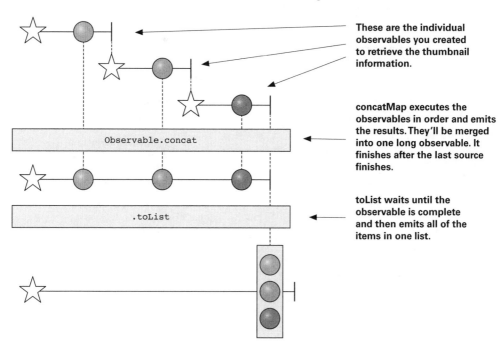

These are the individual observables you created to retrieve the thumbnail information.

concatMap executes the observables in order and emits the results. They'll be merged into one long observable. It finishes after the last source finishes.

toList waits until the observable is complete and then emits all of the items in one list.

The complete solution

Now that you've seen all of the parts of the processing chain, you're able to draw the full picture. It starts with `buttonClickObservable` and ends with a subscriber that receives the final list of type `PhotoWithThumbnail`.

The middle part is the most complicated, and here you leave out `concatMap` for simplicity. You'll see how it works in code on the next page.

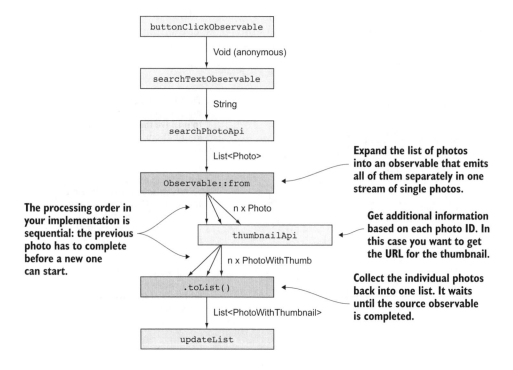

This time, you haven't yet written much code. The reason is the code is very short—but hard to read without understanding what's behind it.

The critical code in the middle of the graph

Because we didn't cover it yet, you'll first list the thumbnail processing code. You'll use a combination of flatMap and a nested concatMap combined with toList. Notice that all of the list expansion and processing is inside flatMap.

```
Observable<List<PhotoWithThumbnail>>
  photoWithThumbnailListObservable =
    photoListObservable
      .flatMap(photos -> {
        return Observable.fromIterable(photos)
          .concatMap(photo -> getThumbnail(photo))
          .toList()
          .toObservable()
      });
```

Inside flatMap is all the code to handle the list of thumbnails. This is after switchMap, so the "multiple click" scenario where you need to unsubscribe the previous operation is already handled.

toList returns a single observable, and you need to convert it into a normal observable so flatMap can accept it.

All together

Finally, with this last piece, you can put all the code together and have a working observable chain. At the end, you switch the thread back to the main thread and pass on the final list to the rendering function.

```
Observable<List<Photo>> photoListObservable =
  buttonClickObservable
    .map(e -> searchTextView.getText().toString())
    .switchMap(searchText ->
      searchPhotos(apiKey, searchText));


Observable<List<PhotoWithThumbnail>>
  photoWithThumbnailListObservable =
    photoListObservable
      .flatMap(photos -> {
        return Observable.fromIterable(photos)
          .concatMap(photo -> getThumbnail(photo))
          .toList()
          .toObservable()
      });

photoWithThumbnailListObservable
  .observeOn(AndroidSchedulers.mainThread())
  .subscribe(updateList);
```

Adding a username from another API

The last thing you're missing is the user who submitted the photo. You'll again go back to the docs to find out that the API that provides that information is called photo.info.

Because you already have a processing step for the thumbnails, you can expand it to do a bit more.

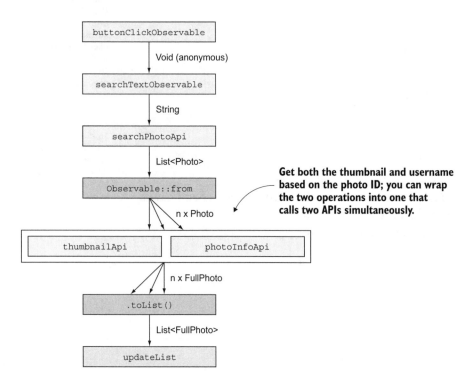

Expanding the processing function

The nice thing about FRP is that we need to touch only the nested processing function and change the `updateList` input type. Instead of getting just the thumbnail, you simultaneously trigger a request to another API that returns the username.

Because you have two network requests per photo that both need to complete, you can use a `combineLatest` with a suitable merge function.

Here you see an expanded processing step from the preceding page:

The source is an observable of a singular plain Photos.

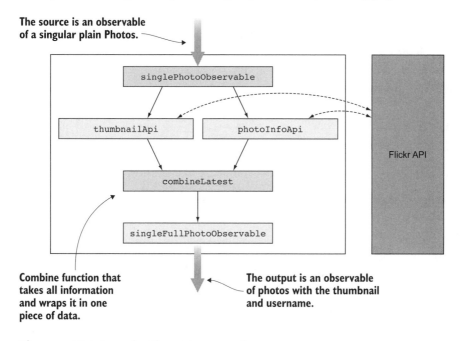

Combine function that takes all information and wraps it in one piece of data.

The output is an observable of photos with the thumbnail and username.

If you put it into code, it's not too complex:

```
Observable<List<PhotoWithThumbnail>>
  photoWithThumbnailListObservable =
    photoListObservable
      .flatMap(photos ->
        Observable.fromIterable(photos)
          .concatMap(photo ->
            Observable.combineLatest(
              getThumbnail(photo),
              getPhotoInfo(photo),
              FullPhoto::create
            )
          )
          .toList().toObservable()
      );
```

Takes the thumbail and the photo info to create the final FullPhoto data structure

Summary

In this chapter you saw how to efficiently deal with a tricky network API with RxJava. In real life, making two additional requests per data item probably wouldn't be acceptable for capacity and performance reasons, but in numerous cases these cascading strategies are necessary. You won't always be in a position to change the API to suit your needs or to build an intermediate server for your purposes.

Regardless, by making all data operations asynchronous with observables, you allow yourself to use any number of APIs (and any amount of time) to perform a step in your chain. This modularity creates resilience to change, as you saw in the last addition of the username. You needed to change only the function that processes the items, leaving the rest of the chain untouched.

Chaining operations

You learned to use the most important operations for creating real-world observable chains.

- `switchMap` is commonly used as the beginning of the chain. It makes sure you execute only one thing at a time, usually based on a user interaction.

- `flatMap` is the simplest way to combine observables, though you have to be careful not to expect to retain the order of what it produces.

- `concatMap` is slightly more exotic and doesn't usually have the best behavior because it prevents simultaneous execution. The same functionality can be achieved by using `flatMap` and making a specific ordering step after the results are ready. This way, the requests don't have to wait for each other.

Advanced RxJava | 5

Advanced
RxJava | **5**

In this chapter

- Creating your own observables

- Threading with RxJava

- Understanding subjects and what they're good for

- Cleaning up subscriptions

Observables and subjects in detail

You've seen observables in many forms, but in this chapter you'll learn how to create your own. Seeing the internals can help you to understand how the system works, even if usually this isn't necessary for the applications you'll build.

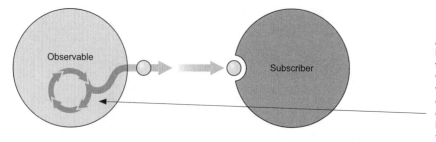

An observable has internal logic to determine when it emits and what. This logic is dependent on the desired behavior. In this chapter, you'll see how this logic can be constructed.

The second important topic we'll discuss is threading. You've already switched the execution back to the main thread in order to update the UI, but you never quite saw how it works. This time, you'll see what RxJava provides to freely manipulate the thread of execution, starting from the internal logic of the observable itself.

We'll also cover a new matter called *subjects*. A subject is a fusion of an observable and a subscriber, combining the best and the worst of both. You need to know how to use subjects, though it's perhaps even more necessary to understand why most of the time you shouldn't use them.

A value goes into the subscriber as it normally would. This happens either through a subscription or manually by invoking its methods.

Usually, the same value goes out with possible logic in between.

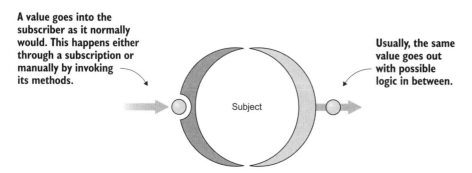

The preceding image is a simple abstract to help you get an idea of what I'm talking about, and we'll get into the details later in the chapter. You'll also see the valid use cases for subjects.

Example: File browser

As before, let's start with an example. This is a simple file browser that lets the user browse the external storage of their device. By clicking the directories in the list, the user can go deeper, and with the navigation buttons, the user also can move either one directory up or back to root.

File operations

There's no existing observable wrapper for the filesystem operations, so it's a very good example for you to see how to create your own. You'll create a utility that allows you to use file operations without blocking the main thread and integrate them seamlessly into your observable chains.

For this application, you need only the ability to list the contents of a folder. This operation isn't a particularly expensive one but serves as a good example. By creating observables for the operation, you're free to easily push them into a background thread while waiting for the results.

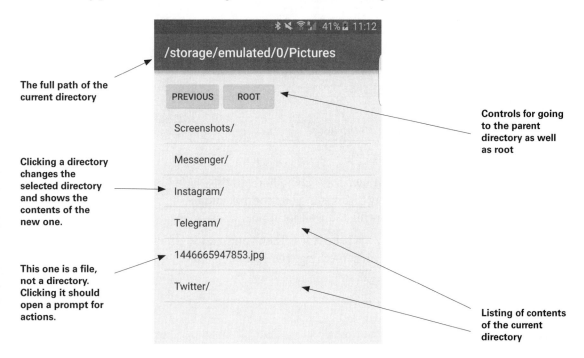

The full path of the current directory

Controls for going to the parent directory as well as root

Clicking a directory changes the selected directory and shows the contents of the new one.

This one is a file, not a directory. Clicking it should open a prompt for actions.

Listing of contents of the current directory

User flow of the File Browser app

The high-level description of this application is divided into two parts: the UI as presented by the platform, and the reactive logic that you'll construct. The logic deals with only data. The interaction points between the two are carefully defined, because you want to keep them conceptually separate.

In this diagram, the left side contains what's shown on the screen by the operating system. The right side shows the pure logic you use to process the data and input.

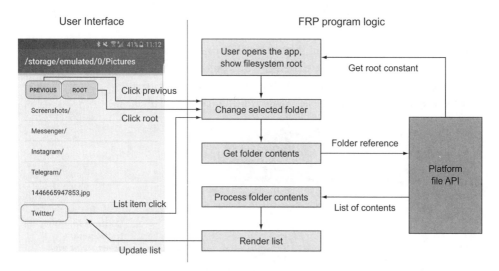

You can start to see the borders of our own logic chain here. In this graph, everything that happens in gray boxes is in your control, and in specific locations you let go of the control and wait for inputs.

First you do everything needed to draw a list of files. Then you sit and wait for further input—you react only if something changes.

Analysis of the file browser graph

You can break the graph on the previous page into different responsibility areas. In the middle, you have your own code that's the core logic. The other areas are either providing input or are targets for your output (side effects).

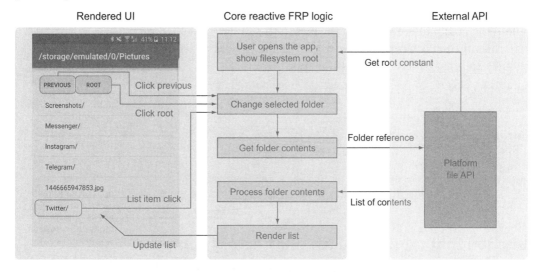

Here are the highlights of the input and output. The ones that start an operation that you expect to complete are a bit of a special case.

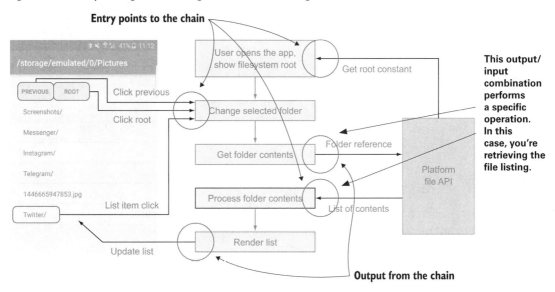

Getting the file listing for a directory

The easiest way to start is by seeing how the directory listing works on Android systems. This is an implementation detail, but we'll cover it briefly to set the context.

You'll first retrieve just the root of the filesystem and show its contents without the possibility of browsing the files in the UI. For this purpose, you'll this time make a *custom observable* that can be created based on a directory and that emits a list of its contents.

This is the operation you'll implement as an observable. It's intended to occur in the background thread.

The rough graph looks like this:

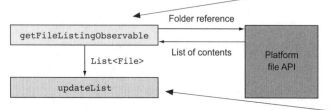

updateList knows how to draw a list of File objects. It'll render directories slightly differently.

Function that returns the list of directory contents

The code to get the contents of a directory is simple. Here's the needed function in its entirety:

This function is potentially expensive. It's probably a good idea to put it into a background thread.

```
List<File> getFiles(File file) {
    List<File> fileList = new ArrayList<>();
    File[] files = file.listFiles();

    for (File file : files) {
        if (!file.isHidden() && file.canRead()) {
            fileList.add(file);
        }
    }
    return files;
}
```

Don't show hidden or prohibited files.

Android permissions

In newer versions of Android, you need to request special permission for filesystem access during runtime. You can find a template that has everything set up in the online code repository.

Custom observables with Observable.create

As you saw before, observables have a few rules to abide by:

- An observable may emit any number of data items, or none at all.

- An observable may complete or error, but only one, and the observable isn't allowed to emit any data items afterward.

Emitters

At the core of each observable is an emitter. It's used to trigger the different events the observable can emit. The basic emitter is this:

```
public interface Emitter<T> {
    void onNext(T value);
    void onError(Throwable error);
    void onComplete();
}
```

onNext is where you can emit the values (marbles) from the observable.

Observable.create

Your aim is to create a function that receives an emitter and calls the appropriate methods within the rules defined. This function is given to `Observable.create`, which creates the observable around the emitter.

You use it like this:

```
Observable o = Observable.create(emitter -> { ... });
```

The point of interest here is what you do in the function, which you have to define. The function is of this signature:

```
void observableOnSubscribeFunction(Emitter<T> emitter)
```

The signature looks a little unusual, but next you'll see how it's used so you can better understand it. At this point, just remember, *the* `subscribe` *function is the function that is called every time a new subscription is made.*

Which part of this is your responsibility to implement?

The only thing you need to define is `onSubscribeFunction`. This function fully defines what the Observable does and when. You'll see an example next, so don't worry if you feel like you're missing something.

Wrapping the file listing function into FileListingObservable

Now that you know how `Observable.create` works, you can wrap the file listing function into an observable. The code for this is shown here:

```
Observable<List<File>> createFilesObservable(File file) {

    // Create a new observable based on the file we
    // received in the arguments
    return Observable.create(emitter -> {
        try {

            // Retrieve the list of files
            final List<File> fileList = getFiles(file);

            // Give files to the subscriber
            emitter.onNext(fileList);

            // Signal the subscribers we are done
            emitter.onComplete();

        } catch (Exception e) {

            // An exception was thrown, let the subscriber
            // handle it as it sees fit
            emitter.onError(e);
        }
    });
}
```

This is the new emitter that you can use with the new subscription. The work starts now!

You use the function you created previously. It's executed in this subscribe function.

This is where you pass the results to the subscriber through the emitter.

Any potential errors are inserted into the chain through onError.

It's important to notice that what you emit here goes to the next subscriber, which might not be the final one. The graph, or the chain, of observables is based on stacked subscribers and emitters, and you can provide events for only the *next processing operation*.

It's worth mentioning that your `Observable.create` doesn't support canceling, which could be a desired behavior. Even if the subscriber unsubscribes, you continue to execute, and the notifications you produce would be thrown away. You can find examples online of how to do this.

Lifecycle of the files list observable

Now that you have an observable, let's look at how it behaves over the course of the program execution:

1 Create a new observable based on a directory:

2 Subscribe to the freshly created observable. In this case you create the observable on the spot and subscribe immediately. The subscriber would be as follows:

```
filesObservable =                         getFileListingObservable
    createFilesObservable(
        directory                             directory
    )
                                          subscribeFunc(emitter) {
filesObservable                               ...
    .subscribe(                           }
        emitter
    )
```

3 Execute the internal logic of the observer, possibly in another thread.

```
getFileListingObservable

        directory

subscribeFunc(emitter) {              directory          Platform
    files =                                              file API
        getFiles(directory)
    ..                                    files
}
```

4 Pass the results to the subscriber, which might in reality be the next step in the processing chain.

```
getFileListingObservable              subscriber {

        directory                         onNext(files) {
                                              // do something with
subscribeFunc(emitter) {                      // files
    files =                               }
        getFiles(directory)           }
    emitter.onNext(files)
}
```

Threading basics

Next you'll look at how to push the file operations into a background thread. To understand the threading a bit better, however, you'll first take a little detour under the surface and see what threading means in the context of functional programming.

What is threading, anyway?

The computer (processor, CPU, core) is able to execute only synchronous instructions, much like a calculator. In terms of code, the computer goes though it line by line.

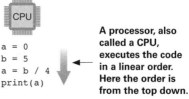

A processor, also called a CPU, executes the code in a linear order. Here the order is from the top down.

Because increasing the speed of a single processor is difficult, smart people came up with the concept of *parallel computing*. The idea is simple: instead of having one processor running one set of instructions, let's have two or four— and get double or quadruple speed.

Simultaneous execution

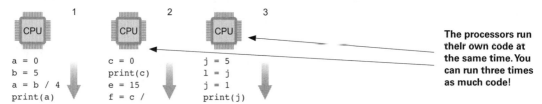

The processors run their own code at the same time. You can run three times as much code!

The idea is that all these processors run parts of *the same application*. After all, usually a human user wants to use only one at a time. Usually, each processor represents a different *thread*. That's why two threads can run physically at the same time: they run in different CPUs.

Thread #1   Thread #2   Thread #3

Problems in paradise

What's the problem, then? Why isn't threading the holy grail of performance?

The short answer is state manipulation. If two pieces of code are run simultaneously on different threads, they still need to update the same UI and use the same system resources. You end up with situations such as this:

A classic situation of code interleaving. The code on the left is executed at the same time as the code on the right, but they use the same variable file. You receive a new file while you're still processing the old one, ending up with strange effects.

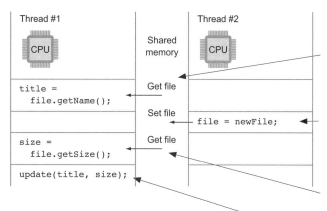

First you read the title from the variable file.

Whoops! A new file has been selected in another thread. The old one is replaced immediately.

The file has been changed in another thread! You didn't even notice.

Now the title will be from the old file, and the size from the new one.

Functions with inputs and outputs

What you saw in the preceding example is bad—you can't trust that a variable stays the same even while executing a single code block. It's also known as a *race condition*, where two threads are competing over whose changes remain.

The traditional mitigation of this is called *thread locking*. It protects a variable from being accessed from another thread while you're working with it. This is otherwise great, but can cause performance problems and something called a *deadlock*. In a deadlock, two threads are forever waiting for each other to finish whatever they were doing.

With Java, the threading challenges also get worse: values between threads aren't even guaranteed to synchronize immediately unless the variable is declared as `volatile`. How often have you seen that keyword used? Anything else works *most of the time* between threads.

Anyway, enough of the horror stories. We'll next see how to solve this.

Threading in functional programming

Functional programming is a special style of programming that has principles that makes it easy to do threading. FRP uses a subset of these functional programming principles.

You've already seen how to do your calculation using *immutable* data objects. This completely eliminates the issues of another thread messing up your state or the way it's updated in other threads.

The aim is to create functions that take input and produce output—without changing any variables outside of their scope.

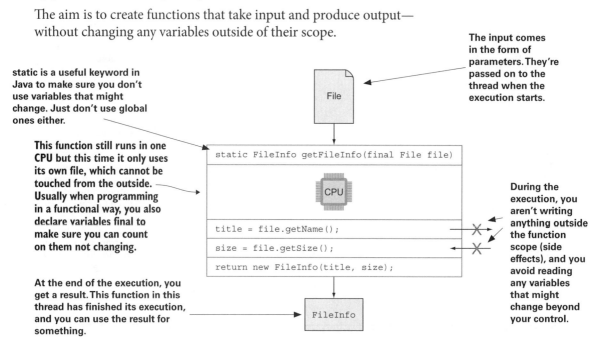

static is a useful keyword in Java to make sure you don't use variables that might change. Just don't use global ones either.

This function still runs in one CPU but this time it only uses its own file, which cannot be touched from the outside. Usually when programming in a functional way, you also declare variables final to make sure you can count on them not changing.

The input comes in the form of parameters. They're passed on to the thread when the execution starts.

During the execution, you aren't writing anything outside the function scope (side effects), and you avoid reading any variables that might change beyond your control.

At the end of the execution, you get a result. This function in this thread has finished its execution, and you can use the result for something.

```
static FileInfo getFileInfo(final File file)

                    CPU

title = file.getName();
size = file.getSize();
return new FileInfo(title, size);
```

This kind of a function is called a *pure function*. It's a bit like mathematics, just calculating things. It can do something complex, but the key is to be careful not to interfere with other functions that might be running at the same time in different threads.

Pure functions are an important concept to understand, because they're the most modular building blocks of a program. You can always call a pure function from wherever you want, and you know it won't cause anything bad. You also don't need an instance of a class to call it, making it much easier to use elsewhere.

Function chaining in reactive

As you saw already, you can have a chain of these simple functions, with the next function consuming the outputs of the last. The CPUs (using threads) become processing lines for individual functions. The functions share information only when they're finished or starting, so that data can always stay immutable.

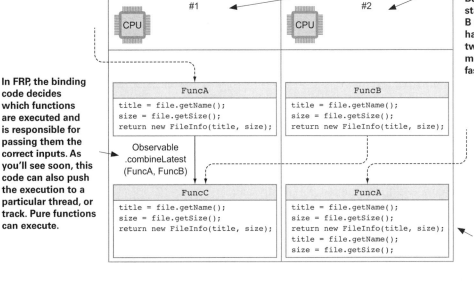

In FRP, the binding code decides which functions are executed and is responsible for passing them the correct inputs. As you'll see soon, this code can also push the execution to a particular thread, or track. Pure functions can execute.

The number of "tracks" could be as many as you want, because your operations are pure. But here you can't start C until A and B are completed, so having more than two CPUs wouldn't make the execution faster.

FuncA is executed again on the second track, but with different input. Its simultaneous execution doesn't influence FuncC in any way.

Showing results with side effects

But how do you get anything done with immutable data? In the end, do you want to have changes made?

This is where you need to cause *side effects*. A side effect is something that causes changes in parts of the program that aren't in the scope of the function. The most common side effect is drawing in the UI. It could also be logging, networking, or even closing the whole application.

In RxJava, you normally try to execute all side effects in subscribers. There are some exceptions, but generally it's good to delay side effects until the end.

Changing the thread by using getFileListingObservable

Using the `createFileObservable` function is nothing you haven't seen before. You call it with a suitable file, and it returns a brand new observable.

For now, you'll use the filesystem root as a hardcoded point of entry:

```
final File root = new File(
    Environment.getExternalStorageDirectory().getPath());


createFilesObservable(root)
    .observeOn(AndroidSchedulers.mainThread());
    .subscribe(this::updateList);
```

Thread changes

To get an understanding of which code is executed in which thread, let's look at a generic example. Here you can see a list of custom functions that are part of the chain, excluding the RxJava boilerplate:

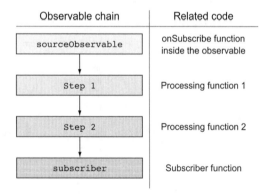

You've seen others before, but the `onSubscribe` function of the observable is new. It's important to notice that it's part of the chain, even if you wouldn't usually create it yourself, but use a source such as the button clicks observable.

With RxJava operators, you can arbitrarily change the thread for any of the steps.

Thread changes with observeOn

You've already seen `observeOn`, but you haven't been formally introduced. It usually reads *as all operations after `observeOn` are in the thread it defines*. In this example, you ensure that the thread is the main thread:

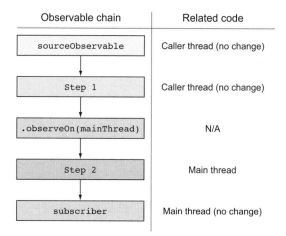

Here's another example of `observeOn` with two separate thread changes: the latter overrides the former.

Observable chain	Thread
sourceObservable	Caller thread (no change)
.observeOn(IO)	N/A
Step 1	I/O thread
.observeOn(mainThread)	N/A
Step 2	Main thread
subscriber	Main thread (no change)

Thread changes with subscribeOn

But what if you want to change the thread of the *observable* itself?
In this case, you'd run the file operations on the I/O thread to avoid
possible blocking of the UI.

The answer is the `subscribeOn` operation, which defines the thread
for this particular code. However, it works a bit differently from
`observeOn`:

- The observable `onSubscribe` function is executed in the thread
  `onSubscribe` defines.

- The first `subscribeOn` in the chain prevails.

The second point is important, even if a little unintuitive. You can
define the observable thread only once, and all further ones are *ignored*.

Here's an example of the most common case. The thread of the source is
changed, resulting in the whole chain staying on it (usually operations
don't change the thread):

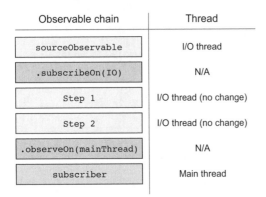

Observable chain	Thread
`sourceObservable`	I/O thread
`.subscribeOn(IO)`	N/A
`Step 1`	I/O thread (no change)
`Step 2`	I/O thread (no change)
`.observeOn(mainThread)`	N/A
`subscriber`	Main thread

At the end, you return to the main thread, because you can't manipulate
the UI from the I/O thread. A couple of rules of thumb for threading:

- Start the chain in a thread that's suitable (usually the background
  thread).

- Change the thread to the main thread just before subscriber.

In RxJava, `subscribeOn` is a special operator that's arguably a little inconvenient. There's no real "right" place for it in the chain; its placement all depends on your application logic.

In general, if you have a heavy or a long operation, such as networking, timers, or data queries, it sometimes makes sense to immediately change the thread already at the source. These kinds of observables can be expected to run in other threads, and the consumer can switch the thread back to something else if necessary.

But, the other side of the argument is that all code should be as modular as possible, enabling different threading configurations from the side of the caller. Enforcing a thread in the lower levels of the application should be done only for expensive operations, and not "just in case."

Using subscribeOn in your code

With our new operator we can easily change the thread of the file operation that's inside your custom observable:

```
createFilesObservable(root)
    .subscribeOn(Schedulers.io())
    .observeOn(AndroidSchedulers.mainThread());
    .subscribe(this::updateList);
```

Make sure you start the chain from the I/O thread.

Notice that you *could* define `subscribeOn` at any point, as long as there's only one.

Here's the same illustration you saw before, though there are no operations in between yet.

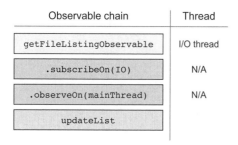

Observable chain	Thread
getFileListingObservable	I/O thread
.subscribeOn(IO)	N/A
.observeOn(mainThread)	N/A
updateList	

Making the file listing dynamic

Your implementation so far isn't useful with the hardcoded root as the path:

```
createFilesObservable(root)
   ...
```

The root here
never changes.

You'll change this now and make a proper dynamic chain. The user's interactions will change the options presented by feeding them back into the chain.

Switching to fileObservable as the source

Because you're always showing the contents of a single folder, it seems logical to use that as the source for what you're showing. Because this will change when the user clicks a file, it should be an observable.

Here you have a simple user journey in which the user is first shown the list of the files and folders at the root of the filesystem. The user then clicks the folder Instagram, causing an update of the file listing shown on screen.

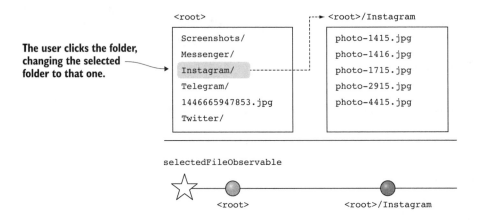

Shaping the full chain

In the end, your chain should look something like this:

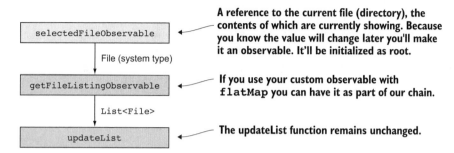

selectedFileObservable ← A reference to the current file (directory), the contents of which are currently showing. Because you know the value will change later you'll make it an observable. It'll be initialized as root.

File (system type)

getFileListingObservable ← If you use your custom observable with `flatMap` you can have it as part of our chain.

List<File>

updateList ← The updateList function remains unchanged.

But to get started quick and dirty, you can make a simple change: instead of hardcoding the root into the function invocation, you hardcode it into a separate observable that emits only that one item.

Observable.just

The way to create an observable from a single data item is called `Observable.just`. It takes a piece of data and returns an observable that emits only that item and completes. You can use it as the start of your chain.

Because you're switching to use an observable as a source, you also have to trigger the file operation based on the new selected folder. You'll use `switchMap` to do the chaining—at this point, the selected folder won't change, but you'll get to that in a bit.

```
Observable.just(root)
  .switchMap(file ->
    createFilesObservable(file)
      .subscribeOn(Schedulers.io())
  )
  .observeOn(AndroidSchedulers.mainThread())
  .subscribe(this::updateList);
```

You also move `subscribeOn` to be immediately after the observable creation. It would work outside `switchMap`, but this way it's clearer that you want to move precisely this operation to the I/O thread.

Making the list click

Now the interesting part: adding handling for clicking the list items to go deeper in the file tree. Because you already have an observable to represent the selected file, you probably want to insert the new one there as well. This observable would have an initial value of the root of the filesystem and then be changed whenever the user clicks.

Before you go into the implementation, here's an illustration of what you want to accomplish:

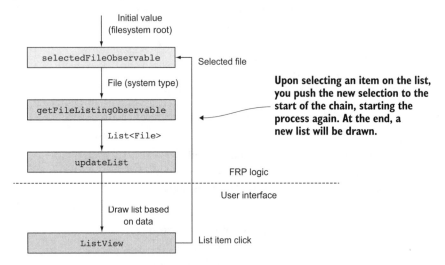

You've expanded the graph from before to include the UI. You need to react to changes coming from there and insert them back into your chain. The dashed line signifies the border between pure program code and the representation to the user. From the logic point of view, you don't care how the information is presented, as long as you get the necessary feedback in the form of a new selected file.

A first implementation with subjects

As usual, you'll make a rough implementation first to get an idea of what's necessary. You'll then clean it up to make it more robust and easier to maintain.

What you want now is to somehow make `selectedFileObservable` emit a new value when a list item is clicked. The `Observable.just` you put in place emits one value and completes.

Subjects

As we briefly discussed before, a subject is at the same time a subscriber and an observable. Those two halves of it are connected with subject-specific logic that determines what happens when either the subscriber part receives a notification or someone subscribes to the observable.

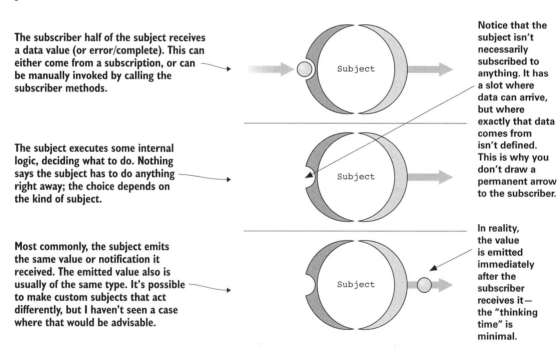

The subscriber half of the subject receives a data value (or error/complete). This can either come from a subscription, or can be manually invoked by calling the subscriber methods.

Notice that the subject isn't necessarily subscribed to anything. It has a slot where data can arrive, but where exactly that data comes from isn't defined. This is why you don't draw a permanent arrow to the subscriber.

The subject executes some internal logic, deciding what to do. Nothing says the subject has to do anything right away; the choice depends on the kind of subject.

Most commonly, the subject emits the same value or notification it received. The emitted value also is usually of the same type. It's possible to make custom subjects that act differently, but I haven't seen a case where that would be advisable.

In reality, the value is emitted immediately after the subscriber receives it— the "thinking time" is minimal.

Different types of subjects

To see how subjects work in practice, you can have a quick look at a
simplified base class declaration:

```
class Subject<T>
    extends Observable<T>
    implements Observer<T> {

    '''
}
```

Every subject is an observable with added functionality.

The observer interface is the tube into which you can throw notifications.

Because the `Subject` class extends `Observable`, you can use it as one.
The `Observer` interface (same as `Subscriber`), on the other hand,
provides the access function:

```
public interface Observer<T> {
  void onNext(T t);
  void onComplete();
  void onError(Throwable e);
}
```

PublishSubject

The most straightforward of subjects is `PublishSubject`. You put an
item in, and it emits that item to all of its subscribers.

`PublishSubject` is a bit like an event dispatcher: once an event has
been emitted, it's gone. New subscribers see only notifications that
occur after they subscribe (notifications also include `onError` and
`onComplete`).

`PublishSubject<String> subject =` `  PublishSubject.create();`	Creates a new PublishSubject
`subject.onNext("black");`	Emits value "black" to no one
`subject.subscribe(color ->` `  log("Color: " + color));`	Creates a subscription that logs all values emitted by the subject
`subject.onNext("yellow");`	Prints "Color: yellow"
`subject.onNext("green");`	Prints "Color: green"
`subject.onComplete();`	Completes the observable and releases subscriptions

BehaviorSubject

In FRP, *behavior* has a special meaning. In our terminology, it's *an observable that emits the last value it emitted for all new subscribers immediately upon subscription.* Some argue that in pure FRP, you have only behaviors. In Rx programming, however, a behavior is just one special kind of an observable, though an extremely useful one.

`BehaviorSubject` is akin to a variable that holds its last state and informs new subscribers of it. You can, in fact, also read its last state with `getValue()`, but this should be used in only extreme cases, as it breaks the whole point of an observable being a stream of data.

Initializing with an initial value

`BehaviorSubject` can either be initialized empty, like `PublishSubject`, or with an initial value. In previous versions of RxJava, the initial value was compulsory, but the restriction was removed later.

> BehaviorSubject always holds the latest value as a "memory," much like a normal variable.

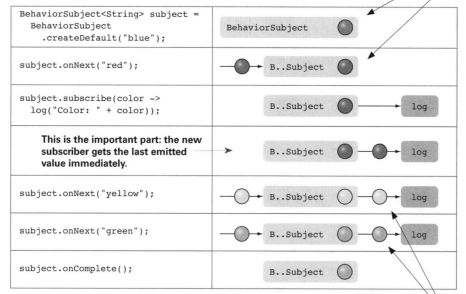

> This is the important part: the new subscriber gets the last emitted value immediately.

> Here BehaviorSubject acts like the normal Publish one. At the same time, it emits the value immediately and saves it as the last emitted one.

In most cases, it's better to use `BehaviorSubject`. The only reason not to use it would be for events, such as mouse clicks, which do not constitute a state change. It wouldn't make sense to have the last mouse click emitted to new subscribers.

Using a subject as the FileObservable

Of the two kinds of subjects you saw, `BehaviorSubject` seems to fit
better. You always have a select file, and changing it doesn't resemble an
event.

```
BehaviorSubject selectedDir =
  BehaviorSubject.create(root);
```

At this point,
BehaviorSubject
does the same as
Observable.just did
before.

```
selectedDir
  .switchMap(file ->
    createFilesObservable(file)
      .subscribeOn(Schedulers.io())
  )
  .observeOn(AndroidSchedulers.mainThread())
  .subscribe(this::updateList);
```

Up to this point, nothing has changed. But next you'll add a listener
to the list in order to capture the selection of a new folder. From the
listener, you can push a new value to the `selectedDir` subject.

**The user clicks the Instagram folder, and you
push the new value to the selectedDir subject.**

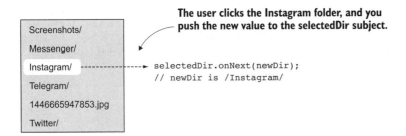

```
selectedDir.onNext(newDir);
// newDir is /Instagram/
```

The listener itself is within a custom adapter, so you can keep track of
the `File` values you're showing. On Android, the `View` class has a
handy property called a *tag*, which can contain any associated
information. You'll use this to save a reference to the original data value
the list item represents.

```
listView.setOnItemClickListener(
    (parent, view, position, id) -> {
        final File file = (File) view.getTag();
        Log.d(TAG, "Selected: " + file);
        if (file.isDirectory()) {
            selectedFile.onNext(file);
        }
    });
```

**Update the selected
file if the user clicks
a directory.**

This is all you need to do at this point. When you push a value to the subject, it automatically triggers the whole chain that updates the contents! Now you add more details into your graph from before:

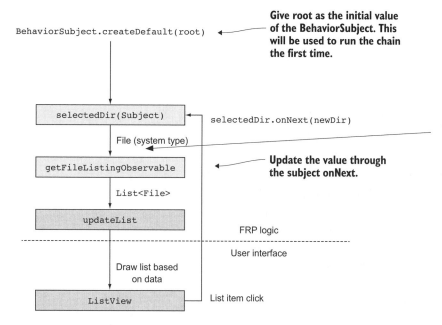

Here you can see that there are now two ways to "enter" the chain— the initial value of `BehaviorSubject`, and `onNext` that's called from the click listener of the list. *The exact same process happens from both triggers.*

The principle of disposing of unnecessary data

As seen in this example, as soon as you enter the chain, you no longer know where the selected directory originated. This information is irrelevant to the way you display the directory listing, so the rest of the chain is agnostic of fit. *By losing unnecessary information immediately when we don't need it, you can write more modular and reduced code.*

Coffee break

You can try creating observables and using subjects yourself. They're not too difficult to use after you get the hang of it.

Here are a couple of exercises to get you going. You can find the solutions online:

- Create a custom observable that emits `true` 5 seconds after subscription. (Tip: You can use the standard Android `Handler` class.)

- Create one `BehaviorSubject` for the first name and one for the last name. Set the defaults and subscribe to print the combined output of both. Add buttons for users to choose from fixed options.

- Add `.doOnNext` in parts of the chain and log the current thread name with `Thread.currentThread().getName()`. `doOnNext` doesn't actively participate in the chain, but is used only for side effects, such as logging. It's useful for inspecting values as they travel through the graph. The following is a brief introduction.

Logging with doOnNext

`Observable.doOnNext` is a decorator that performs an action based on the emitted item but doesn't change the stream in any way. It can be used to cause side effects (things that aren't related and don't influence the chain). Logging items is one good example: it creates an effect in an external system, but doesn't modify the values in any way.

You can take an example from earlier and add logging. Because you're not very far into this example, the logs will show only root.

```
selectedDir
  .doOnNext(dir -> Log.d("Selected dir " + dir))
  .switchMap(file ->
    createFilesObservable(file)
      .subscribeOn(Schedulers.io())
  )
  .doOnNext(files ->
    Log.d("Found " + files.size() + "files"))
  .observeOn(AndroidSchedulers.mainThread())
  .subscribe(this::updateList);
```

Log the selected directory. Notice that the directory is unaffected by logging.

Log the number of files found in the directory. Again, the list is unaffected.

Adding buttons for Previous and Root

You can now use the app to go deeper in the file hierarchy by clicking the files, but there's no way to go back! To alleviate this usability problem, you'll add buttons for going back to the root of the filesystem as well as the parent folder.

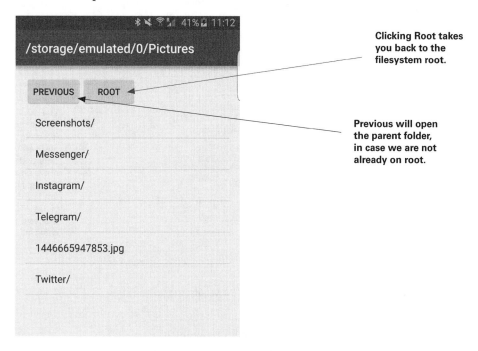

Clicking Root takes you back to the filesystem root.

Previous will open the parent folder, in case we are not already on root.

This is pretty standard file browser functionality. Some add the folder "…" as the first item on the list, but for clarity you've created a button for it. You could later change this functionality, though the code would end up with a lot of special case handling for this list item.

Expanded graph for Previous and Root

With the two new buttons, you get two new entry points to the chain.
The idea is starting to become clear: you define the FRP processing
pipeline once and attach all external inputs to it.

For now, you're still using the subject to aggregate all directory
changes. We just call `onNext` whenever you want to change the selected
directory, and the subject emits the new value into the chain.

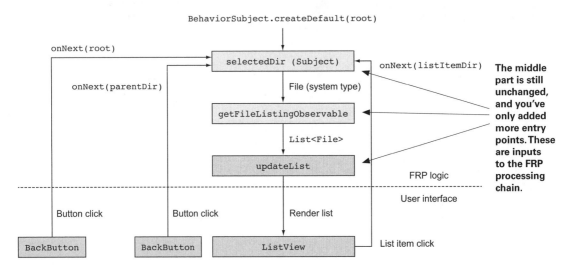

Notice that the graph is a closed cycle only for the rendering of the
`ListView`. Changes to the selected directory don't affect the *appearance*
of the Previous and Root buttons (at least not yet).

Coding the two new buttons

As with the `ListView`, you'll add listeners to the buttons and update the subject from there. The only problem is, how do you get the parent directory? You have only a subject now.

As before, you first want to get things working so you'll take a little shortcut. You may remember I mentioned `BehaviorSubject` has a way to relieve its "current" value, which is typically the last one it emitted. It's called `getValue()` and you'll use this to get ahold of the parent directory.

This is the saved value of BehaviorSubject. You can retrieve it with the getValue() function.

Let's see how this works in action. You'll use the RxBinding library to get an observable of clicks from both buttons. The syntax looks a bit different, but it's nothing else than a click handler at this point.

First the Root button:

```
RxView.clicks(findViewById(R.id.root_button))
    .subscribe(event -> selectedFile.onNext(root));
```

The root variable is still the same one you had before. It'll never change during the execution of the problem, so you can safely use it inside Rx chains.

The Previous button is where you need `getValue()`:

```
RxView.clicks(findViewById(R.id.back_button))
    .subscribe(event -> {
        File currentDir = selectedDir.getValue();
        File parent = currentDir.getParentFile();
        selectedDir.onNext(parent);
    });
```

It also isn't too scary. The only special thing here is that you read the last value of the selected directory subject and use it to calculate the new one.

First version ready!

That's it; the little app is now functional. It features a way to navigate through the filesystem of the device with a shortcut back to the root. But this app can be made more elegant, and you'll see how next.

Improved version with cleaner observables

You might stop here for a simple application, because it works. But because you want to learn how to make clean and scalable code, you'll take a moment to refactor the code.

It's often a good strategy to make the FRP chain work in some way and to seal it when it's ready. By *sealing* I mean to remove possible inconsistencies that could cause problems later. These include the following:

- Reading variables inside the FRP chain (constants are fine)

- ~~Writing to variables scoped outside of the FRP chain~~   ◄────────

- Exposing subjects as an entry point to the chain

- Having unnecessary data passed along the chain

- Having unnecessary `.subscribe()` calls (usually one is enough)

This isn't acceptable even for a rough implementation. It's potentially broken code that should be done in some other way from the start.

In your code, you clearly have the third one as well as the last. These consistencies aren't inherently wrong, but usually mean that something isn't as modular as it should be. Ideally, each part of the app should know as little as possible and create a subscription only when causing side effects, such as UI rendering. You can examine the code of the Root button to see what the problem is:

```
RxView.clicks(findViewById(R.id.root_button))
    .subscribe(event -> selectedFile.onNext(root)); ◄────────
```

The Root button is a source of data of type File. It shouldn't have information about where the data goes (the subject).

The code is simple, but it violates the principle of "knowing as little as possible." It doesn't need to know what you do with the data file. What you can do instead is make it an observable:

```
Observable<File> rootButtonObservable
  = RxView.clicks(findViewById(R.id.root_button))
    .map(event -> root);
```

You also removed the subscribe here, postponing it to a later time. Because you update the UI at only one point, you should be able to combine all subscriptions into one that does it all.

The other inputs

You were using a subject to take a shortcut and aggregate multiple inputs into it. But, it's better to create observables for all of the inputs and use the observable tools to combine the results—a subject makes it harder to track who changed what.

If you look at the inputs to the chain, you can identify the missing three input observables that use the same subject.

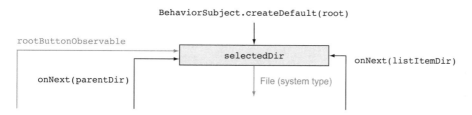

What you need are the three: initial value, Previous button, and the one you get from list item selection.

List selection observable

For the list selection, you can use a custom observable. Instead of passing the value to the selected directory subject, you use the subscriber in the custom observable. This way, the subscriber isn't exposed, and the observable does know where the value it's emitting goes.

```
Observable<File> listViewObservable =
  Observable.create(emitter ->
    listView.setOnItemClickListener(
      (parent, view, position, id) -> {
        final File file = (File) view.getTag();
        Log.d(TAG, "Selected: " + file);
        if (file.isDirectory()) {
            emitter.onNext(file);
        }
      }));
```

Wrap the listener into a custom observable. The selectedDir is replaced with the emitter.

There's still an onNext, but you've made the code more modular by not using the external scope selectedDir. You also don't need to subscribe here yet; you just create an observable.

Only a couple of lines have changed here, though semantically it was a big change. Instead of subscribing to click events, you've created a source of `File` objects—whenever the user clicks a directory on the list, this observable emits the associated file.

The Previous button

The Previous button is similar to the Root button, but with one exception: its action depends on the selected directory. We have a minicycle here, because the last emitted directory of `selectedDir` affects the behavior of this button.

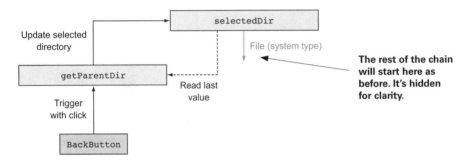

What does this mean? It means that in this case you need the subject to enable this kind of cycle. But you can still use the observables you created before and improve that part.

The code for `backButtonObservable` becomes like this:

```
Observable<File> backButtonObservable =
  RxView.clicks(findViewById(R.id.back_button))
    .map(event -> {
      File currentDir = selectedDir.getValue();
      File parent = currentDir.getParentFile();
      return parent;
    });
```

As you can see, `selectedDir` is still there. You could make the code a bit prettier with an operator called `.withLatestFrom`, but at this point it wouldn't make the code much better. Later chapters cover the operator, but it's effectively `combineLatest` for two observables in which the second one doesn't cause an emission of a combined item.

Putting it all together

The one thing about subjects you haven't seen yet is their ability to act as *subscribers*. The way to write cyclic reactive graphs is as follows:

1 Declare a subject.
2 Define observables that depend on the subject (without using its `onNext`).
3 Subscribe the subject to the observables created.

You'll do exactly this. You can keep the initial value for `BehaviorSubject` because you're forced to use a subject anyway.

The cyclic graph code

You'll now expand the list we just outlined and write it in code:

1 Declare a subject.

```
BehaviorSubject<File> selectedDir =
  BehaviorSubject.createDefault(root);
```

2 Define the observables that depend on the subject, as shown before. For instance:

> You need the last value of the selectedDir subject to identify the parent directory.

```
Observable<File> fileChangeBackEventObservable =
  backEventObservable
    .map(event ->
      selectedDir.getValue().getParentFile());
```

3 Combine the observables and subscribe the subject to the resulting merged observable.

```
Observable<File> fileChangeObservable =
    Observable.merge(
      listItemClickObservable,
      previousButtonObservable,
      rootButtonObservable);

fileChangeObservable
  .subscribe(selectedDir);
```

> The selectedDir subject is used as a subscriber here. Subjects are special in that they can adopt either role.

The detailed graph

To wrap up the chapter, let's draw one more graph that contains some of the details explaining our decisions. All illustrations of graphs or chains are approximations, and depending on which aspect you're planning to depict, you always choose the parts to include.

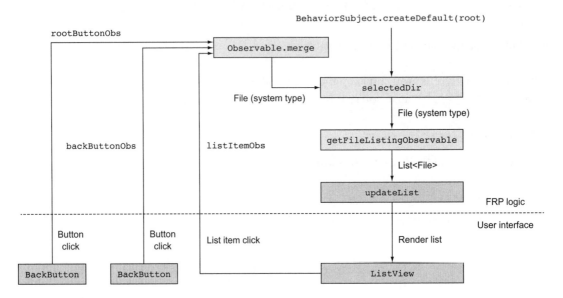

The full code so far

As briefly mentioned, on Android you have to ask for permissions for filesystem access when the application is already running. That's why instead of onCreate we have another function that contains your initialization code. You call it initWithPermissions.

First you'll set up all the needed observables and the simple ListView. You also create a function for the creation of listItemClickObservable, but the code remains the same.

MainActivity.java initWithPermissions

```java
private void initWithPermissions() {
  final ListView listView =
    (ListView) findViewById(R.id.list_view);
  FileListAdapter adapter =
    new FileListAdapter(this,
      android.R.layout.simple_list_item_1,
      new ArrayList<>());
  listView.setAdapter(adapter);

  final File root = new File(
    Environment
      .getExternalStorageDirectory().getPath());
  final BehaviorSubject<File> selectedDir =
      BehaviorSubject.createDefault(root);

  Observable<File> listItemClickObservable =
    createListItemClickObservable(listView);

  Observable<File> fileChangeBackEventObservable =
    backEventObservable
      .map(event ->
        selectedDir.getValue().getParentFile());

  Observable<File> fileChangeHomeEventObservable =
    homeEventObservable
      .map(event -> root);
```

The reactive logic of part of the code

After everything is ready, you can use RxJava logic to combine the observables with your dedicated logic. This is the end of the `initWithPermissions` function.

```
Observable.merge(
  listItemClickObservable,
  fileChangeBackEventObservable,
  fileChangeHomeEventObservable)
  .subscribe(selectedDir);

selectedDir
  .switchMap(file ->
    createFilesObservable(file)
      .subscribeOn(Schedulers.io()))
  .observeOn(AndroidSchedulers.mainThread())
  .subscribe(
        files -> {
            adapter.clear();
            adapter.addAll(files);
        },
    e -> Log.e(TAG, "Error reading files", e));
}
```

There's nothing new in this code, but it's good to see it all together. If you're thinking the function has too many dependencies, you have a point: you could split it. You'll look into the process of doing that in the next chapter, as there are some best practices around splitting functions.

Next in this chapter you'll see how to properly clean up after yourself.

Saving and releasing the subscriptions

As usual, you've created subscriptions in the initialization method, such as this one. You currently aren't doing anything with the subscription that's returned by the `subscribe` function.

```
Disposable subscription = selectedDir
    .subscribe(
        files -> {
            adapter.clear();
            adapter.addAll(files);
        });
```

Before you had just internal logic, but now you have an asynchronous operation with the filesystem that could complete at any time—even after you've closed the activity.

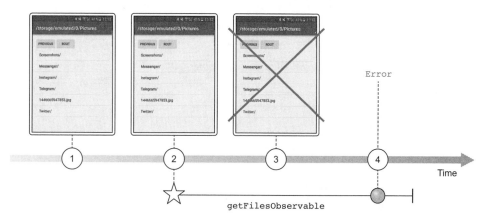

The preceding image shows the four steps that illustrate the problem:

1 User opens an Activity in the app.
2 Async filesystem operation is started.
3 User closes the Activity.
4 The async operation finishes and tries to update a view that isn't there.

Collecting subscriptions

The idea is to save all subscriptions you create into one container and then release all when the activity is closed. The activity here could be any kind of a platform container that has an `onDestroy` method—or something similar. Any subscriptions created *within* that container are then managed by it.

The way you can do this is with a class called `CompositeDisposable`. It has methods for adding subscriptions and for clearing them when you're done. This way, after the activity is destroyed, there are no more subscriptions that depended on it.

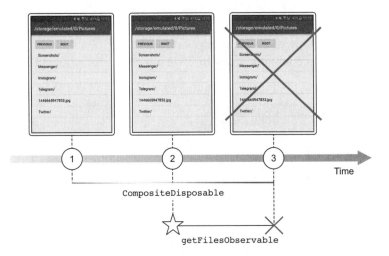

The following are the steps depicted in the preceding picture. With `CompositeDisposable`, you can end the operations when the activity closes.

1. User opens an Activity in the app
   - Create `CompositeDisposable`

2. Async filesystem operation is started
   - And added to the `CompositeDisposable`

3. User closes the Activity
   - `CompositeDisposable` is cleared

The way you accomplish this is with a class in the RxJava library. It has convenient methods that you can use. Notice that it implements the `Disposable` interface, but you won't need that here. You'll use only the additional methods for collecting and clearing the subscriptions.

RxJava CompositeSubscription

```
CompositeDisposable implements Disposable {
  void add(final Disposable s);
  void remove(final Disposable s);
  void clear();
  ...
}
```

To use this, you create one `CompositeDisposable` that you use through the activity:

MainActivity.java

```
private final CompositeDisposable subscriptions =
  new CompositeDisposable();
```

This is kind of a stack where you can put all of the subscriptions that have been created during the lifetime of this activity. It'll be purged in the `onDestroy` method, releasing everything that's no longer needed.

MainActivity.java onDestroy

```
@Override
 protected void onDestroy() {
  super.onDestroy();
  subscriptions.clear();
}
```

Saving the subscription references

The only thing left is to save the subscriptions you create. All of the reactive logic is in the `initWithPermissions` function, which is called after the filesystem permissions have been accepted by the user.

MainActivity.java initWithPermissions

```java
Disposable selectedDirSubscription =
  Observable.merge(
    listItemClickObservable,
    fileChangeBackEventObservable,
    fileChangeHomeEventObservable
  ).subscribe(selectedDir);

Disposable showFilesSubscription = selectedDir
  .subscribeOn(Schedulers.io())
  .flatMap(this::createFilesObservable)
  .observeOn(AndroidSchedulers.mainThread())
  .subscribe(
    files -> {
      adapter.clear();
      adapter.addAll(files);
    });

subscriptions.add(selectedDirSubscription);
subscriptions.add(showFilesSubscription);
```

The logic isn't new; you just save the created subscriptions into variables. On the last two lines, you add them to the managed `CompositeSubscription` to be released when they're no longer needed. Notice the code doesn't need to know exactly when they're *garbage collected*. That's left for the container and its `onDestroy` method.

A final note on subjects

Subjects are a controversial topic: be prepared for a variety of extreme opinions. In pure functional languages, it can be argued that subjects should be abolished, but in Java, they sometimes act as a good bridge between traditional code and FRP.

The biggest problem and temptation when using subjects is that any part of the code that has access to a subject can push more values into it—or complete or error it.

Generally speaking, this is bad, because it reduces your understanding of what the code does. If you know exactly where the values come from, why do you need subjects? Laziness is one excuse, but in the long run, it ends up being a bad one.

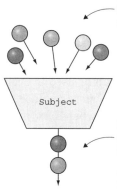

A subject allows anyone to insert values into it. These include onError and onComplete (not depicted).

The inserted data items are usually emitted immediately, retaining the order.

To the outside, a subject appears as an observable. It emits whatever was inserted into it.

But with subjects, you can easily try out how your chain works without being too formal with the sources of data. This is good for trying different approaches.

When to use subjects?

The simple rule about using subjects is that in most cases, there's a better way.

If you end up with a subject in your code, it often means the code isn't yet finished. Think carefully about where the data comes from and use those observables instead of exposing the entry point with a subject.

Subjects are great for quick prototyping, but be careful to replace them with proper observable chains after you know what the program should do—in other words, after you know who is putting the values in the subject.

Summary

This chapter presented a cursory look at many new topics. You saw briefly how observables can be constructed and how they work internally. This isn't such a common need when you're writing your own applications, but is useful to know particularly if you want to wrap existing code into a more modular package. Observables are always a source of data, and thus can be reused easily.

You also had a look at threading and how threading changes work in RxJava. They're specific for the implementation of RxJava, but typically it's easy to manipulate threading in any Rx or FRP library. The key takeaway here is to change the thread to either reduce load on the main thread or to return to a specific thread when you want to cause side effects (such as change the UI).

The last topic covered was subjects and how they can be used in cyclic graphs. Usually, you should try to stay away from subjects because they encourage bad coding habits, but they're useful when drafting the solution and in a few isolated cases. You encountered one of these, and decided to leave the subject in place—while cleaning up the surrounding code.

End of part 1

You've ended the first part of the book and have a basic understanding of how to read graphs describing a reactive application as well as how to construct them.

If you didn't understand all the details of some operators don't worry, we'll have another look at the more complicated ones as they appear again.

The most important thing at this point is to understand that reactive programs are constructed by defining relationships between different observables and, finally, subscribing to the results. This is how all of our applications will work.

Next you'll see how to solve more complex problems with different graphs, while keeping the code as modular as possible. You'll start learning on a more abstract level, so feel free to return to these chapters if the construction of graphs starts to seem tricky.

Architectures in RxJava | part 2

In this part

Now that you have the foundation of RxJava in place, you can start looking into more abstract topics.

RxJava is a powerful tool, but it requires more planning in terms of where the data comes in and where it ends up. You'll use containers called *view models* to encapsulate this logic.

In chapter 6, you'll restructure the example started in chapter 5 in order to create smaller components with clear responsibilities.

You'll continue on to other key parts of reactive architectures: the model in chapter 7, and the view model in chapters 8 and 9. Part 2 ends with chapter 10, which presents techniques for unit testing RxJava code.

 By failing to prepare, you are preparing to fail.

—Benjamin Franklin

Reactive view models | 6

In this chapter

- Working with view models and the view

- Using view models in the file browser example

- Working with view models as sources of view data

- Using view models on the Android platform

The view layer

UI programming has come a long way in recent years with different kinds of architectures and paradigms. The only thing that doesn't change is separating the logic from the rendering. On a practical level, you usually put the code that determines what the program looks like visually in one file, and the information to display in another file.

The line is sometimes admittedly blurry, but let's look at a few examples of what's considered rendering and what's considered logic:

Rendering	Logic
• The size and color of a spinning loader	• The visibility of a loading spinner
• The position of a thumbnail of a list item	• The logic to get the necessary data to show on a list
• The positions of circles and crosses on a grid of tic-tac-toe	• Game rules that determine what a player is allowed to do

Typically, you try to put these two responsibilities into different places (classes, files of code). The rendering part is called the *view*.

View

Here are the key characteristics of a view:

- Occupies a part of the visible screen
- Decides how the pixels it contains are rendered
- Represents the endpoint of data processing
- Can contain light logic, such as drop-down states

It's well worth mentioning that *view* is a generic name for a layer that represents all the components of the app that match the preceding description

The view and the file browser

To get a better idea of what the view is, look at the file browser example from the preceding chapter. In that example, you used a filesystem API to get information about the filesystem itself, a reactive system that handles the logic, and a UI that consists of buttons and a list.

If you put these three parts side by side, you can see that the view is probably all of the Android UI components that render the list of files as well as the buttons. In this case, it's not much of your own code, except for the layout.

Structure of the file browser example

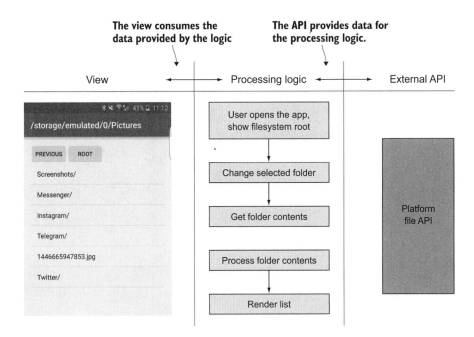

Usually, the view is indeed what you see on the screen. It's like the canvas of a movie projector—without it, no one could see the movie.

You'll next have a deeper look at the way these parts interact in our example application and then proceed to refactor your code to reflect the defined responsibilities.

Platform containers

Until now you've been writing your code in whichever file is convenient. This is fine when there isn't much of it, but after the number of lines increases, so does the code's complexity.

In terms of classes, most of our examples have consisted of a *master* class, which contains pretty much everything, and a declaration for the view layout. On Android, this is typically a static XML file.

We'll call this container class an *owner*. It's a container for your code that the platform (in this case, Android) provides.

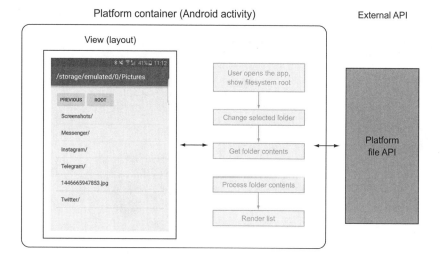

Platform container

Here are the key characteristics of platform containers:

- A platform container is created and managed by the platform operating system.

- The owner could be the application itself, a single screen inside of the application, or an independent component on a screen.

- On Android, the owner is usually `Application`, `Activity`, or `Fragment`.

Platform container lifecycle

You'll get back to the lifecycles of platform containers later, but it should be noted that you can usually recognize them by their overloaded methods.

The lifecycle methods are ones such as `onCreate` and `onDestroy`, which allow you to initialize the container as well as release resources when it's destroyed.

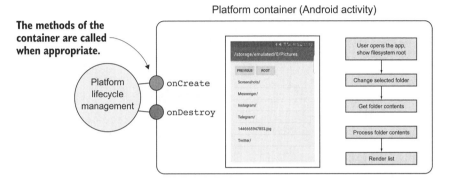

For our reactive purposes, what you've been doing is putting everything in the `onCreate` function itself:

onCreate

- Create the layouts and UI components to be presented to the user (create the view layer).
- Set up necessary reactive chains and subscriptions.
- Make sure the view is updated based on the arriving data.

onDestroy

- Unsubscribe subscriptions that were created in the `onCreate` function.

> ### Is there always a platform container?
>
> All of the code is started by something in the platform. Even a program with just one method needs someone to call it. This kind of program would conceptually have only a *create* method.

View models

As a program grows, you want to isolate the logic in its own module (basically a class). We'll call this extracted logic the *view model*.

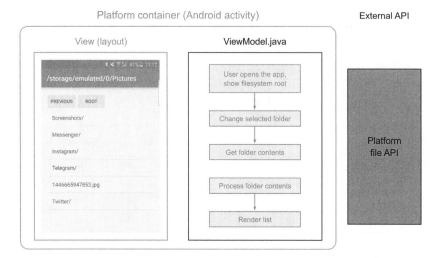

You'll explore exactly what this means soon, but to understand the motivation, you can think of a unit test.

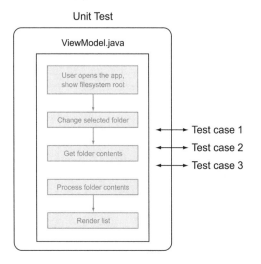

A *unit test* is a piece of code that tests whether another piece of code does what it's supposed to do.

Platform containers are always a little difficult to test because of their heavy initialization requirements, but because you have a new class, testing *outside the platform container* is relatively easy.

Here you've taken just the `ViewModel` class and instantiated it inside the unit test. The unit test acts as a sort of container here.

What are the dependencies of the reactive logic?

A view model needs to encapsulate all the logic needed to run the UI. You'll look at the file browser as an example of what this entails.

File browser logic

In the file browser you have the core processing logic and its dedicated input and output points in one file. The user is allowed to choose a folder to go deeper in the hierarchy and, on the other hand, you have APIs to retrieve the listings of those folders.

The logic in the middle is your reactive part, and it has distinct inputs and outputs, usually illustrated with arrows. These are the points where your internal logic is interacting with the "outside world."

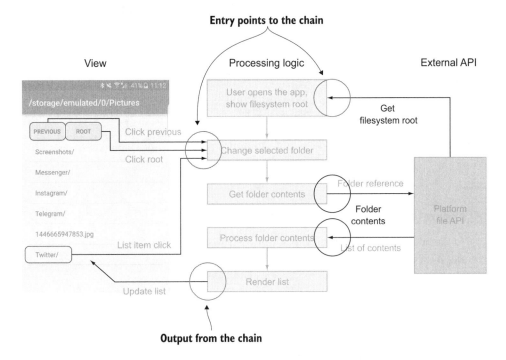

In the context of Android, you usually put all the logic in the `Activity` class with the rest of the initialization code. It works, but as discussed, it tends to make the class long and the code difficult to unit test.

Now that you've created a new class, the `ViewModel`, it needs to be able to take these inputs and produce the desired outputs.

The blueprint of a view model

Conceptually, a view model isn't much more than an isolated block of code that has a defined (reactive) interface with the outside world.

You won't be making big changes to your existing file browser, because the logic itself stays the same. You create a new class into which you move the reactive chain. You'll call this class a *view model*.

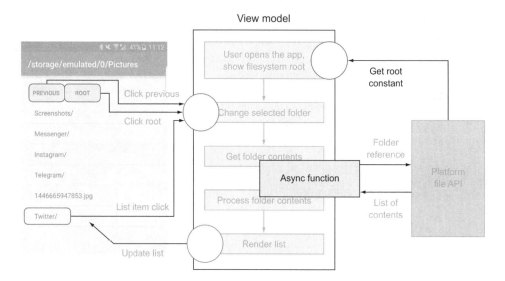

The characteristics of a view model

A view model is like a treasure chest where you put the most important parts of the code. It's a container that holds the pure logic, or the core, of your application. You'll do everything to keep it clean and safe.

Here are a few guidelines for view model housekeeping:

- Doesn't contain *references* to any platform-specific components
- Exposes as few inputs and outputs as possible
- Doesn't directly use external parts of the code

Migrating existing code into a view model

The abstract concept is all nice and clean, but how do you write a view model? There's no absolutely right way of doing this, but commonly you have a few guidelines to code by:

- The view model can take dependencies in constructor parameters. These include input sources and handles to external APIs.

- The outputs of the view model are typically getter functions that return an observable of the data they wish to expose. But it's important that the observables emit the last value immediately, much like BehaviorSubjects covered before.

- Thread changing is usually done outside of the view model, because it can make testing more difficult. But you'll learn more about that later.

Constructor arguments

A simple way to pass inputs to the view model is to use constructor arguments. They're a good way too, because they establish a clear relationship between the view model and its creator.

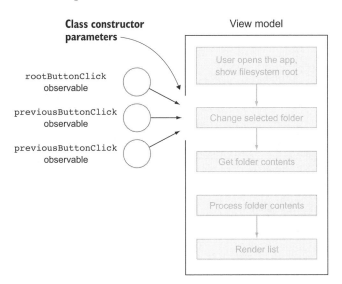

Getting external data in the view model

To encapsulate the filesystem API without calling it directly from the view model, you can pass it a single asynchronous function. Whenever the logic in the view model needs the functionality it can call that function.

getFiles function

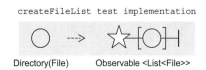

```
createFileList test implementation
```

Directory(File)   Observable <List<File>>

The function takes a directory (of type `File`) and returns an observable that emits the contents of that directory when the operation is ready.

You can see the function used in the chain in the middle.

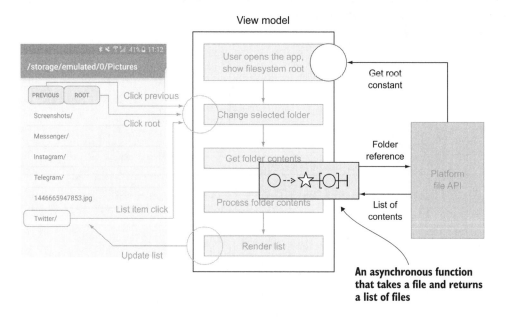

You can declare the function as type `Func1<File, Observable<List<File>>` and hand it over in the constructor arguments.

The full constructor of the view model

With the filesystem API function, your dependencies are fully defined.

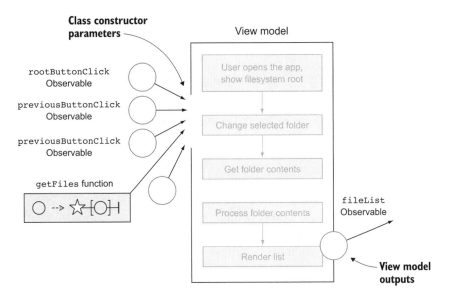

You also add the filesystem root as an external parameter, though it's just a variable and not an observable. In this picture, the circle denotes a dependency rather than an observable.

Here you take the parameters and save them for later use:

FileBrowserViewModel.java

```
. . .

public FileBrowserViewModel(
        Observable<File> listItemClickObservable,
        Observable<Object> previousClickObservable,
        Observable<Object> rootClickObservable,
        File fileSystemRoot,
        Func1<File, Observable<List<File>>> getFiles) {
  this.listItemClickObservable = listItemClickObservable;
  this.previousClickObservable = previousClickObservable;
  this.rootClickObservable = rootClickObservable;
  this.fileSystemRoot = fileSystemRoot;
  this.getFiles = getFiles;
}
```

Connecting views and view models

The name *view model* comes from the idea that it provides the data, or the *model* for the *view*. The view in this case isn't necessarily an instance of the Android `View` class, but rather any part of the application that's able to *present data*.

The view model is the part of the application that *provides up-to-date data*.

The view model is responsible for giving the initial data and replacing it whenever newer data is available.

Setting up the view and the view model

In the beginning, you create the view model and view independently of each other. It helps to remember that they don't really know of each other. One view isn't usually tied to a particular type of a view model— just as long as that view can provide the right kind of data.

Here's a depiction after the two have been created: they aren't connected in any way yet.

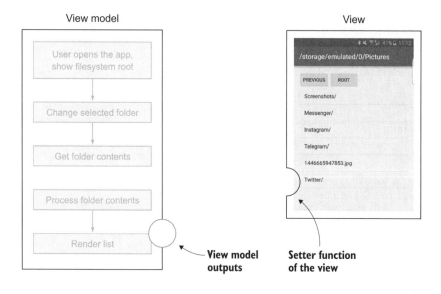

Exposing outputs from view models

In this application, you have just one thing to show on the screen: the list of the files in the selected directory. Therefore, you create a getter for just that.

What you want to expose is a `BehaviorObservable` that gives the last value immediately and subsequent ones as they're updated.

It's usually safest to create the output as a `BehaviorSubject` and to subscribe it to the desired value.

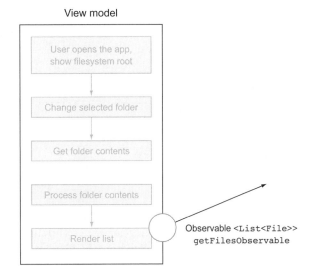

View model

User opens the app,
show filesystem root

Change selected folder

Get folder contents

Process folder contents

Render list

Observable <List<File>>
getFilesObservable

FileBrowserViewModel.java

```
private final BehaviorSubject<List<File>> filesOutput
  = BehaviorSubject.create();

...

public Observable<List<File>> getFilesObservable() {
    return filesOutput.hide();
}
```

Subject.hide() makes sure the receiver can't push more events in the subject. It used to be called .asObservable().

The subject is final and has to be initialized only one time. This ensures that whoever subscribes to that subject can be sure it will stay the same as long as the view model exists.

Binding view models to views

You'll sometimes use the word binding to refer to a specific coupling of a view model and a view. Before doing that, you'll have to create the view model with its dependencies:

MainActivity.java initWithPermissions

```
FileBrowserViewModel viewModel =
  new FileBrowserViewModel(
    listItemClickObservable,
    backEventObservable,
    homeEventObservable,
    root, this::createFilesObservable
);
```

Here you give the view model everything necessary from the `MainActivity`. The `createFilesObservable` function takes a folder and returns a list of its contents. You give the view model a function reference with the lambda notation—so the view model can call the function when required.

Binding with a subscription

Next you'll create a subscription between the output of the view model and that setter function of the view. You'll switch the thread to the UI thread to be sure.

You'll also need to release the created subscriptions. For this, you'll save them in a `CompositeDisposable` called `viewSubscriptions`.

MainActivity.java initWithPermissions

```
viewSubscriptions.add(
  viewModel.getFileListObservable()
    .observeOn(AndroidSchedulers.mainThread())
    .subscribe(this::setFileList)
);
```

The list of subscriptions represented as Disposable instances

When you're finished with the activity, you'll release the created subscriptions:

MainActivity.java onDestroy

```
viewSubscriptions.clear();
```

Disposes of all subscriptions on the list you collected

What you end up with is a continuous stream of values from the view model to the view. The view becomes a projection of the view model.

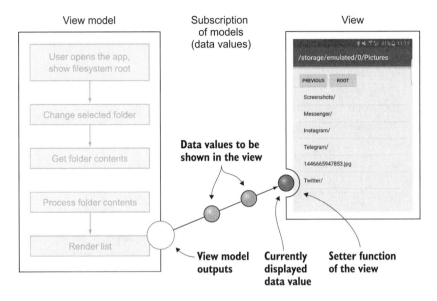

The basic idea of binding is to keep the data processing and its presentation separate. At the end of this chapter, you'll have a more in-depth look at how to conceptually separate an application into distinct layers.

Can binding be done without RxJava?

The action of binding isn't necessarily a job for reactive logic or RxJava; binding is a plain connection that synchronizes the view model and the view without processing the data any further. This binding could be done with another library as well, though because you've already learned about observables and subscribers, you can keep using them.

The important thing to keep in mind, though, is that the view model's output should be considered final, and it's not advisable to base new reactive chains on it. If you need to share parts of view models it's better to share the internal reactive chains than to stack view models to depend on each other.

The whole picture

You can now see everything the platform container (the *owner* of the view model) is responsible for:

- Create the dependencies for the view model
- Create the view model
- Establish a connection between the exposed properties of the view model and where they're displayed (in this case, the ListView)

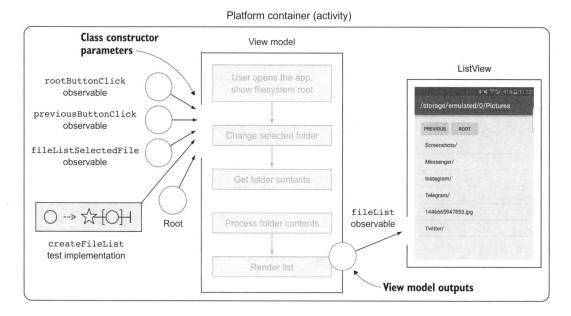

You can already compile the app, and it runs fine, though the list will be empty because the middle part is still missing. Now that you have the container ready, you'll put in the logic.

View model lifecycle

Next we need to put the actual code in. The problem is that a part of it creates subscriptions that we were saving in a `CompositeDisposable` in the Activity. For instance, this line connects the `getFiles` operation to the `filesOutput`:

```
subscriptions.add(selectedFile
        .flatMap(createFilesObservable)
        .subscribe(filesObservable::onNext));
```

Now if you move the code in the view model, what do you do with the subscriptions?

Saving subscriptions in a view model

To manage our subscriptions, add another `CompositeDisposable` to the view model instance that will keep track of all subscriptions that it has created.

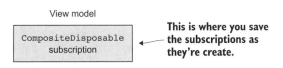

Normally, you try to follow this principle: whoever created it is responsible for cleaning up. In this case, that's the view model.

View model subscribe and unsubscribe

You'll add functions for the view model to create the subscriptions as well as to release them. This just means that you'll postpone the creation of the subscriptions until the `subscribe` method is called.

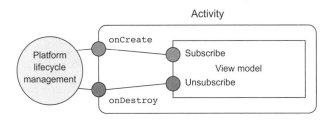

The code of the view model

As discussed, you'll have two functions: one to create your
subscriptions and another one to release them.

For this logic you'll create a new function in the view model called
subscribe. It'll contain the creation code that was previously in the
onCreate main activity.

FileBrowserViewModel.java subscribe function

```java
public void subscribe() {
  final BehaviorSubject<File> selectedFile =
          BehaviorSubject.createDefault(fileSystemRoot);

  Observable<File> previousFileObservable =
          previousClickObservable
                  .map(event ->
                          selectedFile.getValue()
                                  .getParentFile());

  Observable<File> rootClickObservable =
          rootButtonObservable
                  .map(event -> fileSystemRoot);

  subscriptions.add(Observable.merge(
          listItemClickObservable,
          previousFileObservable,
          rootFileObservable)
          .subscribe(selectedFile));

  subscriptions.add(selectedFile
          .switchMap(getFiles)
          .subscribe(filesObservable::onNext));
}
```

This might look a
bit strange, but it
means that you
want to emit the
fileSystemRoot
every time the user
clicks the Home
button.

Here you use the
function that was
given to you. It takes
a file (folder) and
returns its contents
asynchronously.

The most complex logic lies in the middle with the
previousFileObservable and the merge function.

The unsubscribe function is short, and can also be moved into a super
class. Currently, there's no actual library to create view models, but it's
just a bit of boilerplate you need to live with.

FileBrowserViewModel.java unsubscribe function

```java
public void unsubscribe() {
  subscriptions.clear();
}
```

Coffee break

Try creating your own simple view model.

Make a button that changes the color of the background to a random one. You an either create a new application or add a button to an existing one.

Where to use a view model

Use a view model to encapsulate the logic from click to color. You need to create an activity with a button and then set up a custom view model as we did.

Solution

This solution has three parts: the button that acts as an input to the view model, the view model logic, and an exposed color from the view model. After the view model is created, you'll "bind" this color to the background color of the whole activity layout.

Let's start with the activity code that handles the initialization. You'll assume here that the layout has been set up with a `my_button` button.

The color randomization uses a bit of a shortcut, but you're free to replace it with a more complex implementation—it could even be given to the view model as a function parameter of type `Func0<Integer>`.

Activity onCreate:

```
// Initialize view model
View button = findViewById(R.id.my_button);
MyViewModel vm = new MyViewModel(
  RxView.clicks(button));

vm.subscribe();

// Bind view model outputs to be displayed
View contentView = findViewById(android.R.id.content);
subscriptions.add(
  vm.getColor().subscribe(
    contentView::setBackgroundColor);
  )
);
```

The view model code is a little longer. You'll save the `clickObservable` and create the subscriptions in the `subscribe` function. You might get away with doing everything in the constructor, because it's a simple view model, but it's usually better to use the `subscribe` and `unsubscribe` methods.

MyViewModel:

```
public class MyViewModel {
  private CompositeDisposable subscriptions
    = new CompositeDisposable();

  BehaviorSubject<Integer> color =
    BehaviorSubject.createDefault(Color.WHITE);

  Observable<Void> clickObservable;

  public MyViewModel(Observable<Object> clickObservable) {
    this.clickObservable = clickObservable;
  }

  public void subscribe() {
   subscriptions.add(
     clickObservable
       .map(event -> getRandomColor())
       .subscribe(color::onNext);
   );
  }

  public void unsubscribe() {
    subscriptions.clear();
  }

  private static Color getRandomColor() {
    if (Math.random() < .5f) {
      return Color.RED;
    } else {
      return Color.BLUE;
    }
  }

  public Observable<Integer> getColor() {
    return color;
  }
}
```

View models and the Android lifecycles

You'll make one closing inspection of view model lifecycles. In the example, you end up with two separate `CompositeDisposables`: one that's inside of the view model and one that's kept for the connections that the container makes between the view model and the view.

View model subscribe/unsubscribe

Calling the view model `subscribe` essentially makes it alive—it'll start processing its inputs and produce the desired outputs. It might trigger network requests doing that, or whatever it's designed to do.

Typically, the view model `subscribe` would be called on `onCreate` and `unsubscribe` on `onDestroy`. We'll keep it like that.

View model to view bindings

In our approach, the platform container (on Android `Activity` or `Fragment`) connects the view model to its presentation layer, the view. This can be done on `onCreate`/`onDestroy`, but a more convenient place for it is usually `onResume`/`onPause`.

On Android there's a state called *paused*, and in this state you usually wouldn't want to update the view. But you'd like to have the view model process the data and present it again after you resume. *The view model will in this case give the latest available data to the view immediately upon resuming.*

MainActivity.java onResume function

```
@Override
protected void onResume() {
  makeViewBinding();
}
```

MainActivity.java onPause function

```
@Override
protected void onPause() {
  releaseViewBinding();
}
```

The improved view model lifecycle

The code change needed isn't large. You'll move the lines that create the view subscriptions to the `makeViewBinding` function for clarity and its pair to `releaseViewBinding`:

MainActivity.java makeViewBinding function

```java
private void makeViewBinding() {
  viewSubscriptions.add(
    viewModel.getFileListObservable()
      .observeOn(AndroidSchedulers.mainThread())
      .subscribe(this::setFileList)
  );
}
```

MainActivity.java releaseViewBinding function

```java
private void releaseViewBinding() {
  viewSubscriptions.clear();
}
```

The full picture

You can include your improvements of the lifecycle in the graph you drew for the view model `subscribe`/`unsubscribe` before.

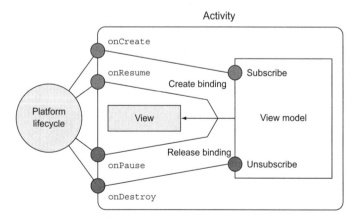

View model phases on Android

What does this all mean in practice? You can see the different parts of the activity lifecycle and what happens to the view model here:

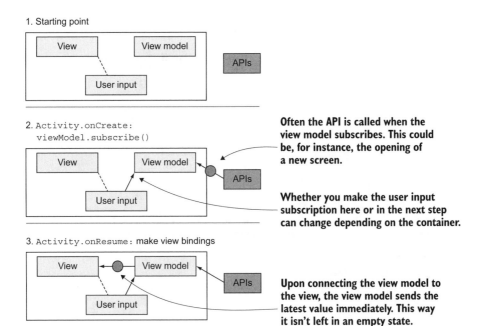

1. Starting point

2. `Activity.onCreate:`
   `viewModel.subscribe()`

Often the API is called when the view model subscribes. This could be, for instance, the opening of a new screen.

Whether you make the user input subscription here or in the next step can change depending on the container.

3. `Activity.onResume:` make view bindings

Upon connecting the view model to the view, the view model sends the latest value immediately. This way it isn't left in an empty state.

After the view bindings are made, the app is ready to use. Here you'll start receiving the user inputs and are free to use the API as well.

4. User uses the app

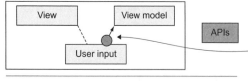

The user starts interacting, thus producing input to the view model. This might trigger new API operations as well.

5. `Activity.onPause`: release view bindings

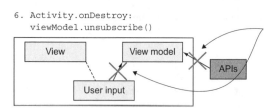

After disconnecting the view binding you can still receive updates from the API. They just wouldn't be shown in the view (UI) until possibly rebinding the view.

6. `Activity.onDestroy`:
   `viewModel.unsubscribe()`

All remaining subscriptions are released. This is important to prevent possible memory leaks.

Code for onResume and onPause

Before you can move the view bindings to `onResume` and `onPause` you need to change the initialization. Currently, the problem is that `onResume` will be called the first time before the `initWithPermissions`—and thus the view model would not have been created yet.

You'll move the view model creation code to `onCreate`, and let it sit idle until `initWithPermissions` is called. In this function, you can finally activate the view model with its `subscribe` method.

Postponing the activation (subscription) of the view model

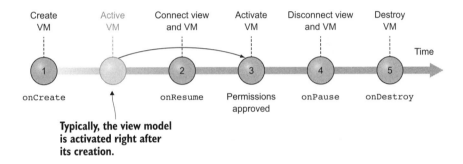

We call the unusual method `initWithPermissions`, but you can handle it quite nicely with the view model lifecycle.

Is it good to change the "standard" lifecycle of a view model?

Usually, it makes sense to stick to conventions, and indeed moving the subscription method of the view model out of `onCreate` isn't a great idea.

But here you have a special case, because the file permissions dialog box blocks the app until you can continue. In this way, you could say that the lifecycle has been altered.

The view affinity of the code

You've seen many kinds of code already: code that gets data from the network, code that populates lists in the view, as well as code that sorts those lists.

These pieces of code, sometimes functions, all have different, distinct, responsibilities. In terms of a reactive application, you can roughly identify sections that are more about just data and ones that center around showing something to the user.

You start from data, such as filesystem information, and go toward putting a list of filenames into the view. The more our code is affected by the view, the stronger is its *view affinity*.

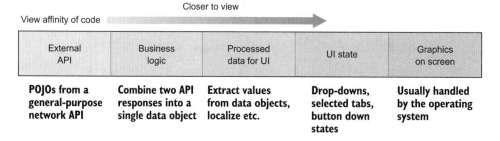

Closer to view

View affinity of code

External API	Business logic	Processed data for UI	UI state	Graphics on screen
POJOs from a general-purpose network API	**Combine two API responses into a single data object**	**Extract values from data objects, localize etc.**	**Drop-downs, selected tabs, button down states**	**Usually handled by the operating system**

Notice that this is by no means a definite spectrum, and sometimes it's hard to place a particular piece of code on it. In general, you can see that you start with the input and go toward the outputs, with different sections handling the data on the way.

The Reactive UI Application with a View

Notice, though, that this is a spectrum toward the view—the UI. This spectrum is meant to address and describe issues that come with the demands of the view.

Where do view models fit on our spectrum?

As mentioned, view models are containers for the reactive logic, which can be everything from external APIs to the final view itself. Typically, a view model, however, covers a big chunk right before the view, and the rest is considered generic data/business logic.

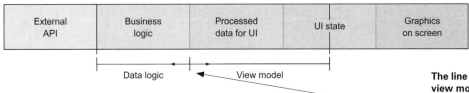

The line where the view model ends and generic data logic starts is flexible and depends on the use case. You'll see examples later.

For our simple example with only one activity, you can be more liberal with this definition, and you'll put everything reactive we have in the view model. In later chapters, you'll see other modules that enable more fine-grained control. The goal is always to keep the responsibility of a module clean and the length short.

It's good to remember that the different parts of the application in reactive systems are just guidelines and holders to keep the classes smaller and the code reusable.

What about presenters?

On Android, an architecture called the Model-View-Presenter recently has become popular. Where does the presenter fit in our picture?

You'll return to more complex architectures in the last part of the book, but in general the presenter is somewhere between a view model and a view, possibly overlapping both. It could be seen as a refinement to the view logic, extracting further functionality away from the platform classes (such as `View` or `Fragment`).

Summary

After spending a lot of time learning reactive chains, you're now seeing where to best put them. In simple cases, you can be more relaxed, but as the number of code lines increases, you need to start paying attention to the architecture.

Next steps

This part of the book focuses on exploring how to keep the reactive logic clean and separate from the specifics of rendering. You'll also learn some new tricks on the way, but the focus will be on how to structure the code in a way that's not going to fall apart after the moving parts become too many.

In the next chapter, you'll dive into view models as containers for the reactive chains you've already been building. You'll also see how to start testing the reactive logic in a deterministic way.

In this chapter

- Introduction to the model and stores

- Changing the file browser to use a model

- Basic implementations of a model

- Persisting app state with a store

Fundamentals of reactive architectures

You've seen how it's possible to make reactive chains to refine data from observables. But before you go further, let's look at how reactive applications can be structured in a scalable way on a higher level.

Data change, process data, render

All modern reactive applications work roughly in the same way. You have some kind of storage for data, or a *database*, and you react to changes in it.

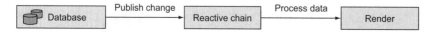

On the other hand, you have mechanisms for updating the database. These include incoming data from the network, user input, or something read from the disk.

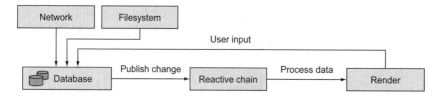

Notice that in this picture, the database is the only place where the data is stored. The reactive chain is processing only the data that originates in the database. This may sound restrictive, but you'll see later the benefits and compromises that you'll end up with.

Model-View-View model

If you go back to the picture from the preceding page, you can see that your state is contained in the store.

What you have in the middle, then, is the reactive code. So far, you've just put that code inside a container, such as `Activity`, but now you'll name it and see how to define it as a separate part of the architecture.

The idea is to separate the reactive chain from the store as well as the view. You'll call the rendering part the *view* from here on, and the reactive chain becomes the *view model*.

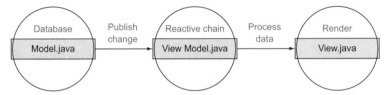

Splitting classes

The reason for this separation is simple: you want to decouple the parts into different classes with clear responsibilities.

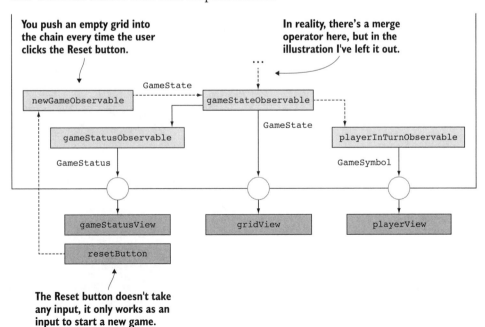

Internal relationships of the model

You can also put in some processing logic that's invisible to the
consumer of the database. This could be considered to represent
relationships between different parts of the database.

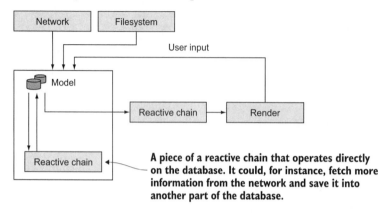

You'll see concrete examples later, but for now it's just to show that
reactive chains usually either prepare data for rendering, or retrieve
more of it.

Is the database mentioned a real database?

The database in the context of a UI app isn't usually a traditional SQL
database but rather a term used for a generic place where you can store
data.

In reactive applications the actual database is more often referred to as the
store or *repository*. The model can in reality contain more than one of them.

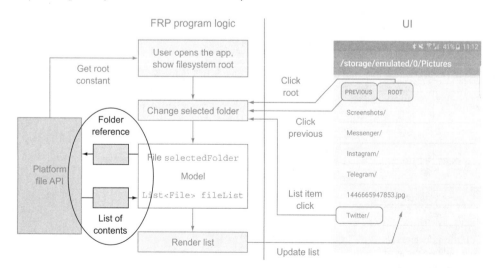

Reactive model

Now that you have a basic idea of what the elements of architectures look like, let's see how to go about using them.

On Android, there are currently no strongly opinionated popular frameworks to start doing reactive programming. Instead the approach is to take bits and pieces from libraries that fit what you want to do. You already saw RxJava, which is the cornerstone of what you're planning to build. It provides the glue between different parts of the architecture, as well as a way to conveniently create the processing chains.

Web server as a repository of entities

To better understand the role of the model, let's look at a REST server. If you query data from the internet, you always need a URL, an identifier. But as information updates, *the data returned with the same URL will be different over time.*

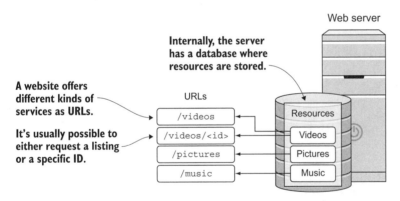

Web request flow

The way a web server works is that it's given information about the resource you'd like to have. This is done through the URL structure: for instance, here the client wants a listing of (potentially) all videos.

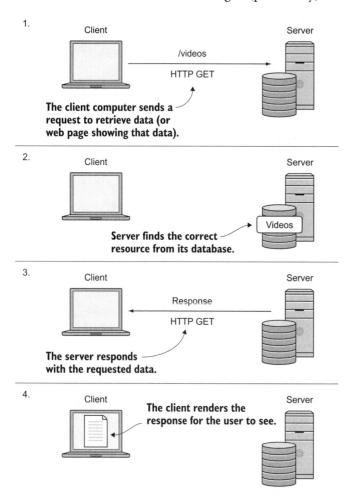

1.

Client   Server

/videos

HTTP GET

The client computer sends a request to retrieve data (or web page showing that data).

2.

Client   Server

Videos

Server finds the correct resource from its database.

3.

Client   Server

Response

HTTP GET

The server responds with the requested data.

4.

Client   Server

The client renders the response for the user to see.

For a specific video, the request would be something like www .manning.com/videos/2514 for a video with ID 2514.

Model as a web server

"I already know how the web works," you might think. The reason you revise the basics of the web is to find the parts that relate to the way your store works. In fact, that store is like a *little web server inside of the application*. Here's how the interface might look:

```
interface VideoModel {
  public Observable<Video> getVideo(int id);
  public Observable<List<Video>> getVideos();
  ...
}
```

We'll get back to the details in a bit, so don't worry if it looks complicated with the observables.

If you draw this into a picture, you'll have the model on the right side, and the way to access it on the left. Inside the model is a store.

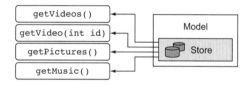

Where is the model?

Even though we were just talking about physical web servers, the model is really an instance inside one device.

It'll be, at one point, created with something like this:

```
Model model =
  new Model(...);
```

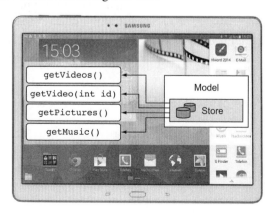

Model as a repository of entities

If you look at the comparison between the web server and the model, you can see similarities: they both have a database and an API for accessing it.

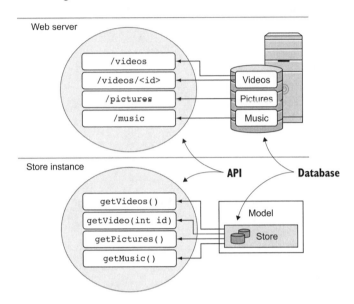

Notice, though, that our mental model is purely on the level of abstraction: the model is just an instance inside the application.

If you get back to the reactive application, you have everything inside one device. The logic and the store can interact directly by calling functions.

You can imagine a singleton store that serves data of certain types. You'll expose observables to also keep track of changes. This way of thinking of the store expands quite far, and you'll continue using it through the book.

Retrieving data from the model

If you look at the process of accessing the model, you can roughly identify a sequence in which the logic that requires the data asks for an observable and then subscribes to it.

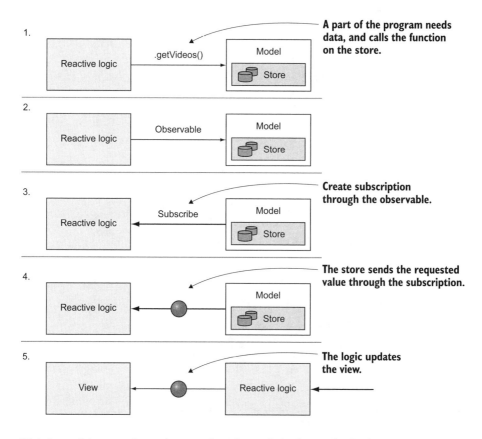

This is nothing you haven't seen already, and that's good. The key here is to define the model as a predictable source of observables and therefore data. It's the universal resource container, from which you can always ask for the latest data (as well as updates to it).

A piece of code as a "client"

The scenario of retrieving data from the model is similar to our case with a server, but *the logic is now acting as the client*. The job of the store is to provide data, and nothing else.

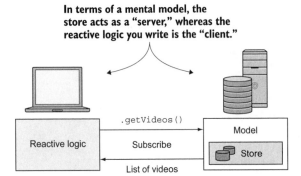

In reactive applications, we often talk about a "single source of truth" principle. This means that within an application, there needs to be one place where any part of the application will get the latest and most correct data.

Aren't singletons bad?

You might have been discouraged from using singletons, or at least from overusing them. It's true that usually they don't promote good programming principles, especially in combination with static members.

But in the case of the store, a singleton is conceptually important. The same way the web server can be accessed through a single URL, a store has only one reference through which it's accessed.

The reason behind this is simple: at any given time, there's one and only one right version of a particular resource. To not make the store a universal singleton (or singleton-like) instance is asking for trouble.

Coffee break

Try to construct a simple `VideoModel` that allows you to add a video as well as to subscribe and return a full list of all of the videos added as an observable. You need to provide only a stream of the full list, and no order or removal of duplicates is necessary.

Make it fill the interface:

```
interface VideoModelInterface {
  void put(Video video);
  Observable<List<Video>> getVideoListStream();
}
```

> **TIP** You can use a `BehaviorSubject` as the internal store mechanism to save the latest value and expose an observable.

Solution

To get an idea of what a model can be, this example hides the implementation of the `BehaviorSubject` behind its interface:

VideoModel.java

```
public class VideoModel implements VideoModelInterface {
  private BehaviorSubject<Video> videoList
    = BehaviorSubject.createDefault(new ArrayList<>());

  public void put(Video video) {
    List<Video> updatedList
      = new ArrayList(videoList.getValue());
    updatedList.add(video);
    videoList.onNext(updateList);
  }

  public Observable<List<Video>> getVideoListStream() {
    return videoList.hide();
  }
}
```

BehaviorSubject is a convenient first implementation in a model. It can provide a stream as well as store the last value for updating.

Take a copy of the previous list and append the new item in the end. In a real-life scenario, you'd probably need to maintain a map based on the ID of the video.

Make sure the subject isn't exposed outside VideoModel.

Revising the file browser

To understand what all this means, you can have another look at the file browser you were working with before. Here's the FRP graph we sketched for it.

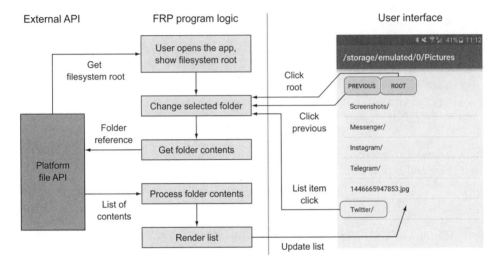

The user can browse the list of files, digging deeper into the folders. The selected folder signifies the current location of the user.

On the other hand, based on the current location, you get a list of files that you present to the user. This is shown in the simple `ListView`. There's also a possibility to go to the root or to the parent folder (in case you're not already at root).

File browser graph with a model

You'll start by adding a small model to the file browser. The model extracts the state you need to deal with and wraps it into a suitable container.

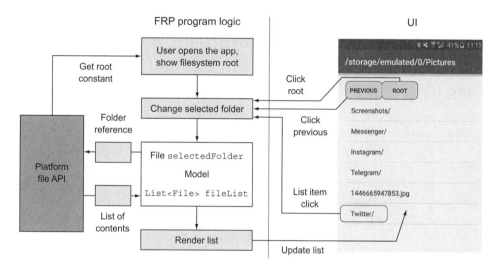

There are many arrows, but it's more important to focus on where the store is placed—it isn't part of the reactive logic, but rather a source and a destination for it.

Split chains

The reactive chain has been split around the store. This is intentional and a good thing, as the separate parts *don't depend on one another*.

Constructing the model for the file browser

You won't use any formal framework, but you'll start building a store yourself. On Android, often it's a good approach to start small and include libraries when it becomes necessary—and the simplest model is easy to implement.

The existing file browser view model

In the file browser you have two main observables for state: the selected file (folder), and the list of files within that folder. These two observables were linked together in the view model in a way that calculates the `fileList` based on the `selectedFolder`.

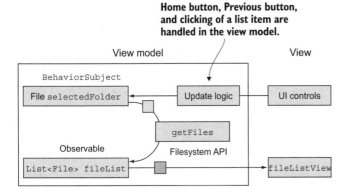

Now what you'll do is move some of the logic outside the view model and into the model. This way, you could potentially reuse it.

Where's the line between the view model and the model?

Where to put the code is more about (a) grouping code of similar responsibility together and (b) making sure there's not too much code in one file. Here the view model is accessing a filesystem API, which is quite low level. It's to handle the low-level operation outside the view model in a more concrete model.

There are no hard rules, though, and often the only real difference between view model and model is that the view model is directly connected to the view.

Moving state from view model into the model

You'll move all of the state from the view model to the model. This includes the selected folder and the resulting file list.

But you also have a dependency between two parts of the model. The selected folder and the file list aren't directly connected to anything except the model.

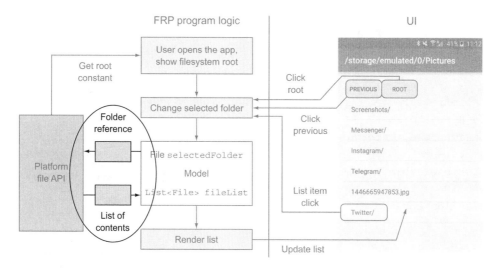

This means you can take this part out of the view model as well and move it into the model instead. It's a better place for the logic because it doesn't have much to do with the view.

Our proposed architecture will thus be a Model-View Model-View with divided responsibilities.

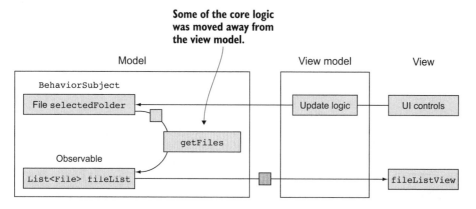

FileBrowser model implementation

You can now define the model in your code. You need a way to set the one selected folder the user has chosen and link it to an output of a list of its contents:

```
public class FileBrowserModel {
  private final BehaviorSubject<File> selectedFile
    = BehaviorSubject.createDefault();
  private final Observable<List<File>>
    filesListObservable;

  public FileBrowserModel(
      File fileSystemRoot,
      Function<File, Observable<List<File>>>
        getFiles) {
    filesListObservable = selectedFile
      .switchMap(file ->
        getFiles.apply(file)
          .subscribeOn(Schedulers.io())
      );
  }

  public Observable<File> getSelectedFile() {
    return selectedFile.hide();
  }

  public void putSelectedFile(File file) {
    selectedFile.onNext(file);
  }

  public Observable<List<File>> getFilesList() {
    return filesListObservable;
  }
}
```

The model contains selectedFile as a mini "store." The BehaviorSubject from the view model was moved here.

I omitted error catching here; you can see the full code in the online examples.

You don't expose the subjects directly from the model. It has full control over its data.

The reason you say "put" instead of "set" is semantics: you don't "set" the value of the selected folder but "push" another value that will replace it.

Notice that the model is more of a facade pattern than a logic container. The model combines different data containers (such as BehaviorSubject) to store all of the application state and can define how they interact on a low abstraction level.

Using the model

The initial switch to a model isn't too complex: you take the parts that use the behavior subjects and replace them with the respective model methods.

But how do you go about using the model in the view model? Who creates the model?

Creating the model

Where you create the model depends on who needs to use it and how long it needs to exist. In our case, you have only one Android activity, so you can create your model there. It just shouldn't be created in a view model—that would be strange, considering the view model is its consumer, not the owner. The activity (owner) makes the connection.

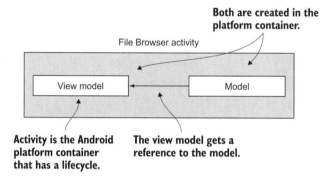

Both are created in the platform container.

File Browser activity

View model   Model

Activity is the Android platform container that has a lifecycle.

The view model gets a reference to the model.

In terms of code, you can connect the view model to the model in the `onCreate` function of the `MainActivity`. (The view model will be activated later in `initWithPermissions` because you first need to ask for filesystem privileges.)

MainActivity.java onCreate

```
fileBrowserModel =
   new FileBrowserModel(this::createFilesObservable);


viewModel = new FileBrowserViewModel(
   fileBrowserModel, listItemClickObservable,
   backEventObservable, homeEventObservable,
   root
);
```

The getFiles function was moved from the view model to the model. The view model no longer has a direct reference.

Updating the model from the view model

Instead of running your logic internally, you'll now update the model and hope it'll do its job. This isn't always typical, and sometimes you can restrict which parts of the model the view model sees. In our simple example, though, you'll leave Java interfaces alone and pass along the entire model.

Code changes in the view model

Let's first look at the old code with behavior subjects. It uses `selectedFolderSubject` for calculations and puts the results back into it:

```
// Somewhere in the initialization code
BehaviorSubject<File> selectedFolderSubject = ...;
...
Observable.merge(
        listItemClickObservable,
        fileChangeBackEventObservable,
        fileChangeHomeEventObservable)
        .subscribe(
          selectedFolderSubject::onNext
        );
```

This is the code that aggregates all possible changes of the selected file. You can change this to use the model instead:

```
// Somewhere in the initialization code
Observable<File> selectedFolder
  = fileBrowserModel.getSelectedFolder();
...
Observable.merge(
        listItemClickObservable,
        fileChangeBackEventObservable,
        fileChangeHomeEventObservable)
        .subscribe(
          fileBrowserModel::putSelectedFolder
        );
```

This creates the loop from the view model to the model and back.

Removing the logic from the view model

The model is a two-way system, so you'll also change the parts that consume values from the model. Here you start to see an emerging division between putting things in and getting things out—they're ultimately separate concerns in reactive programming and should be kept reasonably apart. In the view model they don't directly interact (they interact through the model).

Here's the old code in the view model with a subject:

FileBrowserViewModel.java subscribe method

```
subscriptions.add(selectedFile
  .switchMap(file ->
    getFiles.apply(file)
      .subscribeOn(Schedulers.io())))
```

The view model now becomes a consumer of the model. It still has its place to stand between the model and the view, but now in this case it only passes the files on to the view. This is where you could add things such as localizations that relate to the presentation of the data.

FileBrowserViewModel.java subscribe method

```
subscriptions.add(fileBrowserModel.getFilesList()
  .subscribe(filesSubject::onNext));
```

It wasn't that big of an effort to migrate functionality into a model. But this applies only *if done early on*. As the amount of code grows, so does the difficulty in switching to using a model.

Should you put all state in a model?

It's useful to put at least the data that's shared within the app into a separate model instance. This makes it easier to track who has access and to what. But not every step or state has to go into a model instance, and we'll discuss later in this chapter what makes sense.

Rules of the model and its consumers

You already saw a model, but let's list some principles to follow when dealing with them. The principles apply to all reactive frameworks, though the number of models and the exact updating mechanisms vary.

The model is the only source of truth

The model refers to the whole data layer. There has to always be only one correct place from where to get the data.

The model gives the latest value first

The model behaves in a way that allows new subscribers to get up-to-date as soon as possible. Typically, the model uses an internal store to cache previous values and serve them immediately to new subscribers.

All consumers of the model have to be ready to receive updates

The deal is, if you use data from the model, you have to be prepared to process possible updates that the model pushes later. This way, there's ideally no stale part of the application that isn't updated at the point when new data is available.

Can a store in the model be an SQL database?

In addition to keeping the model contents in the application memory, we can use one that's able to persist itself on another medium, such as a local SQLite database on the device. Whether you want to directly use the database depends on its performance, but as an abstraction, the store enables changing the persistence strategy fairly easily.

Google Firebase is even trying the ambitious approach of synchronizing the database to a remote server transparently.

`ContentProviders` on Android can be considered as stores, though we would still want to wrap them into store interfaces/observables.

Single source of truth

Of these principles, the first one is one of the cornerstones of reactive architecture: the store *always* has the latest data. But what does this mean?

The model is the Wikipedia of your app

If you had a question a few years ago, you'd likely find the answer in Wikipedia.

Likewise, inside the app you have a model that's able to give you the latest version of the data. If you look up the answer to your question again the data might have been updated, so your version would be stale, but you have a place where you can always go and ask for the latest data.

If you want to read about the latest health recommendations for eating carrots, you can open the page on Wikipedia about that topic.

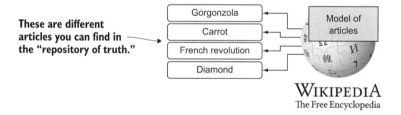

Subscriptions to the truth

The nice thing about our reactive stores is that you don't need to constantly go and check whether the data has changed. In our model, though, you can make a subscription and keep up-to-date as long as the data (the truth) is needed.

Coffee break

BehaviorSubjects are great for doing internal implementations, but sometimes you need more fine-grained control. For the sake of this exercise, see if you can make the same model implementation, but using a PublishSubject for selectedFolder.

Solution

You can also find this solution online, but we'll go through it here.

The starting point is with the BehaviorSubject:

```
private final BehaviorSubject<File>
  selectedFolder = BehaviorSubject.createDefault();
```

This subject does two things: it publishes updates to all subscribers and caches the last value (accessible through selectedFolder.getValue()). Because you want to get more control, though, you'll replace it with a PublishSubject and a separate cached value. The BehaviorSubject thus splits into two.

FileBrowserModel.java

```
private final PublishSubject<File>
  selectedFolderSubject = PublishSubject.create();
private File selectedFolder = null;
```

The default value of selectedFolder is null, whereas for BehaviorSubject it was undefined, but you'll see what to do with it soon.

Saving the last value

The next thing to do is save the last value and publish an update:

```
public void putSelectedFolder(File file) {
  selectedFolder = file;
  selectedFolderSubject.onNext(file);
}
```

Exposing getStream with an initial value

A bigger change is needed at a point when someone requests the observable. You can still use `selectedFolderSubject.hide()` to get the stream of future values. But to get the cached value, first you need to add to the stream yourself. This can be done with the `.startWith` operator that adds the given value to the start of the observable:

```java
public Observable<File> getSelectedFolder() {
  if (selectedFolder == null) {
    return selectedFolderSubject.hide();
  }

  return selectedFolderSubject.hide()
    .startWith(selectedFolder);
}
```

There's a slight difference in this implementation as compared to the `BehaviorSubject` you had before. If someone subscribes to this observable at a much later time, they'd still get the same `selectedFolder` first, even if it had changed in the meantime.

Delayed subscribers to the getSelectedFolder observable

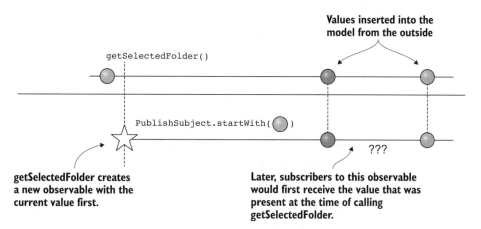

Values inserted into the model from the outside

getSelectedFolder()

PublishSubject.startWith( )

???

getSelectedFolder creates a new observable with the current value first.

Later, subscribers to this observable would first receive the value that was present at the time of calling getSelectedFolder.

Caching the latest value

The last thing to do is to save the last value when you receive it. You save it for future use and then publish it to any previous subscribers:

```
public void putSelectedFolder(File file) {
  selectedFolder = file;
  selectedFolderSubject.onNext(file);
}
```

The order of these two operations isn't hugely significant, though with this implementation it isn't thread safe. Someone could call the getSelectedFolder from another thread between these two lines, which would cause unexpected behavior. In production code, you could, for instance, use a synchronized block to queue the execution.

Benefits of using an explicit cache

With a single item (the selected folder) in the cache, our revised strategy doesn't seem too beneficial. But it can be useful with more complex requirements.

Having the cached values not tied to a single BehaviorSubject allows you to do different things:

- Clear a cached value by setting it back to null

- Create PublishSubjects for different kinds of updates (single item, full list, and so forth)

- Define the "last value" strategy by returning a custom observable

---

Isn't it bad to save the cached value plainly?

In reactive programming, you do try to keep everything as observables. But the state is always "somewhere" and sometimes needs to be synchronously accessible to update it. The model or a store inside of the model is a common place to find it.

But notice that usually the cached value isn't directly exposed. You want to enforce the clients of your model to handle updates, so you'd typically provide only an observable, even if you have the value cached. The cached value becomes an internal implementation detail.

Persisting app state

To understand the motivation for isolating state from the logic, you can expand the File Browser app to persist its state on the disk. To see how to go about it, let's look at the model again—this time, you already have the key state there.

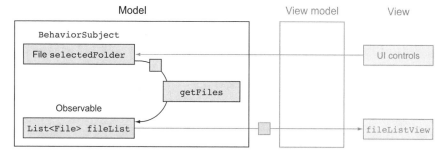

The question you need to ask is, what information is required to initialize the app? This will be the state you'll want to persist to reload the app.

The answer depends on the app, and in our case it's a file browser. Because you're showing a single directory, you can just save that, and the list of contents will be recalculated automatically when the app is opened.

Atomic state

You'll name this information that can't be calculated from anything else *atomic state*. The list of files in the selected folder isn't atomic state because you can always retrieve it again through the API.

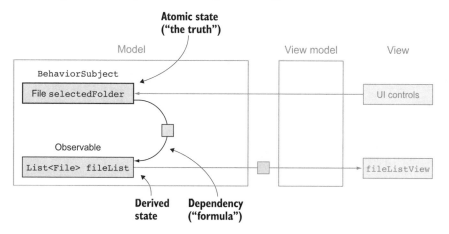

Saving the model state

First you'll try your hand at saving the `selectedFolder` as it's changed. You can do this by taking a "snapshot" of the `BehaviorSubject` whenever it emits a new value. This value is written onto a file on the disk.

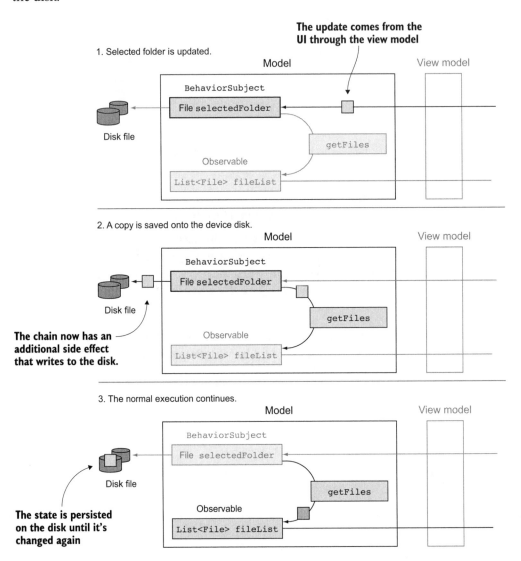

Code for saving the model state

On Android a simple way to save state is with `SharedPreferences`.
A `ContentProvider` would be a more scalable way, but for many
purposes, the amount of boilerplate code isn't justifiable.

Using SharedPreferences

What you want to do is write a copy of the `selectedFolder` file path
whenever it's changed. To do this, you can subscribe to it a function
that does this:

FileBrowserViewModel.java

```
public FileBrowserModel(
    Function<File, Observable<List<File>>>
      getFiles,
    SharedPreferences sharedPreferences) {    ◄───────
  selectedFolder
    .observeOn(Schedulers.io())
    .subscribe(folder ->
      sharedPreferences.edit()    ◄
        .putString(
          SELECTED_FOLDER_KEY,
          folder.getAbsolutePath()
        )
        .commit());
. . .
```

SharedPreferences is given as a reference from outside. This could be changed into a function that writes to disk.

You use the edit command of SharedPreferences to open a writer. In the end, you commit the changes to affect the operation.

How is this different from saved bundled state on Android?

On Android, there's indeed a platform way to save the state of the
application upon its closing. But persisting state in the UI containers
(such as activities or fragments) is problematic. Often many parts of
the application share the same state, as you've defined in the model,
and in this case the persisting would be duplicated.

With reactive applications on Android, it's a good idea to disable the
platform restoration entirely. Re-creating the view hierarchy from
the model state when the app starts isn't too expensive or slow on
modern devices if done correctly.

Loading the model state on startup

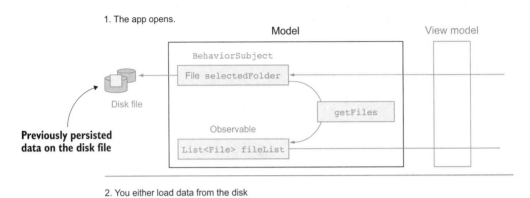

1. The app opens.

Previously persisted data on the disk file

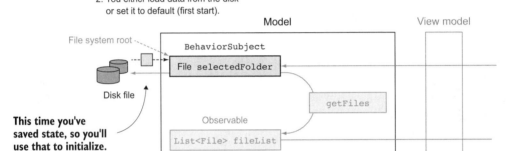

2. You either load data from the disk or set it to default (first start).

This time you've saved state, so you'll use that to initialize.

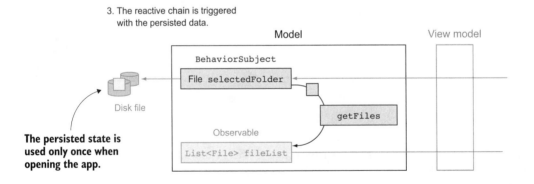

3. The reactive chain is triggered with the persisted data.

The persisted state is used only once when opening the app.

Code for loading the model state

For the code that reads the initial state, you'll add it at the beginning of the `FileBrowserModel` constructor. You'll also pass the default value for the selected folder, in case no value on the disk is available.

The signature of the `getString` function allows you to define the default value in the second parameter, so you can use that for our purposes.

```
SharedPreferences.getString(
  String key, String defaultValue);
```

With the added code, the beginning of the constructor first loads the state and then proceeds with the rest of the initialization.

This particular code will result in one extra write operation as the `BehaviorSubject` emits its value immediately, but because it doesn't cause a loop, you'll leave it as a further improvement.

FileBrowserModel.java

```
public FileBrowserModel(
    Function<File, Observable<List<File>>> getFiles,
    String defaultPath,
    SharedPreferences sharedPreferences) {

  // Load previously persisted value or use the default
  String persistedSelectedFolder Path = sharedPreferences
    .getString(SELECTED_FOLDER_KEY, defaultPath);

  File initialSelectedFolder =
    new File(persistedSelectedFolderPath);

  selectedFolder = BehaviorSubject
    .createDefault(initialSelectedFolder);
  ...
```

Provided as a dependency from the owner. In our case, it's the activity, but you could start using a dependency injection framework too.

A string for the default folder to use in case no persisted one is available

This is the part that loads the value or uses the default folder path given.

BehaviorSubjects and stores

You may remember that I mentioned that a model uses a store to persist data. Why aren't you using one here?

The answer is you created a simple ad hoc store with the `BehaviorSubject` + `SharedPreferences`.

The simple one-value store

Perhaps the most reduced persisted store on Android can be constructed from a `BehaviorSubject` and a disk backing.

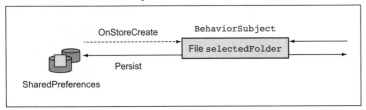

BehaviorSubject + SharedPreferences Store

What you have is essentially a mini-store that can be wrapped into its own class. On the next page, you'll see an example implementation.

Do you need a better store?

You'll continue using lightweight stores in this part of the book. The reason is the store implementation doesn't affect the rest of the application much—you can implement the full architecture and change the store later.

There is also nothing wrong with these kinds of stores as long as the filesystem performs well enough for your purposes and you don't need to share the state between processes. You'll explore "heavier" stores later in the book.

Simple SharedPreferencesStore

There are many kinds of stores, but here you'll make one that works in only one process (no widgets or other parts that need to share data between Java VMs). It also supports only a single value: in our case, the selected folder.

You'll look into more sophisticated stores in later chapters, but this one is a good starting point for exploring encapsulation.

SharedPreferencesStore.java

```java
public class SharedPreferencesStore<T> {
  private final BehaviorSubject<T> subject;

  public SharedPreferencesStore(final String key,
      final String defaultValue,
      final SharedPreferences sharedPreferences,
      final Function<T, String> serialize,
      final Function<String, T> deserialize) {
    T initialValue = deserialize.apply(
      sharedPreferences.getString(key, defaultValue)
    );
    subject = BehaviorSubject
      .createDefault(initialValue);
    subject.subscribe(value ->
      sharedPreferences.edit()
        .putString(key, serialize.apply(value))
        .commit()
      );
  }

  public void put(T value) {
    subject.onNext(value);
  }

  public Observable<T> getStream() {
    return subject.hide();
  }
}
```

This is the subject you previously had directly in the model code. Now you'll replace it with an instance of a store.

Because you use strings as a format for persisting, you need to add functions to tell the store how to change from file to string, and vice versa.

You don't save the subscription at this time. Usually stores live so long that their internal subscriptions are released as the app is completely shut down.

Using SharedPreferencesStore

The model you have will now internally use the store as a way to store the `selectedFolder`. Notice that to the outside, it looks exactly the same as before.

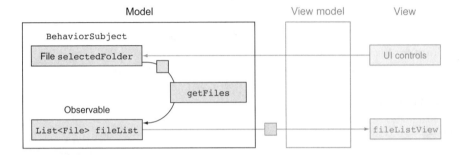

In terms of code, you just need to change the initialization of the model. The model will give the store everything it requires to know how to handle its values and persist them.

FileBrowserModel.java constructor

```
selectedFolderStore = new SharedPreferencesStore<>(
    SELECTED_FOLDER_KEY,
    defaultPath,
    sharedPreferences,
    file -> file.getAbsolutePath(),
    path -> new File(path)
);
```

Arbitrary string that will be used as the filename for SharedPreferences

These two are the serializing and deserializing functions between strings and files.

Summary

In this chapter, you saw the remaining key parts of reactive applications used in this book. You can arrange them on a spectrum to see which are more concerned with rendering and which are concerned with pure data.

View affinities of architectural parts

External API / persistence	Business logic	Processed data for UI	UI state	Graphics on screen

Model

Store

View model

View

In general, stores are the heart of the application and contain and persist key data. There's also state in the view models and the view, but only *derived state* can be re-created based on the store.

Model as a source of truth

The key takeaway of this chapter is that a reactive application needs a definite source of truth for any data. If it's used in only one place, the source of truth can be "local." But, if another part of the application starts using the same data, it needs to be shared—this sharing mechanism we call the model.

The model isn't a new invention, but in a reactive application it becomes even more important than before. It's also inherently reactive, exposing observables to keep the data up-to-date.

Other possible parts of reactive architectures

Later in the book, in chapters 11 and 12, you'll see the presented architecture divided into small components with different responsibilities. But the ones listed so far are the ones you'll use the most. Typically, if one of them becomes too large, though, you can create a module with a different responsibility to keep the code manageable.

Developing with view models | **8**

....

In this chapter

- Architectural views and view models

- The view drawing cycle and reactive programming

- View models with multiple outputs

....

View models and the view

In the preceding chapter, you had a first look at view models. You learned that they're vessels for the business logic, isolating it in a way that allows it to be scrutinized and unit tested. At the end of the day, *view model* is just a clear name for encapsulation of functional logic needed to show something on the screen.

What's left in the presentation layer of the application after you remove this business logic is called the *view layer*. In the architectural sense of the term, the view layer shouldn't be confused with the Android View class—the view layer usually contains instances of Views, but isn't limited to them.

The view layer is everything and anything that displays the processed data to the user.

This defines the view as the endpoint of the factory line, where everything is ready and you can finally send the product to the customer. You have all the information you need and you just need to display it to the user.

In this drawing, you can see the relationships between view models and view—as well as the fact that the view doesn't see the APIs at all because they're all hidden in the dedicated view model.

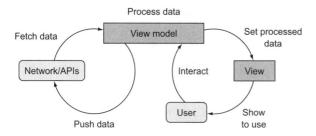

In this chapter, you'll explore view models further and learn some new Rx tools on the way. It's a long chapter, so hang tight.

Example: Tic-tac-toe

To inspect where to draw the line between business logic and the drawing of data, let's use the simple example of tic-tac-toe.

In case you aren't familiar with this game, two players take turns drawing either a cross or a circle on a 3 × 3 grid. The one who gets three in a line wins—or, when that isn't possible anymore, the game ends in a tie.

Here's a game that has been played for three rounds. The players can place their icons in only the empty squares.

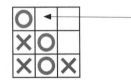

Because the circle always starts, in this particular game the circle is about to win.

A tie   Circle wins

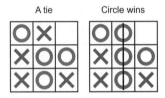

At this point, we're sticking with a hot-seat version, in which the players have to play on the same device. There's no internet connectivity in this application.

The different moves of tic-tac-toe

Different approaches exist for breaking down a problem and creating an application, but in this case you'll use one that starts from what you want to be drawn on the screen.

In the game of tic-tac-toe we have a two-dimensional grid of three kinds of states: empty, a circle, or a cross. In the simplest form, this can be done with an enumerated type and a 3 × 3 array.

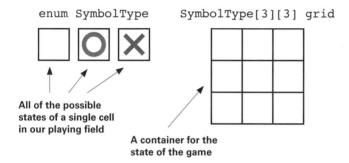

enum SymbolType

All of the possible states of a single cell in our playing field

SymbolType[3][3] grid

A container for the state of the game

You're getting somewhere. All data at this point is of type `SymbolType[3][3]`. With this you can draw the grid and the symbols. You'll create a view that knows how to draw data of this type. It'll have a setter `setData(SymbolType[][] data)` that accepts the data. As soon as new data is given, the view is redrawn to represent the new information.

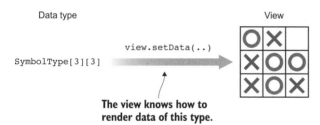

Data type

View

`view.setData(..)`

SymbolType[3][3]

The view knows how to render data of this type.

At this point, the process is still a little abstract, but it'll be clearer after you get to the drawing part.

Drawing the game grid

Before you get into the reactive part, you still need to have the premises set up for your game. You'll start with drawing the grid on the screen.

There are many ways to construct a view that's able to show the user the game board. You'll opt for a rather low-level approach by drawing the graphics directly on the screen canvas.

The lifecycle of using canvas graphics on the screen is similar in all UI platforms, though you'll use Android as an example of how it can be done.

Here are the steps to draw and update the game grid:

1. Create

- The owner creates the interface component.
- The interface component is initialized with an empty grid.

2. Call setData() to trigger update

- `setData` invalidates the state of the view.
- The redraw is scheduled.
- The old graphics are cleared and updated with ones based on the new data.

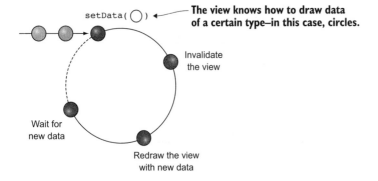

The draw function

If you use a basic view, you can implement all of your drawing logic into the view's `onDraw` function. In that function you get a canvas that lets you use basic functions, such as drawing lines, circles, or bitmaps.

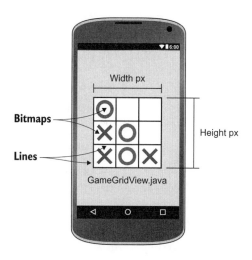

The `View` class is an Android platform component that occupies a certain amount of space on screen. Most UI platforms are built in this fashion.

When you make some operations in the class `GameGridView.java` the only area you can affect is the one dedicated for the view component. Therefore, the draw function can assume the top-left corner of the coordinate system is always (0, 0), even if the view is in the middle of the device screen.

The custom view class

The first thing you'll do is create the new class. Everything related only to drawing will be kept there:

GameGridView.java

```java
public class GameGridView extends View {
  private GameSymbol[][] gameState;
  ...
```

You also added a `gameState`, which will hold the data you use in your drawing function. You'll see soon why this is necessary.

Notice that the drawing of the view isn't reactive per se, but what you're learning are techniques to keep the drawing separate from the logic.

Updating the data that the view presents

You need to add a way to tell your custom view that it has something
new to show. After setting the data, you call the platform way of
notifying the drawing system it needs to redraw. The drawing function
will then use the data you saved for its drawing.

GameGridView.java

```java
public void setData(SymbolType[][] gameState) {
  // Save data for drawing
  this.gameState = gameState;   ◀————————————————————————

  // Schedule redraw
  this.invalidate();
}
```

This is a member
variable you created
for the View class.
Notice that it's just
a holder for the data
and shouldn't be
exposed outside
this class!

The drawing function is a separate platform function. It isn't advisable
to directly call it, and thus you need to save the data until you need it
here. You can see the full code in the online example.

```java
@Override
protected void onDraw(Canvas canvas) {
  // Clear the old drawings
  clearCanvas(canvas);   ◀————————————————————————

  // Draw background
  drawGridLines(canvas);   ◀————

  // Draw symbols by looping through them
  for (int i = 0; i < 3; i++) {
    for (int n = 0; n < 3; n++) {   ◀————————
      Symbol symbol = this.data[i][n];
      if (symbol == Symbol.CIRCLE) {
        drawCircle(canvas, i, n);
      } else if (symbol == Symbol.CROSS) {
        drawCross(canvas, i, n);
      }
    }
  }
}
```

You're skipping
some more
straightforward
code, but you can
see it in the online
code example.

This is a double loop
that goes through
your entire 3 × 3
array. Using magic
numbers in the code
instead of constants
is bad, but you'll
change that later.

Trying out the view with hardcoded values

Before you get to user interaction, you can quickly see whether the view you created renders as specified. The good thing about the components in a reactive application is that they assume little about where the data comes from. You can therefore give the `setData` function of the component a bunch of hardcoded data, and it should render the view correctly.

MainActivity onCreate

```
GameGridView gameGridView =
  (GameGridView) findViewById(R.id.grid_view);

gameGridView.setData(
  new GameSymbol[][] {
    new GameSymbol[] {
  GameSymbol.CIRCLE, GameSymbol.EMPTY, GameSymbol.EMPTY
    },
    new GameSymbol[] {
  GameSymbol.CIRCLE, GameSymbol.CROSS, GameSymbol.EMPTY
    },
    new GameSymbol[] {
  GameSymbol.CROSS, GameSymbol.EMPTY, GameSymbol.EMPTY
    }
  }
);
```

This code produces a static view of the game grid that can't be changed.

It's usually good to check at every point that the code you just wrote does what it's intended to do. An application's much more difficult to debug later, after you have a big pile of code.

Making it interactive

You're getting closer to the reactive part of the app. The interaction will be done with an Rx chain, but let's see what you plan to do.

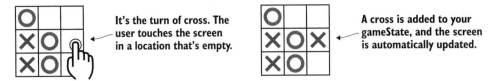

It's the turn of cross. The user touches the screen in a location that's empty.

A cross is added to your gameState, and the screen is automatically updated.

Rules determine how this works in detail, but you'll get to those later. For now, let's focus on how to get the correct symbols showing on the tiles that the user touches.

Getting the touch events

You'll again use the RxBinding library to get a wrapper that gives you the touches on the view as an event observable. Normally, you'd register a listener for touch events, but this way, you can use the event processing capabilities of RxJava.

MainActivity.java onCreate

```
// Retrieve a reference to the created view
GameGridView gameGridView =
  (GameGridView) findViewById(R.id.grid_view);

// Get an observable with the RxBinding wrapper
Observable<MotionEvent> userTouchObservable =
  RxView.touches(gameGridView);
```

This observable will now emit all of the events that you usually receive in `setOnTouchListener`.

The reactive processing chain

When the user clicks on the playing grid, you want to insert the correct symbol into that location and then change the turn.

To know which grid tile the user clicked, you run the click event through a simple processing chain. The steps are roughly as follows:

1 Start with the relative (x, y) coordinate of where the user clicked inside the grid view.

2 Determine into which tile the click landed and emit this simplified coordinate. Instead of screen coordinates, these are indexes for the grid array you have.

3 Update the grid by placing a new symbol in the location you determined.

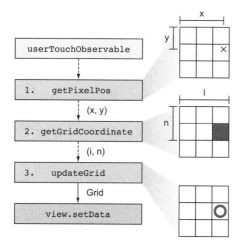

We've covered only the part of the chain that's interesting, but you'll later see how it fits into the big picture. A few questions are left unanswered, such as how do you get the physical size of the view on the screen or a reference to the last grid in order to update it—after all, we're talking reactive programming, where you don't want to magically access variables outside your chain.

Grid coordinate resolving code

To get back to the touch processing, in step 2 you have to identify
which grid tile the user touched. Here you need a bit of mathematics,
but don't worry; you'll go through the algorithm in detail.

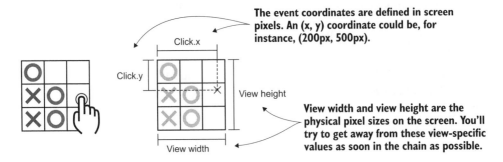

The event coordinates are defined in screen pixels. An (x, y) coordinate could be, for instance, (200px, 500px).

Click.x

Click.y

View height

View width

View width and view height are the physical pixel sizes on the screen. You'll try to get away from these view-specific values as soon in the chain as possible.

For the horizontal grid position, you first divide the x coordinate of the
click by the width of the whole view on the screen. You'll get a number
between 0 and 1, 0.5 being in the middle.

1 You multiply the number from the first step by the number of
tiles in the grid on the horizontal axis, which in this case is 3.
Rounding down the number, you get the horizontal grid position.

2 What you'll have is a function that takes pixel coordinates and
produces `GridPositions`. To distinguish these two you create a
new data type that holds these values. In this case they range from
(0, 0) to (2, 2). Indexing here starts from 0.

```
class GridPosition {
   int x
   int y
}
```

Code for resolving grid positions

You'll create a new function that takes a pixel position on the screen and returns a `GridPosition` instead. A pixel position of (125 px, 63 px), for instance, might be converted into a `GridPosition` of (2, 1), depending on the screen pixel size.

MainActivity getGridPosition

```
private static GridPosition getGridPosition(
        float touchX, float touchY,
        int viewWidthPixels, int viewHeightPixels,
        int gridWidth, int gridHeight) {

  // Horizontal GridPosition coordinate as i
  float rx = touchX /
    (float)(viewWidthPixels+1);
  int i = (int)(rx * gridWidth);         ◄─────────────────

  // Vertical GridPosition coordinate as n
  float ry = touchY /
    (float)(viewHeightPixels+1);
  int n = (int)(ry * gridHeight);        ◄─

  return new GridPosition(i, n);
}
```

You sometimes use i and n to make a distinction that these aren't pixel coordinates. But it's easier to remember that x is horizontal and y is vertical, so we won't stick to them all the time.

> ## Pixel coordinates vs. GridPositions
>
> Both the pixel coordinates and `GridPositions` are pairs of numbers. Mixing them up can be easy.
>
> When dealing with these kinds of values, it's helpful to name them with a custom data type. This way, at least the compiler will warn you if you try to pass a function in pixels instead of positions on the grid—even if both might contain x and y.

Now for the part of the code that uses this function.

You'll listen to the events you get from the RxView touches stream, and you'll filter that stream to contain only events for which the user lifts a finger. This can be done directly on the observable with a common filter.

MainActivity onCreate

```
// Get the touches
Observable<GridPosition> userTouchEventObservable =
  RxView.touches(gridView, motionEvent -> true)
    .filter(ev ->
      ev.getAction() == MotionEvent.ACTION_UP);
```

With this event observable, you can resolve a stream of GridPositions that allow you to later update the game grid.

```
// Get the GridPosition from the pixel coordinate
Observable<GridPosition> gridPositionEventObservable =
  userTouchEventObservable
    .map(ev ->
      getGridPosition(
        ev.getX(), ev.getY(),
        gameGridView.getWidth(),
        gameGridView.getHeight(),
        GRID_WIDTH, GRID_HEIGHT
      )
    );
```

Finally, until you have the grid updating function ready, you can see whether it works by logging the events. You'd expect values between (0, 0) and (2, 2).

```
// For starters just log the results
gridPositionEventObservable
  .subscribe(gridPosition ->
    Log.d(TAG, gridPosition.toString()));
```

The extended graph structure

To complete the graph on the previous page, you can observe that to update the grid, you need the last grid as well. Otherwise, you'll always be making the first move and forgetting the previous ones.

You can use the technique you saw in the preceding chapter, in which you make a cyclic graph that uses the previously emitted data value to calculate a new one.

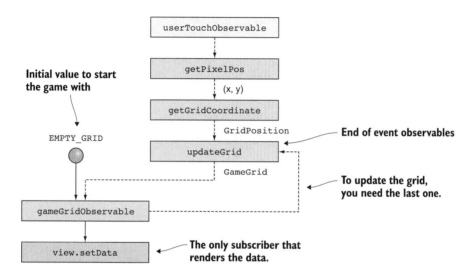

Notice that you have only one subscriber. The `setData` should be called only at the end of the chain, and there shouldn't be more than one. If you started updating the data from many parts of the application, you'd lose the clarity of where things are supposed to happen.

Converting event observables into normal ones

If you observe carefully, you'll notice that the arrows change from dashed to solid at this point. This is a transition point from events to solid reactive state. Before going forward with the implementation, let's take a detour to talk about that.

Events vs. reactive state

You might have noticed that you used a new kind of arrow in the preceding graph—one that looks like a dashed arrow. The difference between the two is purely semantic: the solid arrow is used to describe a *dependency* between the state of different entities. Think about the credit card example in which the validity is calculated from the input fields.

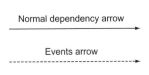

Normal dependency arrow

Events arrow

The events arrow, on the other hand, is for events that don't signify any *permanent* state change, such as mouse clicks. They're relevant at only one point in time.

Drawing the line between events and state

What's the difference between an observable that emits state changes and an observable that emits pure events?

You can test it by asking, "Are the emitted values of the observable communicating state change or are they one-off events?" Or, "Would the last value the observable emitted be potentially useful in five minutes?" If the answer is yes, you have a real observable that represents reactive state. If no, you're dealing with an event observable.

In our case, `gridObservable` represents reactive state. If you reload the view, you can use the last value it emitted to redraw it.

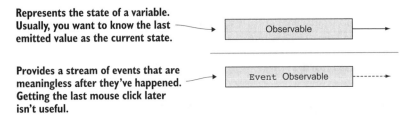

Represents the state of a variable. Usually, you want to know the last emitted value as the current state. → Observable

Provides a stream of events that are meaningless after they've happened. Getting the last mouse click later isn't useful. → Event Observable

In general, you want to deal with "real" solid arrows as much as possible. Dependencies between reactive entities are easier to understand and maintain than events.

RxJava observables work technically for both, though, so you can use that to your benefit and process events as well. You just have to remember which ones you're dealing with and try to get to real reactive state as soon as possible.

Examples of different observables

A real-life metaphor of a reactive state could be the life of a butterfly.
Here you see the life of a butterfly depicted as an observable.

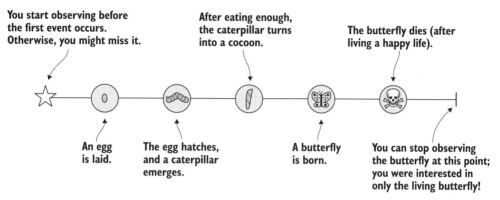

This is a good example of the emitted values being *state changes*. Every
time the "value" of the reactive entity changes, the observable emits
the new value. These kinds of observables are also sometimes called
behaviors, in case you encounter the term in other literature.

An example of an event observable is that of mouse clicks at certain
coordinates. Notice that the click isn't representing any state; it's just a
momentary action in time.

Click at (0,3)	Click	Click	Click	Click

Is event processing reactive programming?

Whether using event observables is functional reactive programming
(FRP), or even reactive programming, it's a debate that has a point,
because events tend to cause issues that are hard to debug.

Reactive programming, as well as RxJava, has been criticized for
not being true FRP. One of the reasons is that event processing isn't
generally considered to be FRP and sometimes makes handling
simultaneous changes complicated. Events are important in UIs,
though, which is why we use the term *reactive* and keep it practical.

To communicate the difference, though, you'll from now on use the
new dashed arrows in cases where you're still in the process of handling
events and interpreting them into a state change. As a rule of thumb,
it's best to get out of the event processing part as soon as possible.

Immutable data and the game grid

To get back to the example, you now have an almost working game that lets you fill the grid with circles. Don't worry: it'll get more playable soon! The only step left is the one where you update the grid with the newly played game symbol.

As you may remember from before, you should never change the existing data value. This is the principle of immutability: for instance, the view might still be drawing itself with the old value when a new one comes. Modifying the old value directly in some other part of the application could cause strange behavior if the grid is updated in the middle of the drawing loop.

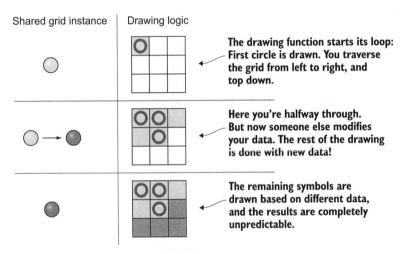

Shared grid instance | Drawing logic

The drawing function starts its loop: First circle is drawn. You traverse the grid from left to right, and top down.

Here you're halfway through. But now someone else modifies your data. The rest of the drawing is done with new data!

The remaining symbols are drawn based on different data, and the results are completely unpredictable.

You could be defensive in the view itself and take a copy of the grid before drawing. But the nice thing about doing proper reactive programming is that you can always *trust* that the variables passed to you won't be modified.

To trust or not to trust?

Why do you need to trust at all if immutability isn't enforced? In a perfect world (or if using a pure, functional language), it would be indeed so, but when doing Rx with Java, you need to exercise self-discipline and make sure you don't change our inputs.

Making a copy of the grid

How do you deal with updating the grid when a player makes a new move? Duplicate the whole grid to make just one change?

In short, yes, at least for starters. Because you don't want to modify the original, the easiest way is to make a copy of it, apply the change, and emit the new grid for the drawing pipeline.

In terms of performance, though, it's possible to optimize the duplication process. There are strategies that retain the parts of the data structure that weren't changed (such as unaffected rows).

It's also possible to make a *stack* of changes with the decorator pattern. You could have the entire game saved as a list of moves that were made. This kind of a stack approach is perhaps the most flexible way, but because it's conceptually more complex, we'll cover it a little later.

Applying a change to the GameGrid

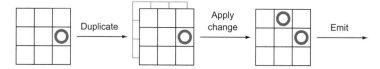

Java provides many ways to copy an array, but for our simple purposes, you can copy each row of the raw array with `System.arraycopy`, which is very efficient. It takes the source array, position in the source, destination, the position in the destination, as well as the total number of items to copy.

Do you always have to make a full copy when handling references?

A *copy* is a misleading name for what you're doing. Later you'll see how to create data structures that can have more efficient internal implementations to reduce the burden of copying. Numerous techniques exist in the field of traditional functional programming.

You need only two things: the original has to remain unchanged, and the new one has to return the right values in the getters. Usually, you wouldn't use raw data, so you're free to do some magic in the getters.

Variable references and primitive data types in Java

How do you know what has to be protected from modification and what not? In most object-oriented languages, such as Java, there's a difference between primitive data types and normal classes. The short version is it isn't possible to modify the primitive data types after they're created and therefore they're inherently safe.

The list of primitive data types in Java is `byte`, `short`, `int`, `long`, `float`, `double`, `char`, and `boolean`. Notice that *they don't have any setter functions*. When you add integers together, you create a new integer.

```
int a = 0;
int b = a;
a = a + 1; // b remains unaffected
```

`String` is a different kind of case. `String` isn't a primitive data type, but at the same time it can't be modified after creation. A string has no setter functions, and so it's also safe.

```
String a = "Once upon a";
String b = a;
a = a + "time"; // b remains unaffected
```

The same applies for all the instance functions of `String`. For instance, `.toUpperCase()` doesn't affect the original one. It just creates a new instance of a string that's uppercase. *This is how you'd want all of your data types to work.*

```
String myString = "foo";
String myOtherString = myString;
myString = myString.toUpperCase();
// Again, b remains unaffected
```

If you look at the code execution in terms of where the variables are stored, you have to look at how the program memory works.

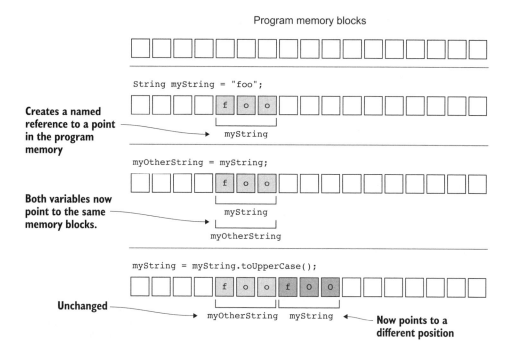

Program memory blocks

String myString = "foo";

Creates a named reference to a point in the program memory → myString

myOtherString = myString;

Both variables now point to the same memory blocks. → myString / myOtherString

myString = myString.toUpperCase();

Unchanged → myOtherString myString ← **Now points to a different position**

This is how creating new values should work; the other variable stays as it was supposed to be.

The class `String` *could* have a method called `.modifyToBeUpperCase()` that modified the original value. In this case, however, the previous instances would be affected and chaos would ensue.

```
String a = "Once upon a";
String b = a;
a.modifyToBeUpperCase(); // b is changed too, confusing!
```

The way the `String` class really works is that the called function
`toUpperCase` returns a modified copy:

```
String a = "Once upon a";
String b = a.toUpperCase();
```

This is an approach more like functional programming, and it better suits
our needs in the reactive chains. The variable `a` remains unchanged.

GameGrid type and functional setters

What you'll create first is a class to hold the entire game grid.
Previously, you had just a two-dimensional array `GridSymbol[][]`,
but to encapsulate more functionality, you'll change it into a type:

```
class GameGrid {
  GameSymbol getSymbolAt(int x, int y)
  GameGrid setSymbolAt(
    GameSymbol symbol, int x, int y)
}
```

Pay attention to this setter. It isn't the traditional kind of Java setter, but made in a functional style. It doesn't modify the original instance.

The unusual part here is that `setSymbol` returns an entire `GameGrid`!
The same way `String.toUpperCase` returns a modified copy of the
string, our setter returns a modified copy of the original `GameGrid`.

The function can be optimized, but in principle it takes a copy of itself
and returns the modified copy:

```
public GameGrid setSymbolAt(
  GameSymbol symbol, int i, int n) {
  GameGrid copy = this.copy();
  copy.grid[i][n] = symbol;
  return copy;
}
```

You can check the full details in the online repository.

Adding the code for interaction

With this information, you're ready to make a first version of the reactive chain in code. This will enable you to place circles on the playing field (taking turns are coming next). It might not sound like much for the time you've spent, but you'll be delighted to see that adding the remaining features will be much faster.

Preparations

You again start with an `onCreate` activity and quickly go through what you already put there. In the end, you'll add a subject to hold the reactive state of the `GameGrid`. This subject will act as a central point of sorts, where you aggregate all updates to the `GameGrid`.

MainActivity onCreate

```
// Find a reference to our GridView
GameGridView gameGridView = ...

// This an empty grid we will use as a reference
GameGrid emptyGrid =
  new GameGrid(GRID_WIDTH, GRID_HEIGHT);

// We already saw how to create this one
Observable<GridPosition> gridPositionEventObservable
  = ...

// Create GameGrid subject with default value
BehaviorSubject<GameGrid> gameGridSubject =
  new BehaviorSubject(emptyGrid);
```

You'll start without a view model and refactor the code to be contained in one when the code grows bigger.

This `gameGridSubject` is quite important to the structure of our application, and we'll be talking about it later more extensively. For now just consider it the place where you can always find the latest `GameGrid`.

Updating the GameGrid Based on events

Now you get to the part where you transition from the events that are generated from the user interaction into updates to the GameGrid as a whole. Remember that the view always wants a complete GameGrid even if just a part of it changed. (Any optimizations in terms of what has changed is up to the view to do.)

For grabbing the last value from the gameGridSubject you'll use a new operator called withLatestFrom. It's a handy tool for dealing with event observables. You'll see the code first and then go into detail about how it works:

MainActivity onCreate (continued)

```
// Process the touches and add them on the gameGrid
touchesOnGrid
    .withLatestFrom(
      gameGridSubject,
      (gridPosition, gameGrid) ->
        gameGrid.setSymbol(
          gridPosition, Symbol.CIRCLE)
    )
    .subscribe(gameGridSubject::onNext);
```

Gets the latest value from another observable, without triggering the chain for a new value coming from it. You'll learn more about withLatestFrom after this.

gridPosition comes from touchesOnGrid.

Creates a new instance of the GameGrid. The naming is a bit misleading, but you know from the FRP context it creates an instance.

On the last line you close the cycle, you make sure changes you make to GameGrid are put back into the gameGridSubject that holds the last state of GameGrid. It will trigger only for incoming events, though, which you'll explore next.

To show the GameGrid in your UI, you'll make a subscription. You'll create a view model for it in a bit, so you won't save and release the subscription at this "prototyping" phase.

MainActivity onCreate (continued)

```
// Connect the View to the latest GameGrid
gameGridSubject
    .observeOn(AndroidSchedulers.mainThread())
    .subscribe(gridView::setData);
```

GridView UI component so that it knows how to draw GameGrid

Cyclic graphs with .withLatestFrom

In some cases, you need the last values from two observables to calculate a third one, but you want only one of them to trigger the chain below. Now you'll see what this means in detail.

You encountered this problem before, but then you were using another method of just accessing a variable from outside the FRP processing step. But this approach isn't always clean because you rely on outside state instead of making pure functions that use only their inputs (and constants). You'll fix it now with our new approach:

Getting the last value of another observable

The observable that you use with `.withLatestFrom` is marked as a thick arrow with a dashed line. The last value that's emitted to the dashed arrow is waiting for the primary observable to trigger the calculation.

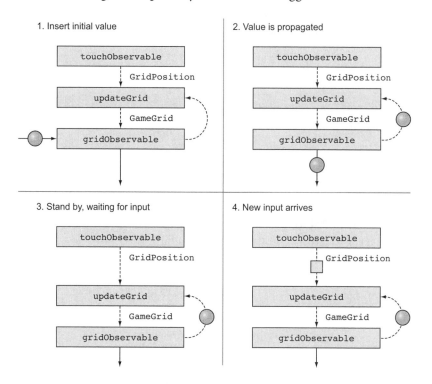

Step 4 is where the `.withLatestFrom` function is doing its thing. It's a lot like `combineLatest`, but *it's triggered on only new values from the primary observable*. In this case, the triggering one is the observable that emits the `GridCoordinates` calculated from the touch events.

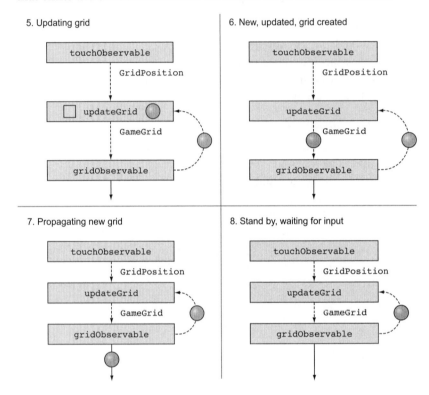

5. Updating grid

touchObservable
GridPosition
updateGrid
GameGrid
gridObservable

6. New, updated, grid created

touchObservable
GridPosition
updateGrid
GameGrid
gridObservable

7. Propagating new grid

touchObservable
GridPosition
updateGrid
GameGrid
gridObservable

8. Stand by, waiting for input

touchObservable
GridPosition
updateGrid
GameGrid
gridObservable

You can think about it like this: you want to update the grid with the touch events only when the user is touching—not whenever you have a `GameGrid` for some other reason (also, in this case, that would create an infinite loop).

You already saw the code, but here it is again:

```
touchesOnGrid
  .withLatestFrom(gameGridSubject,
    (gridCoordinate, gameGrid) ->
      gameGrid.setSymbol(
        gridCoordinate, Symbol.CIRCLE)
  )
```

This lambda function is the combine function that's executed on all new values of the gridCoordinate.

Coffee break

You aren't at a point where you can place circles on the game grid. The game isn't too exciting yet, but often it takes a while to build the foundation to get to the interesting parts.

The `withLatestFrom` operator is something you don't need too often, but it's sometimes good to have, especially when dealing with events.

Exercise: dialog box generator

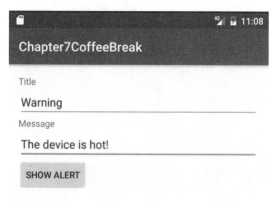

You'll create a little app that can show alerts (dialogs) based on the input written in the text fields. The app isn't complex, but for the exercise's sake you'll go the extra mile and use RxJava for it.

You'll define the inputs as Observables, and it's your job to combine them to produce a dialog box. Keep in mind which observables emit events and which ones represent permanent states. We'll go through this in the solution.

Start with a dialog box that gets only the title from the text input, and then try to include the message as well: this is a little more difficult than it seems, though. Think of which observables represent reactive state and how they can be manipulated.

Showing a dialog box

To show a dialog box on Android, you can use `AlertDialog.Builder`:

```
new AlertDialog.Builder(this)
  .setTitle(dialogContents.first)
  .setMessage(dialogContents.second)
  .show()
```

Preparations for the coffee break

You can check out the starting point of the coffee break from the online repository. Alternatively, you can create a new project for this and add the dependencies as well as enable `jackOptions`. You can refer to the appendix to set up a default project or copy the settings from the Tic-Tac-Toe project.

The layout is standard Android with `TextViews` and `EditTexts`.

You'll define the needed observables without keeping the references to the original view components. This time the task is to figure out how to show the dialog using only these observables as well as operators such as `withLatestFrom` and `combineLatest`.

MainActivity.java

```java
final Observable<String> titleObservable =
  RxTextView
    .textChanges(
      (TextView) findViewById(R.id.title_edit_text))
    .map(Object::toString);

final Observable<String> messageObservable =
  RxTextView
    .textChanges(
      (TextView) findViewById(R.id.message_edit_text))
    .map(Object::toString);

final Observable<Object> clickEvents =
  RxView.clicks(findViewById(R.id.action_button));

// TODO: Show a dialog when an event is emitted from
// the clickEvents Observable
```

Solution

You'll first make the simple version where you use just the title. This works the same way you did before: `withLatestFrom` takes *one event observable and another one that represents permanent state*. It's important to keep this in mind—if you have something else in your hands, you probably should use something other than `withLatestFrom`.

In our case, you have a `clickEvent` observable and a `titleObservable`. Of these, `clickEvent` is used as the trigger; `titleObservable` provides it only *the latest value that the user has typed*. This is exactly what `withLatestFrom` does.

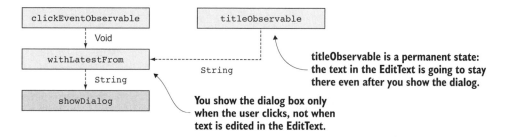

In terms of code, you're basically taking the `Void` objects provided by the `clickEvent` observable and converting them into strings. The string here represents all the information you need to show the dialog box: you'll have to add something later to include information from the message input as well.

You'll first create an observable that can be used to trigger the dialog box with all the information you want. Notice that it's still an event: `withLatestFrom` always takes and produces events. It can be used to add information to those events—in this case the title.

MainActivity.java onCreate

```
final Observable<String> showDialogEventObservable =
    clickEvents.withLatestFrom(titleObservable,
        (ignore, title) -> title);
```

Ignore is used as a placeholder for the Void type. You aren't interested in it, so you ignore it.

When you have this in place, you can set up a subscriber that shows the dialog box when the event comes:

MainActivity.java onCreate (continued)

```
showDialogEventObservable
  .observeOn(AndroidSchedulers.mainThread())
  .subscribe(title ->
    new AlertDialog.Builder(this)
      .setTitle(title)
      .show()
  );
```

In a production application, you'd save and release the subscription, but for our example, this is enough.

Including a message in the dialog box

Now, to include the message, you need some kind of a way to give the dialog box all the information it needs in the subscriber. It's often good to start by thinking about what you need in the subscriber and then find a way to get it.

We need two strings, the title and the message. For this, you could create a new data type, but you can also get away with a `Pair<String, String>`.

You can redefine the subscriber to accept this:

MainActivity.java onCreate (modified)

```
showDialogEventObservable
  .observeOn(AndroidSchedulers.mainThread())
  .subscribe(dialogInformationPair ->
    new AlertDialog.Builder(this)
      .setTitle(dialogInformationPair.first)
      .setMessage(dialogInformationPair.second)
      .show()
  );
```

Let's have a quick look at what `Pair` is, though.

The Pair class

If you want to bundle two values together, you can do that with the `Pair` class that can be found in the Android platform. It's simple, though, containing only two items of arbitrary type: `first` and `second`. They're final after the creation of the pair, meaning they can't be changed.

You could even define the class yourself if you wanted to:

```java
public class Pair<T, U> {
  public final T first;
  public final U second;

  public Pair(T first, U second) {
    this.first = first;
    this.second = second;
  }
}
```

`Pair` is a convenient structure to use when you want to do something quick and potentially temporary. If the code starts getting difficult to read, though, create a custom class with more descriptive names than `first` and `second`.

In our case, `first` will be the title of the message and `second` the message body.

Getting more data into withLatestFrom

You want to keep a similar structure to what you had before, but with added information. Fortunately, you're allowed to do all kinds of operations to the observables that aren't *events*.

> ### Why aren't you "allowed" to use event observables for some operations?
>
> It's not that you aren't allowed to use event observables; it's that it makes conceptually no sense. You have to be clear which observables emit when the user clicks, for instance, and which ones emit when the state it represents is updated.
>
> If you use `combineLatest` with two event observables, for instance, `combineLatest` would trigger when there's an event from either observable—but only after there has been at least one from each. It's a possible scenario, though a rare one. Usually this kind of behavior would be a bug.

You can now expand the graph you had before. You'll take `messageObservable` and combine it with `titleObservable` to create a `Pair<String, String>`. In this case, `withLatestFrom` doesn't make sense, because you want it to always have the latest value from both—title and message text inputs.

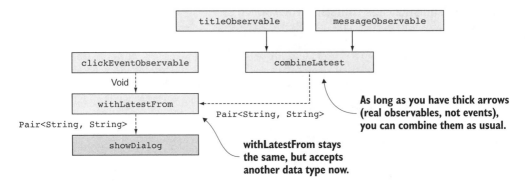

In terms of code, you can modify the previous observable to hold this information instead of the simple string:

MainActivity.java onCreate (modified)

```
final Observable<Pair<String, String>>
  dialogInformationObservable =
Observable.combineLatest(
  titleObservable,messageObservable, Pair::new);
```

`withLatestFrom` stays the same except for the type changes:

```
final Observable<Pair<String, String>>
  showDialogEventObservable =
  clickEvents.withLatestFrom(
    dialogInformationObservable,
    (ignore, dialogInformation) -> dialogInformation
  );
```

Wrapping the logic into a view model

You've already started building the logic for your UI but you didn't yet start with a view model. It's not much more than a container, though, so now that you have a piece of logic it isn't difficult to make a separate view model class for it.

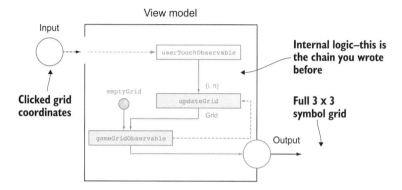

The output would be connected to the setData function of the view that we covered before. The view model provides the data, and the view knows only how to draw it.

The connection is established by the container, such as an activity.

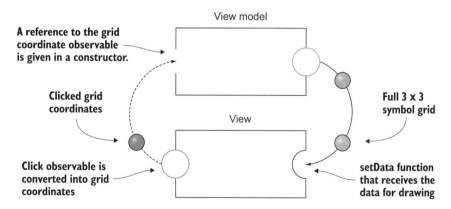

View model code

You'll create a new class called `GameViewModel`. It's, at this point, simple in terms of inputs and outputs:

GameViewModel.java

```java
public class GameViewModel {
  private final CompositeDisposable subscriptions =
    new CompositeDisposable();

  private final BehaviorSubject<GameGrid>
    gameGridSubject = BehaviorSubject.create();

  private final Observable<GridPosition>
    touchEventObservable;

  public GameViewModel(
    Observable<GridPosition> touchEventObservable) {
    this.touchEventObservable = touchEventObservable;
  }

  public Observable<GameGrid> getGameGrid() {
    return gameGridSubject.hide();
  }
}
```

You'll hold the subscriptions you create here. They can then be released with the container lifecycle.

The input is an observable that gives events indicating which GridPosition was clicked.

The output is a behavior that returns the latest GameGrid. It'll be connected to the view that can draw it.

In terms of the reactive chains, you'll add a `subscribe` function that creates it. This is what you already had before:

```java
public void subscribe() {
  subscriptions.add(touchEventObservable
    .withLatestFrom(gameGridSubject,
      (gridPosition, gameGrid) ->
        gameGrid.setSymbolAt(
          gridPosition, GameSymbol.CIRCLE))
    .subscribe(gameGridSubject::onNext)
  );
}
```

Click coordinate processing

You may have noticed that you didn't insert the view dimensions into the view model. They are, though, necessary to convert the raw click coordinate into the position of the grid tile that was clicked.

This is where you need to decide the responsibilities of the different parts of your application. Generally you want to put most of the *business logic* into the view model, which in FRP terms means the logic that decides how the application processes and combines data.

In this case, whether the part of the FRP chain that determines the clicked grid tile is business logic is a good question, but since it doesn't depend on any other data, it can be considered as just a more sophisticated *data source*. On an abstract level, the logic is encapsulated.

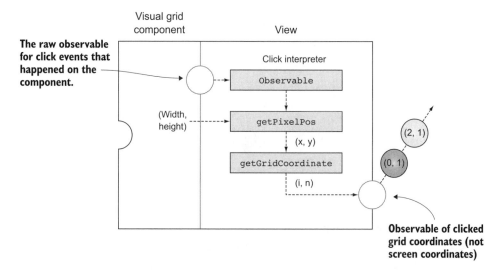

In this illustration, the click interpreter is the part of the chain you kept out of the view model. You can still unit test it individually as long as you don't give it direct references to the view it decorates, but nevertheless the click interpreter can be considered to be part of the view:

- It deals only with data originating in the view it decorates.
- The logic directly relates to the way the view is drawn on screen (in particular, how big the view is in terms of screen pixels).

Moving click processing into the view layer

`MainActivity` is still a little busy, as ideally it should be nothing but a container for creating the parts of the application and connecting them. What you'll do next is cut out the grid coordinate processing and move it into a wrapper around the `GameGridView` class.

GameGridView

`GameGridView` is the class that knows how to draw the grid on the screen. It has a nicely defined responsibility with its `setData` function, so you don't want to pollute it with another one.

You'll extend `GameGridView` and create something called `InteractiveGameGridView`. *Interactive* here means the new `View` class understands where the user is touching in terms of `GridPosition`.

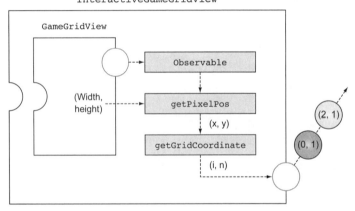

The class structure becomes nested, with `InteractiveGameGridView` using parts of the plain `GameGridView` and adding this function:

```
public Observable<GridPosition> getTouchesOnGrid()
```

This will hold the same code you previously had in `MainActivity`. It registers a touch listener with `RxView.touches` and then figures out the exact `GridPosition` that was touched.

You'll also have to remember to change the type created in the layout.

Changing turns

Until now, you've been able to only fill the game with circles. How can you keep track of which player is taking a turn? Let's start by adding a label in the view, indicating who's playing next.

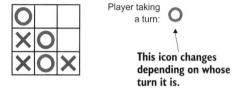

Player taking a turn:

This icon changes depending on whose turn it is.

You have a problem, though, because your view model doesn't have this information yet. It has only the grid itself.

The easy solution is to add another output from the view model that tells you this.

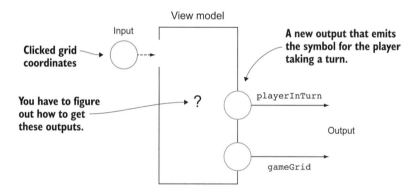

View model

Input

Clicked grid coordinates

A new output that emits the symbol for the player taking a turn.

You have to figure out how to get these outputs.

?

`playerInTurn`

Output

`gameGrid`

Connecting multiple view model outputs

Connecting multiple view classes to one view model isn't very complicated, because all you need is to create two views that consume the data from the two outputs of the same view model.

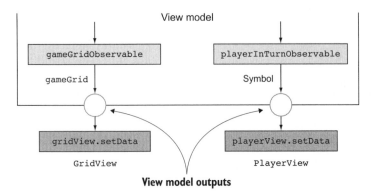

View model outputs

Notice that semantically the two view classes still belong to the *view layer*, which can contain multiple individual views.

Custom PlayerView

In this case, you created a custom PlayerView that knows how to render a symbol. It extends ImageView and adds a method for the custom data type. Custom classes are good to keep MainActivity clean.

PlayerView (extends ImageView)

```
public void setData(GameSymbol gameSymbol) {
  switch(gameSymbol) {
    case CIRCLE:
      setImageResource(R.drawable.symbol_circle);
      break;
    case CROSS:
      setImageResource(R.drawable.symbol_cross);
      break;
    default:
      setImageResource(0);
  }
}
```

If you have the symbol EMPTY, reset to no image at all.

Improved grid data type

When starting to figure out where to get the player who is taking a turn, you start by defining what exactly it is—or by defining the rules of constructing it. This process is a bit like being back in mathematics class, where you'd first draw a picture before even starting to do the calculations.

In the game of tic-tac-toe, the players take turns, with the circle starting. We can describe this as two conditions:

- The first turn is the circle.
- The current turn depends on the last symbol inserted: if it was a circle, the player taking a turn is the cross, and vice versa.

Here you depart a bit from the simple "switch between circle and cross" and instead derive the current player from *the last symbol inserted into the grid*. You should always aim to deduce data based on data you already have, and the last symbol inserted is data you can easily retain.

GameState type for the entire state of the game

Currently, we're saving the last symbol inserted. We'll place your `GameGrid` into a `GameState`, which includes the last played symbol as well.

```
class GameState {
  GameGrid gameGrid
  GameSymbol lastPlayedSymbol
}
```

In general, you want the data type to hold just data, not to contain the rules of the game. You'll define the exact getters later, for now it's enough to know what's inside of the `GameState`.

Updating the playerInTurnObservable

Because you've now saved the last turn in the GameState data type, you can derive the symbol of the player whose turn it is. You do this by first extracting the last symbol from the larger data type (calling the getter getLastPlayedSymbol) and then applying the conversion, as defined in the game rules.

You can take a little shortcut and use the EMPTY type to signify that the game has just started and there's no last move available.

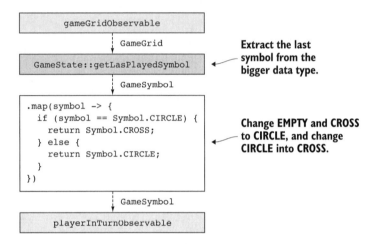

With this little chain you've created playerInTurnObservable that's based on gameGridObservable. Notice that you aren't inserting any other information; the new observable is entirely derived from the one you already had.

After replacing GameGrid with GameState in the view model, you can create playerInTurnObservable in the constructor of the view model.

Inserting player turns into the graph

With your new `playerInTurnObservable` you have all the information you need to insert the correct symbol.

Notice that you again need to "see" only the last symbol, but even if it changes, *it doesn't trigger the chain again after making the move.* This is why you use the dotted line to signify it's only additional information to the processing step.

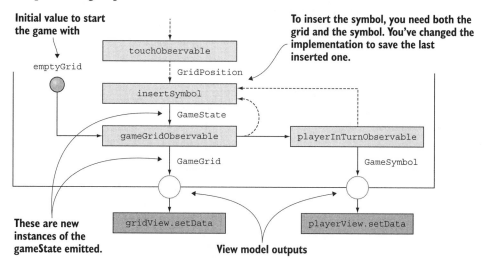

In object-oriented programming, you might create a variable and access it directly, but in FRP you generally don't want to do that for reasons of purity, modularity, and thread safety. As before, you'll use `.withLatestFrom`. See the last coffee break for details of the technique.

```
Observable<Pair<GameState, GameSymbol>>
  gameInfoObservable = Observable.combineLatest(
    gameStateSubject, playerInTurnSubject, Pair::new);

subscriptions.add(touchEventObservable
  .withLatestFrom(gameInfoObservable,
    (gridPosition, gameInfo) ->
      gameInfo.first.setSymbolAt(
        gridPosition, gameInfo.second
      )
  )
  .subscribe(gameStateSubject::onNext)
);
```

Data handling process

When new data arrives, the process is something along the lines of this:

1 Check which tile the user clicked.

2 Get the last grid and the symbol for the player who is taking a turn.

3 Insert the symbol into the grid at the correct location, while saving its type in the same data object.

4 At the end of the observable chain, publish the results from the view model outputs to be rendered in the two views.

GameState structure

You may have noticed that despite switching from GameGrid to GameState, you kept the setSymbolAt the same. This makes sense since we want to indeed update the whole GameState when a new move is played.

But what we need to do now is update the gameGrid as well as the lastPlayedSymbol:

GameState.java

```
public GameState setSymbolAt(GridPosition gridPosition,
                             GameSymbol symbol) {
  return new GameState(
    gameGrid.setSymbolAt(gridPosition, symbol),
    symbol
  );
}
```

Is it clear that you're not only setting a symbol at GridPosition but also changing lastPlayedSymbol?

Here you have to make a choice. In a way, what you're doing is "adding" a played move. A game highly depends on the order of moves played, so it makes sense that you impose the order in which they're played.

You could think of another name, but this function could be used even to load a previous game, as long as you have the moves in the correct order to be inserted.

Coffee break

You have a basic playing ground for inserting symbols, and though the game doesn't yet do much, you can experiment by expanding it.

Building new features and expansions is one of the advantages of reactive programming, and often you'll see that expanding reactive applications is easier than first appears.

Exercise

Add a third player, the triangle, and see how many classes you need to touch. Don't worry about whether the game makes sense, as you haven't even implemented the rules yet. You can get back to this version later and complete a game of three players.

Solution

You'll proceed step by step, keeping the app so it can compile at all times.

First you need to add a new symbol to the type enumeration. If you try to run the app, it hasn't changed at all—the new type is ignored.

.GameSymbol.java

```java
public enum GameSymbol {
    EMPTY, CIRCLE, CROSS, TRIANGLE
}
```

To let the triangle get its turn, next we add it to the player turn rotation. You switch CIRCLE to CROSS, from CROSS to TRIANGLE, and then back to CIRCLE.

You can do the turn rotation by changing the function responsible for the rotation. It's declared as a lambda function, and you'll keep it like that. But you could also define more complex rules for changing the turn, just by modifying this function.

GameViewModel.java subscribe function

```
.map(symbol -> {
    switch (symbol) {
        case CIRCLE:
            return GameSymbol.CROSS;
        case CROSS:
            return GameSymbol.TRIANGLE;
        case TRIANGLE:
        case EMPTY:
        default:
            return GameSymbol.CIRCLE;
    }
});
```

The last step is to add the drawing logic for the TRIANGLE type. You add it to both GameGridView and PlayerView in a similar way:

PlayerView.java

```
public void setData(GameSymbol gameSymbol) {
  switch(gameSymbol) {
    case CIRCLE:
      setImageResource(R.drawable.symbol_circle);
      break;
    case CROSS:
      setImageResoturce(R.drawable.symbol_cross);
      break;
    case TRIANGLE:
      setImageResource(R.drawable.symbol_triangle);
      break;
    default:
      setImageResource(0);
  }
}
```

You can find GameGridView in the online examples, but completing the rest of the drawing logic is a similar process of adding one more option into the drawing code.

Filtering illegal moves

Our game still has a couple of unimplemented features. It's still possible to insert a symbol at any position on the grid, making the game a little pointless. The other unimplemented features are adding the winning conditions and restarting the game.

Blocking non-empty tiles

First things first: you should allow users to play only in the empty tiles.

You could write code directly into the GameGrid and silently block the move. But this would move some of the logic of the game into the data type, which you don't want to do.

What you can do is block moves that aren't allowed by filtering them in the view model based on whether the grid tile is empty. You can do this directly in the processing chain.

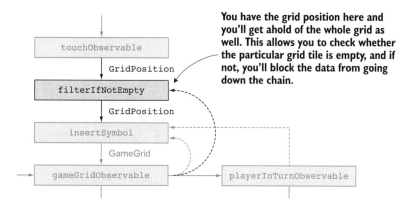

You have the grid position here and you'll get ahold of the whole grid as well. This allows you to check whether the particular grid tile is empty, and if not, you'll block the data from going down the chain.

The filter function itself is a little tricky to implement, because you need the two values, grid and position, but you want to output only the position. Next you'll take a moment to look at the details of this function.

Using pairs to temporarily bundle data

To know whether a move is allowed you need to check the `GameGrid` for an empty location. But if you use a filter you'd have only `GridPosition` itself, not `GameGrid`:

```
touchEventObservable
  .filter(gridPosition -> ???)
```

You might start thinking about `withLatestFrom`, and it's indeed part of the solution. You'll temporarily combine `GridPosition` as well as `GameGrid` into one data structure, do the necessary processing, and in the end simplify the structure to contain only the original data value. The additional `GameGrid` is used only for filtering and is then discarded.

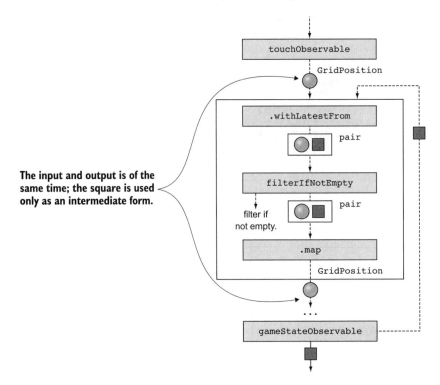

Adding filtering to GameViewModel

You can use this strategy to construct the code that filters clicks on grid tiles that aren't empty:

GameViewModel.java subscribe

```java
Observable<GridPosition> filteredTouchesEventObservable =
  touchEventObservable
    .withLatestFrom(gameStateSubject, Pair::new)
    .filter(pair -> {
      GridPosition gridPosition = pair.first;
      GameState gameState = pair.second;
      return gameState.isEmpty(gridPosition);
    })
    .map(pair -> pair.first);
```

You then use this observable instead of the unfiltered
`touchEventObservable`:

```java
subscriptions.add(filteredTouchesEventObservable
  .withLatestFrom(gameInfoObservable,
    (gridPosition, gameInfo) ->
      gameInfo.first.setSymbolAt(
        gridPosition, gameInfo.second
      )
  )
  .subscribe(gameStateSubject::onNext)
);
```

> ### Isn't it redundant to first use withLatestFrom for filtering and then again for applying the move?
>
> It might seem tempting to combine the two `withLatestFrom` blocks and do everything in one big function that filters and applies the move. But using `withLatestFrom` twice helps keep the individual functions smaller and cleaner. Later you'll see how this helps you when modifying the application.

Winning conditions

A game that simply lets the players fill the grid isn't that interesting. Let's add the winning conditions.

The game can have two statuses: ongoing or ended. If the status is ended, either the game is a tie or one of the players has won.

```
class GameStatus {
  boolean isEnded
  Symbol winner
}
```

The question is, what information do we need to figure out this piece of data? You need only the game grid and you can analyze the situation from it. The process is similar to what you did before, so after you have the algorithm, you can apply what you learned.

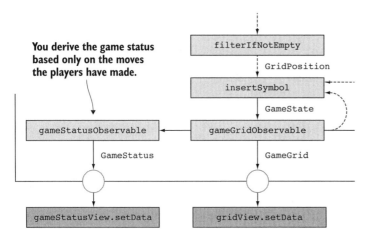

The code for determining GameState

You have a couple of conditions to check: has someone won, and is it possible for anyone to win anymore? This check is relatively straightforward with a small grid.

You can go through all horizontal rows, vertical rows, and the two diagonals, checking whether all symbols are the same (and non-empty). For a tie, you can for now check whether the grid is full and perhaps later introduce a more precise algorithm.

This algorithm is encapsulated in the `getWinner` function, which is a static function that takes the grid and checks whether someone has won or it's a tie.

Adding logic to the view model

In the view model you have most of the logic already, and you'll add the part that derives the `GameStatus` from the `GameState`.

You don't have a couple of parts yet; let's see the `getWinner` function first.

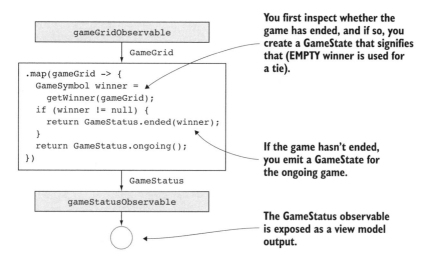

You first inspect whether the game has ended, and if so, you create a GameState that signifies that (**EMPTY** winner is used for a tie).

If the game hasn't ended, you emit a GameState for the ongoing game.

The GameStatus observable is exposed as a view model output.

Making the getWinner function

Although it's more of an implementation detail, you can create a basic winner-checking algorithm by going through all grid tiles and checking for matches originating from each particular tile. This algorithm is adapted based on the example of http://codereview.stackexchange. com/a/127105.

We'll create a new GameUtils class to hold this algorithm:

GameUtils.java

```java
public static GameSymbol calculateWinnerForGrid(
    GameGrid gameGrid) {
  final int WIDTH = gameGrid.getWidth();
  final int HEIGHT = gameGrid.getHeight();
  for (int r = 0; r < WIDTH; r++) {          ◄─── You'll loop through
    for (int c = 0; c < HEIGHT; c++) {     ◄───   each of the grid
      GameSymbol player = gameGrid.getSymbolAt(r, c);      tiles and check
      if (player == GameSymbol.EMPTY)                      whether it's the
        continue;                                          start of a winning
                                                           row.

      if (c + 2 < WIDTH &&
          player == gameGrid.getSymbolAt(r, c+1) &&
          player == gameGrid.getSymbolAt(r, c+2))
        return player;          ◄────────── Three consecutive
      if (r + 2 < HEIGHT) {                 horizontal symbols
        if (player == gameGrid.getSymbolAt(r+1, c) &&      found
            player == gameGrid.getSymbolAt(r+2, c))
          return player;        ◄────────── Three consecutive
        if (c + 2 < WIDTH &&                vertical symbols
            player == gameGrid.getSymbolAt(r+1, c+1) &&     found
            player == gameGrid.getSymbolAt(r+2, c+2))
          return player;        ◄────────── Three consecutive
        if (c - 2 >= 0 &&                   diagonal symbols
            player == gameGrid.getSymbolAt(r+1, c-1) &&     found
            player == gameGrid.getSymbolAt(r+2, c-2))
          return player;        ◄────────── Three consecutive
      }                                     diagonal symbols
    }                                       in the other
  }                                         direction found
  return null;                ◄──────────── No winner yet!
}
```

Displaying GameState in the UI

To let the players know someone has won, you'll add a text in the UI. This is a plain `TextView` that uses a string based on the game state.

You need a function that converts the `GameState` into a `String` that is then inserted into the `TextView`.

You'll also hide or show the panel on top of the game grid depending on the winning state.

Changing GameStatus into a string

You should use text resources in production on Android, but here you have a simpler approach in which the strings are hardcoded.

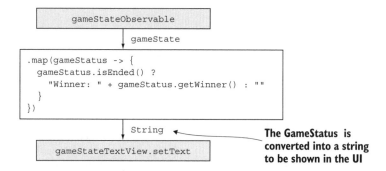

The GameStatus is converted into a string to be shown in the UI

You'll keep this mapping in `MainActivity`, because it's small, but we could also create a custom `TextView` that knows how to render `GameStatus`.

View binding code

As you did with the file browser example, you'll move the code that connects the view model and the view into a separate function. This will again give you more flexibility in terms of the lifecycle—even if this time you won't do anything exotic.

MainActivity.java

```java
private void makeViewBinding() {
  viewSubscriptions.add(
    gameViewModel.getGameGrid()
      .observeOn(AndroidSchedulers.mainThread())
      .subscribe(gameGridView::setData)
  );

  viewSubscriptions.add(
    gameViewModel.getPlayerInTurn()
      .observeOn(AndroidSchedulers.mainThread())
      .subscribe(playerInTurnImageView::setData)
  );

  viewSubscriptions.add(
    gameViewModel.getGameStatus()
      .map(GameStatus::isEnded)
      .map(isEnded -> isEnded ? View.VISIBLE : View.GONE)
      .observeOn(AndroidSchedulers.mainThread())
      .subscribe(winnerView::setVisibility)
  );

  viewSubscriptions.add(
    gameViewModel.getGameStatus()
      .map(gameStatus ->
        gameStatus.isEnded() ?
          "Winner: " + gameStatus.getWinner() : "")
      .observeOn(AndroidSchedulers.mainThread())
      .subscribe(winnerTextView::setText)
  );
}
```

You accumulate all created view subscriptions into a CompositeDisposable

These parts are View logic and could be moved into custom classes. But they're small, so you can keep them here for the time being.

Filtering all moves after the game has ended

The same way you filtered all moves that aren't placed on empty grid tiles, you can also start blocking all moves after the game has ended. To find out whether the game has ended, you can use our newly created `GameStatusObservable`.

You'll be using the pair structure again to create the filter that depends on another observable.

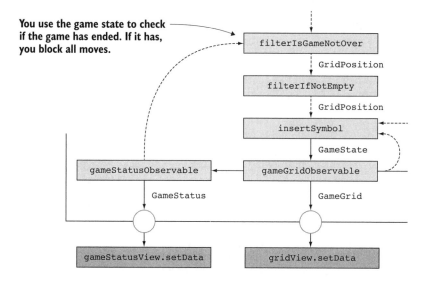

You use the game state to check if the game has ended. If it has, you block all moves.

GameViewModel.java subscribe function

```
Observable<GridPosition> gameNotEndedTouches =
  touchEventObservable
    .withLatestFrom(gameStatusObservable, Pair::new)
    .filter(pair -> !pair.second.isEnded())
    .map(pair -> pair.first);
```

This should do it. You block the whole event processing chain in case `GameStatus` changes to ended. In the following chapters, you'll see how to make the code more modular and testable.

One more thing: Restarting the game

Now you're at the point where the game finally works! But it can't be restarted, which should be fixed.

Restarting the game means doing the following:

- Clearing any symbols from the grid
- Resetting the turn to be a circle (in case it's a cross)
- Clearing any text indicating the game has ended

Normally, this would be a bit of a hassle, but with our chain approach of Rx, you can simply push another value to `GameGridSubject`, and that's it. Every part of the UI will update automatically through the Rx system.

```
subscriptions.add(newGameEventObservable
    .map(ignore -> EMPTY_GAME)    ◄─────────────
    .subscribe(gameStateSubject::onNext)
);
```

Reset gameStateSubject with an empty game every time a click comes from the New Game button.

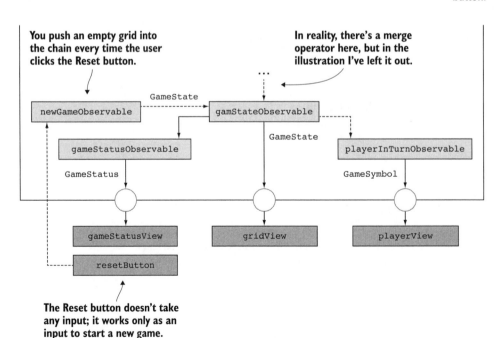

You push an empty grid into the chain every time the user clicks the Reset button.

In reality, there's a merge operator here, but in the illustration I've left it out.

The Reset button doesn't take any input; it works only as an input to start a new game.

Summary

If you take a step back, you can see that you have a view model and a view layer. This difference between the two layers is clear from your drawings if you name the layers and draw a line:

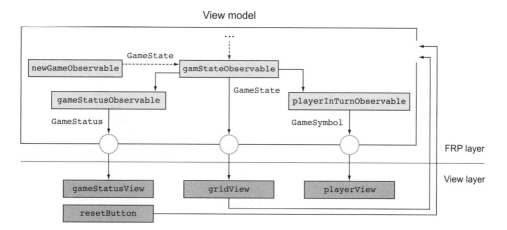

The user is the source of the events coming from the view, but for this diagram you can assume that the UI events "magically" appear for reasons unknown to us. Sometimes the user is drawn to clarify the point.

Tic-tac-toe version 2

What you have is a simple game, and in the next chapter you'll see how to expand it to be more interesting.

You'll also see how the reactive approach gives surprising advantages when handling data—you already got an idea with the Reset button, which you were able to do with just a couple of lines of code. Normally, these kinds of features that are added later require refactoring, but with Rx you've already written the code in a "refactored" way.

Expanding existing Rx apps | 9

In this chapter

- Expanding an existing Rx app to have new features

- Persisting and loading application state

- Moving parts of a view model logic
  into a dedicated model

Working with existing reactive code

One of the advantages of Rx is that adding new functionality to an application is relatively straightforward if the code is structured properly. What you need to do is to carefully think about what you want to change and then reshape the graph accordingly.

In this chapter, you'll take a piece of code you already wrote and identify the points where your new goals diverge from the old ones.

You'll be exploring how reactive programming makes the application modular—the chain is just a combination of independent functions—and how to utilize the existing modules.

Starting from tic-tac-toe

You'll start from a working game of tic-tac-toe, which you already saw in the preceding chapter. Don't worry if you don't remember the details, because you'll revise the implementation before you start applying changes.

This is how the game you already have looks:

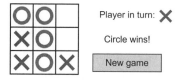

In this simple game, the players in turn insert either a cross or a circle. The player who gets three markers in a line wins.

The game of Connect Four

Let's imagine a real-life scenario: a product owner in their great wisdom has decided that a simple tic-tac-toe game doesn't cut it in the market anymore. What the cool kids are raving about these days is instead the game Connect Four.

Long story short, you need to update your app to be a different game altogether! Fortunately, you built the app in a way that this can be done.

The changes to the rules are as follows:

- Players drop their markers from the top, so it's possible to play the new moves only on top of existing markers (or into empty columns).

- Instead of having three markers in a line, the winner now needs four.

- You'll add a button for saving the game, so if the player closes the app, you can load the game at its previous state.

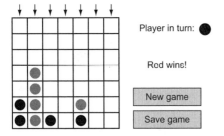

These changes don't sound too complex. But this game does look very different from the tic-tac-toe game you had! Does it even make sense to try to adapt it, or should you start from scratch?

Let's go through the needed changes and see how you could adapt it.

Updating grid size and assets

Before getting to the reactive part, the most prominent thing is changing the grid size from 3 × 3 into a 7 × 7.

You have a couple of magic numbers to change for that, namely, GRID_WIDTH and GRID_HEIGHT. If you've done everything well, expanding the grid should work out of the box, theoretically, by changing these values to 7s.

You know that the view that renders the GameGrid blindly takes whatever it's given and tries to display it. *Therefore, the information indicating the grid size comes with the GameGrid.*

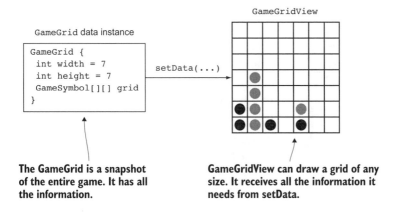

The GameGrid is a snapshot of the entire game. It has all the information.

GameGridView can draw a grid of any size. It receives all the information it needs from setData.

Assets and drawing

The crosses and circles are just pictures and easy to replace. You'll use images designed for Connect Four.

If you replace the assets and the grid size, you'll have a bigger tic-tac-toe grid with red and black markers. At this point, the winner is still the one who gets three in a row, and there are no restrictions on where the markers can be played (apart from not on top of each other).

Black and red

Even though they're just names, you'll change the `GameSymbol` enumeration to reflect the updated symbols. Instead of `CIRCLE` and `CROSS`, you'll have `BLACK` and `RED`. The `EMPTY` value stays because you'll use it for game mechanics.

GameSymbol.java

```java
public enum GameSymbol {
    EMPTY, BLACK, RED
}
```

Dropping the markers

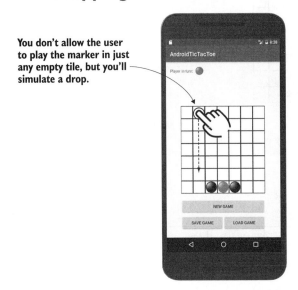

You don't allow the user to play the marker in just any empty tile, but you'll simulate a drop.

If you run the game now, it should work: just as it used to, but with prettier graphics and a bigger grid.

The remaining task, and the trickiest one, is changing the game logic so that the marker is "dropped" at the available location vertically.

The only case when the user can't play the marker occurs when the entire column that the user touches is already full.

Next you'll see how to make this change in the reactive processing chain you made before.

The tic-tac-toe reactive graph

The journey from a touch to an updated game field on screen is represented by your graph.

Many steps are required to get there, and because you built your app in a reactive fashion, you can see the individual steps as parts of the chain. Each step is a modular, autonomous piece of code that doesn't know about its surroundings. The RxJava code connects the little pieces together to create something more out of them—in this case, a game.

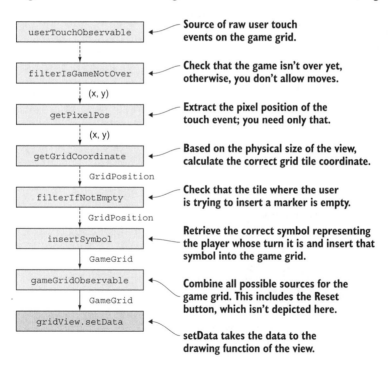

Changing the tic-tac-toe graph into Connect Four

In your new game, you have a slightly different reaction to users clicking on the grid. The symbols fall to the bottom of the grid, which means you need to make changes to the graph.

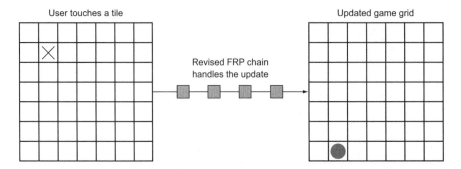

You'll go through the graph step by step, checking at each point whether you can still use the previous implementation or have to make changes to accommodate the new logic.

You could choose to write the new app from scratch, but because the code is modular you'll save time by reusing some parts.

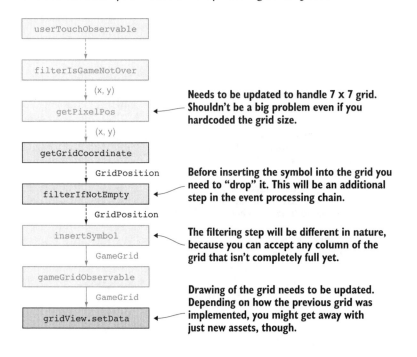

Needs to be updated to handle 7 x 7 grid. Shouldn't be a big problem even if you hardcoded the grid size.

Before inserting the symbol into the grid you need to "drop" it. This will be an additional step in the event processing chain.

The filtering step will be different in nature, because you can accept any column of the grid that isn't completely full yet.

Drawing of the grid needs to be updated. Depending on how the previous grid was implemented, you might get away with just new assets, though.

Dropping the marker in Connect Four

The clearest difference in the game logic is that the marker (or symbol) is going to be dropped from the top and will fall until it hits either the bottom of the grid or another marker.

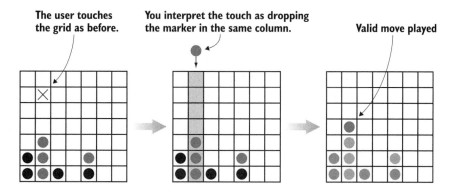

You can implement the function itself as a simple `for` loop along the y-axis of the game grid. Here you use `I` to loop through the y values. As before, this is a generic, pure, function that will be used inside Rx.

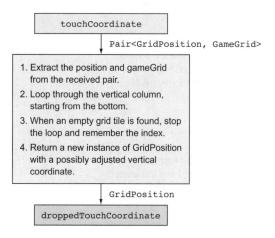

The code for the dropping function

To put the instructions of the preceding page in code, we need a function that takes as input the pair of `Position` and `GameGrid` and returns a new instance of `Position` that's the first available position in the desired column.

Notice that you don't modify the inputs: the clicked position and the grid itself. This is because of the immutability principle. You *could*, however, return the original position, in case the user indeed clicked the "correct" tile in the first place. This kind of optimization is a bit redundant, though, because we're talking about one new object instance per played turn.

The following is a possible implementation of the dropping function. In reality, you'll put it in a separately defined function, not directly in the `.map` operator as shown here.

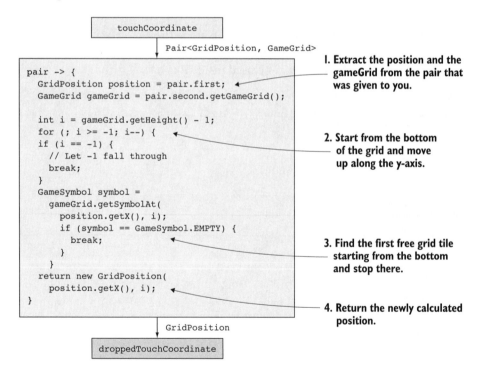

```
                touchCoordinate

                     Pair<GridPosition, GameGrid>

pair -> {                                          I. Extract the position and the
  GridPosition position = pair.first;                gameGrid from the pair that
  GameGrid gameGrid = pair.second.getGameGrid();     was given to you.

  int i = gameGrid.getHeight() - 1;
  for (; i >= -1; i--) {                           2. Start from the bottom
  if (i == -1) {                                      of the grid and move
    // Let -1 fall through                            up along the y-axis.
    break;
  }
  GameSymbol symbol =
    gameGrid.getSymbolAt(
      position.getX(), i);
    if (symbol == GameSymbol.EMPTY) {             3. Find the first free grid tile
       break;                                        starting from the bottom
    }                                                and stop there.
  }
  return new GridPosition(
    position.getX(), i);                          4. Return the newly calculated
}                                                    position.

                     GridPosition

          droppedTouchCoordinate
```

Checking for valid moves

Before, you had a step in the chain that checked if the tile clicked by the user was empty. Now that's unnecessary because you already have an empty tile as found by the algorithm that searches for the next free space.

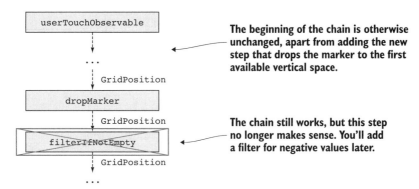

The beginning of the chain is otherwise unchanged, apart from adding the new step that drops the marker to the first available vertical space.

The chain still works, but this step no longer makes sense. You'll add a filter for negative values later.

Allowed moves

To find out exactly what this step should do in the game of Connect Four, let's get back to the drawing board.

The original intention of checking for an empty tile was to filter out the moves that aren't *allowed*. With that in mind, which moves aren't allowed in your new game?

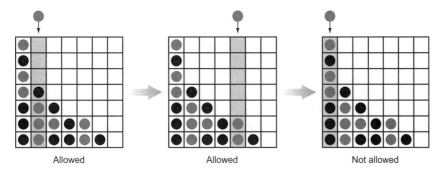

It turns out the only moves that aren't allowed are the ones where the target column is already completely full.

The question is, what kind of values does the `dropMarker` step produce when the column is full?

To find out, you can either run the game and test it, or you can look at your logic again and make an assumption. Either way, you'll come to this conclusion: when the column is full, the loop goes all the way to the top, and over. You get a vertical index of –1.

Of course, we cut corners a bit here, and probably the first version of the function would've stopped at 0; using –1 as the limit for the `for` loop seems a little arbitrary.

Regardless, this is how the algorithm is implemented:

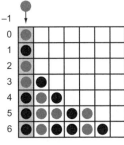

Not allowed

If the column is full, you loop all the way to –1 and return that.

It would seem to follow that you need to filter all emitted data items that are outside the grid, or at least the ones that are vertically in the minus region. At this point, you can choose, but for simplicity's sake, you'll take the shortcut here and assume that all vertical coordinates need to be non-negative.

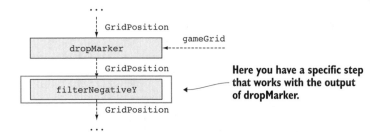

Here you have a specific step that works with the output of dropMarker.

Now that you've decided that the vertical coordinates for the illegal moves will be negative, you can filter those out:

```
.filter(position -> position.getY() >= 0)
```

You drop all positions that are "above" the game grid.

Updated event processing chain

If you place the new processing steps into the original chain, you get a chain that works with the new rules of the game. The only changes are the size of the grid (input and drawing) and the fact that the marker falls in the selected column.

In reactive programming, you can keep most of the code exactly the same. We've been fast-forwarding here, but if you had, for instance, unit tests for some of the previous steps, those could be left intact. Thanks to modularity, you can reuse the code easily.

Notice that most of the graph is still handling events originating from the user clicking the grid. You turn these events into *state changes* in the game grid.

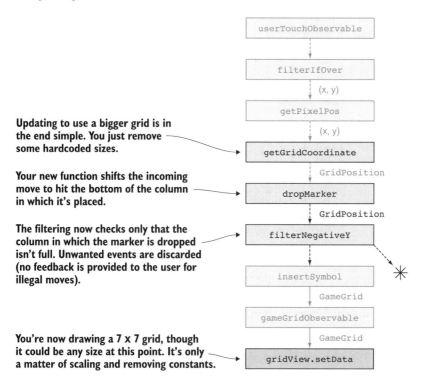

Recap of the steps in event processing

You started with a few illustrations of what you'd like to achieve. Let's get back to those now and see where they fit in your revised event processing chain.

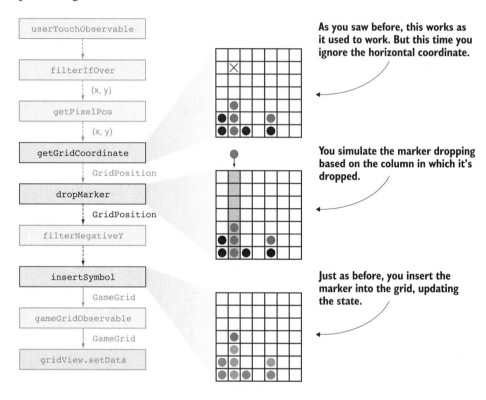

Only the middle part has been significantly changed. Pay attention to the types of data going through the chain. You use `GridPosition` to differentiate between screen coordinates and grid coordinates, but don't let that confuse you. In a way, the grid is an x/y coordinate system in itself too.

We've also left out the rest of the chain, because this page isn't big enough! That part of the chain is unchanged from the previous chapter, though.

Coffee break

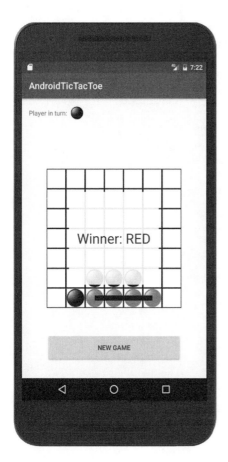

The grid is getting bigger, and it's no longer easy to see where the winning line of four is. To alleviate this situation, try adding a rendering of the winning line to `GameGridView`.

Starting point

This exercise is a little tricky, but its essence is that `GameGridView` now needs more information about what it should draw. It's no longer drawing only the grid but also the winning line.

Start with the code found in the online repository tagged Coffee Break 1 Start. It contains an expanded winning calculation function. It also has the drawing code in `GameGridView` called `drawWinner`.

GameStatus structure

In the starting code, you can find the positions for the start and end of the winning line. The winner is like it used to be:

```
GameStatus {
  GameSymbol winner
  GridPosition winningPositionStart
  GridPosition winningPositionEnd
}
```

Solution

You need to provide the new `GameStatus` data to the `GameGridView`. You could expand the `setData` function of `GameGridView` to accept two parameters, namely, `GameGrid` and `GameStatus`—but for clarity, you'll create a new type to contain these two. You'll call it `FullGameState`.

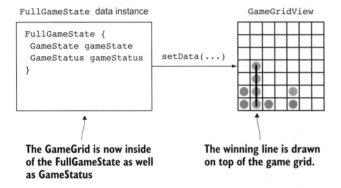

The GameGrid is now inside of the FullGameState as well as GameStatus

The winning line is drawn on top of the game grid.

The code to set the data will change to use the expanded type for the game state:

GameGridView.java

```java
public void setData(FullGameState data) {
  this.data = data;
  invalidate();
}
```

Because the data is provided from the view model, you have to add code to expose it:

GameViewModel.java

```java
public Observable<FullGameState> getFullGameState() {
  return Observable.combineLatest(
    gameStateSubject, gameStatusObservable,
    FullGameState::new);
}
```

Saving and loading the game

Having published the app, some more serious players are requesting a possibility to save the game state to continue later. Although our game is still simple, this request sounds reasonable. Also, by making a save module, you could use it for something like a chess game, for which saving the game is commonplace.

The drawing board

Before you start coding, let's sketch a solution in terms of the UI. You'll have a Save button and another dialog box, or activity, for viewing saved games. From the time-stamped list, the user can choose a desired game to load.

- The Save button writes the current game state on disk.

- The Load button opens an activity, reads the saved games from disk, and shows a list of them. Clicking one loads the game.

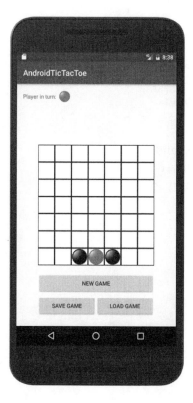

Creating the model

As you saw in an earlier chapter, saving and loading is easier when you have a model in place. This means a place where you keep the data separate from the logic.

The original graph

To decide what data should go into the model, you can have a look at your graph. What you want is to capture the state that fully describes the state of the game.

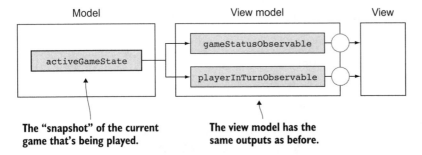

The "snapshot" of the current game that's being played.

The view model has the same outputs as before.

Here you can see that all that's in the middle is the `GameState`. All the events flow into it, and out of it comes only the derived state—things that can be calculated based on the `GameState`, such as the winner.

The GameState

To check what the `GameState` contains, you can open the class and have a quick look. The class has the `GameGrid` as well as the player symbol that was last played. This explains how the player in turn, for instance, can be calculated.

```
GameState {
  GameGrid gameGrid
  GameSymbol lastPlayedSymbol
}
```

Moving GameState to the model

`GameState` is what we call *atomic state*, state that can't be calculated from any other state. It's what we want to save.

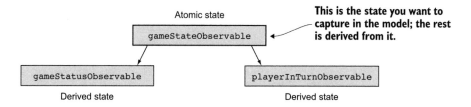

You'll define a model and put the `GameState` there. The view model will then subscribe to that.

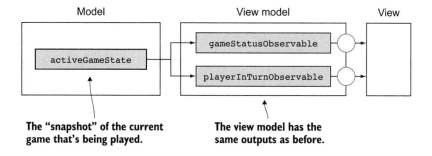

You can place the model in the `Application` scope:

```
public class GameApplication extends Application {
    private GameModel gameModel;

    @Override
    public void onCreate() {
        super.onCreate();
        gameModel = new GameModel(this);
    }

    public GameModel getGameModel() {
        return gameModel;
    }
}
```

The instance of the model can be accessed through this getter from any activity of the Android app.

Code for GameModel

You can start the model by moving the active game there. The application can play only one game at a time, so the active game has a special role. You also move the definitions for grid size there, as well as adding a function to start a new game:

GameModel.java

```
public class GameModel {

  ...

  private final BehaviorSubject<GameState>
    activeGameState = BehaviorSubject
      .createDefault(EMPTY_GAME);

  public void newGame() {
    activeGameState.onNext(EMPTY_GAME);
  }

  public void putActiveGameState(GameState value) {
    activeGameState.onNext(value);
  }

  public Observable<GameState> getActiveGameState() {
    return activeGameState.hide();
  }
}
```

`GameViewModel` will change to use this model instead of keeping its own internal `BehaviorSubject`. You can pass it in the constructor:

GameViewModel.java

```
public GameViewModel(
    GameModel gameModel,
    Observable<GridPosition> touchEventObservable,
    Observable<Object> newGameEventObservable) {
```

Sharing the model

Before moving on to creating the loading dialog box, let's take a step back. One problem with traditional ways is a discrepancy between the data and the way it's drawn. In one typical case, you have a list and a screen that shows details of a specific list item.

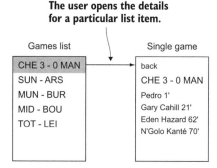

The "keep it too simple" version

You start with the "keep it simple" approach: you simply pass the data around. One screen loads the data and hands it over to the screen it has opened. *This isn't wrong, but it doesn't scale.*

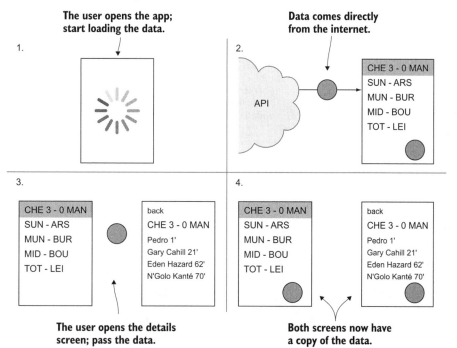

Expanding the too simple version

Everything is fine and simple as long as the data you're passing around isn't changing too much. As soon as one screen triggers an update, though, you have a problem of state: the other one is supposed to update, but you don't want to create a spider web of every screen needing to know all other screens that use the same data!

Update sequence

You can see what happens upon refresh step by step.

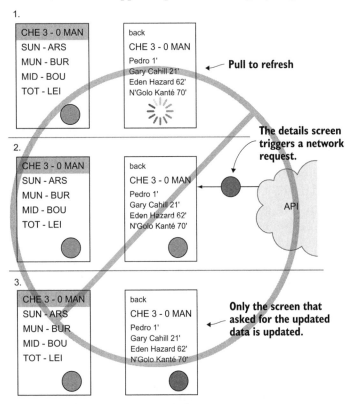

Isn't this how ContentProviders work?

If you are using Android ContentProviders or other centralized solutions for storing and consuming data, you can go ahead and skip the next couple of pages. The principles of the model are exactly the same as with ContentProviders, but after you've covered the fundamentals you'll start building your reactive logic on top of them.

The advantage of reactive programming and RxJava on top of possible ContentProviders is that you get more flexibility in the way you process and consume the data.

Updating the reactive way

In the reactive world, you add a store in front of the application UI code. Your launch sequence changes to be less coupled, because the UI doesn't know where exactly the data came from.

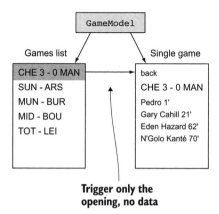

You already learned that the model will give observables, and those observables will then emit the new data as it becomes available.

List of games or a single game?

In this example, the screen on the left has a listing, whereas the one on the right has only a single item displayed. For this kind of setup, you build a special model that has a get interface as follows:

```
interface GameStore {
  Observable<Game> getGameById(String id);
  Observable<List<Game>> getGames();
}
```

The model internally manages how it keeps all observables up-to-date. For the time being, you don't concern yourself with the `put` operations.

The model data load sequence

Here's the previous user interaction, but this time with a store. We've left out some details, such as who handles the network request, but you'll look at that later.

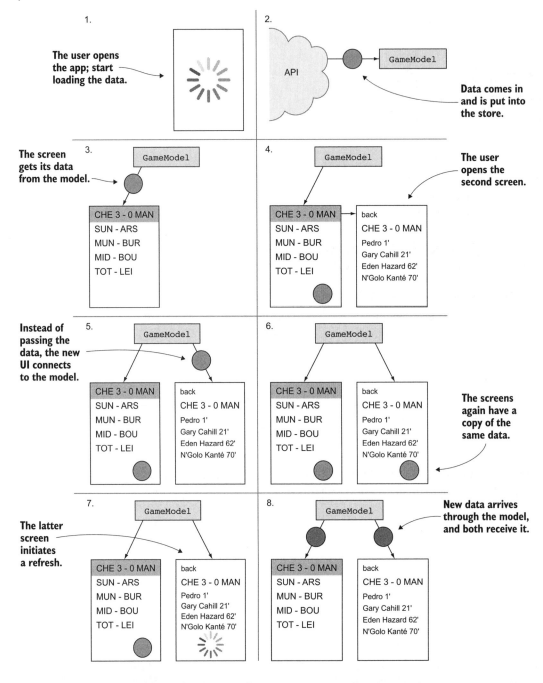

1.
The user opens the app; start loading the data.

2.
API
GameModel
Data comes in and is put into the store.

3.
The screen gets its data from the model.
GameModel

CHE 3 - 0 MAN
SUN - ARS
MUN - BUR
MID - BOU
TOT - LEI

4.
GameModel
The user opens the second screen.

CHE 3 - 0 MAN
SUN - ARS
MUN - BUR
MID - BOU
TOT - LEI

back
CHE 3 - 0 MAN
Pedro 1'
Gary Cahill 21'
Eden Hazard 62'
N'Golo Kanté 70'

5.
Instead of passing the data, the new UI connects to the model.
GameModel

CHE 3 - 0 MAN
SUN - ARS
MUN - BUR
MID - BOU
TOT - LEI

back
CHE 3 - 0 MAN
Pedro 1'
Gary Cahill 21'
Eden Hazard 62'
N'Golo Kanté 70'

6.
GameModel

CHE 3 - 0 MAN
SUN - ARS
MUN - BUR
MID - BOU
TOT - LEI

back
CHE 3 - 0 MAN
Pedro 1'
Gary Cahill 21'
Eden Hazard 62'
N'Golo Kanté 70'

The screens again have a copy of the same data.

7.
The latter screen initiates a refresh.
GameModel

CHE 3 - 0 MAN
SUN - ARS
MUN - BUR
MID - BOU
TOT - LEI

back
CHE 3 - 0 MAN
Pedro 1'
Gary Cahill 21'
Eden Hazard 62'
N'Golo Kanté 70'

8.
GameModel
New data arrives through the model, and both receive it.

CHE 3 - 0 MAN
SUN - ARS
MUN - BUR
MID - BOU
TOT - LEI

back
CHE 3 - 0 MAN
Pedro 1'
Gary Cahill 21'
Eden Hazard 62'
N'Golo Kanté 70'

Stores and observables

The model uses stores internally. In our particular kind of RxJava store, you return observables from the store. The idea is that you first return the latest value and then keep the observable subscribed for subsequent values.

This is the mechanism enabling you to know that all parts of the app that subscribe to the model get their initial state correctly and updates as well.

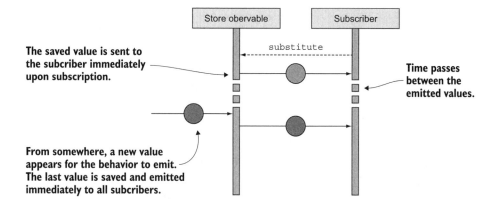

The saved value is sent to the subscriber immediately upon subscription.

Time passes between the emitted values.

From somewhere, a new value appears for the behavior to emit. The last value is saved and emitted immediately to all subscribers.

What if there's no data?

This chapter doesn't cover data fetching strategies, but what happens if you don't have data. There are two strategies here: either you don't return anything until you have data (let's say a network request was triggered), or you give a dedicated empty value.

The former is easier to use, but you can't react to a situation in which no data is available. You can show a spinner, but sometimes you might want to perform an action immediately. The latter, on the other hand, gives more flexibility but introduces a burden of needing to handle the special case when it isn't needed.

Usually you'd go for the option of nothing emitted in the case of no value and add it if it turns out to be necessary.

Loaded games activity

To get back to our example, you'll next create a separate activity for showing saved games and loading one of them. `MainActivity` and `LoadGameActivity` will share the same model, which enables `LoadGameActivity` to change the active game.

`LoadGameActivity` does nothing but enable the user to load a previous game. `LoadGameActivity` receives the list of games from the model. When clicking one of the games, `LoadGameActivity` updates the active game in the model to reflect the change.

In this style of using the model, any part of the app can open `LoadGameActivity` and it will work. The flow of both activities will go through the same model.

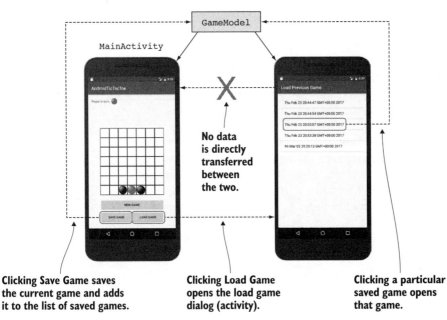

Clicking Save Game saves the current game and adds it to the list of saved games.

Clicking Load Game opens the load game dialog (activity).

Clicking a particular saved game opens that game.

PersistedGameStore

You already have a model and the active game in it, but you need to expand it to contain the saved games as well. In terms of observables that the model exposes, it will be the active `GameState` and a list of saved games.

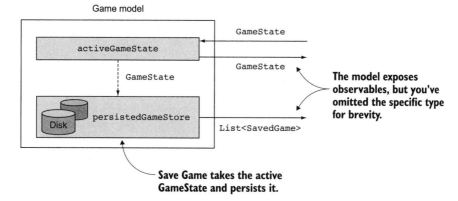

The model exposes observables, but you've omitted the specific type for brevity.

Save Game takes the active GameState and persists it.

You'll create a new type to contain the information indicating when the game was saved. For now, it's our only way of distinguishing between the different saved games.

SavedGame.java

```
SavedGame {
  GameState gameState
  long timestamp
}
```

The model interface gets functions for saving the game and getting a list of all saved games:

GameModel uses an internal store to hold the games.

```
GameModel {
  private PersistedGameStore gameStore
  void putActiveGameState(GameState value)
  Observable<GameState> getActiveGameState()
  Observable<List<SavedGame>> getSavedGamesStream()
  Observable<Object> saveActiveGame() {
}
```

Code for the store

This time, the store will contain a list of items instead of a singular one.

You'll use a combination of a cached list and a `PublishSubject` to manage the state. The list is loaded from the disk on startup and kept up-to-date when new games are saved.

PersistedGameStore.java

```java
class PersistedGameStore {
  private List<SavedGame> savedGames;
  private final PublishSubject<List<SavedGame>>
     savedGamesSubject = PublishSubject.create();
```

> The list of saved games that's kept in memory. It's loaded on startup from the disk.

> You use PublishSubject to inform subscribers of list updates.

The same way as before, you give the last value at the start of the stream with the `.startWith` operator:

```java
  public Observable<List<SavedGame>
     getSavedGamesStream() {
    return savedGamesSubject.hide()
      .startWith(savedGames);
  }
```

What's different is the `put` function. Here you first create an updated list, persist it, and only then publish the new value through `PublishSubject`. We'll not go into all details here, and you can find the code online. This example store uses `SharedPreferences`:

```java
  public void put(GameState gameState) {
    final long timestamp = new Date().getTime();
    final SavedGame savedGame =
      new SavedGame(gameState, timestamp);
    savedGames.add(savedGame);
    persistGames();
    savedGamesSubject.onNext(savedGames);
  }
```

Saving games

Before you can load games you first have to be able to save them. This is rather simple: you take the last `GameState` and move it into the `PersistedGameStore`.

You can do this internally in the model, triggered by the click of the Save button.

The saved game will be added to the list of saved games immediately, though you'd see it only when opening `LoadGameActivity`.

Adding saveActiveGame to GameModel

You'll add a function to the model that will copy the game to the saved games. `PersistedGamesStore` will automatically add a timestamp to it and convert it into a `SavedGame` type.

Take the last **activeGameState** and copy it to the **persistedGameStore**.

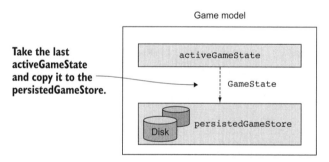

GameModel.java

```java
public void saveActiveGame() {
  persistedGameStore.put(
    activeGameState.getValue()
  );
}
```

persistedGameStore takes care of everything needed to save the game. Internally, it uses Gson to serialize the game.

Why not addSavedGame?

You could also add a function to the model that allows you to save any game on command. But you usually try to keep the interface as small as possible, and in the case of your app, you know the only game you allow to be saved is the active one.

Loading games

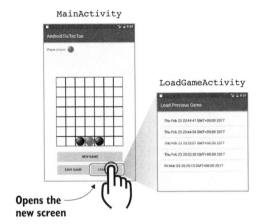

The loading game sequence starts with opening the load game dialog box called `LoadGameActivity`. Just like the other activity, you'll connect it to the model.

The loading sequence

The only special thing about loading games is that technically the game is loaded just before `LoadGameActivity` is closed. This relieves `MainActivity` from the responsibility of handling the outcome.

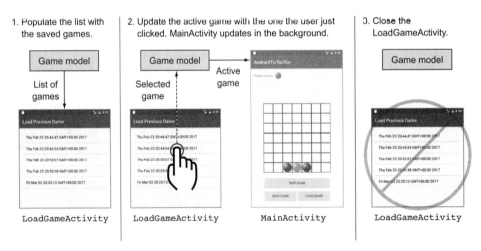

1. Populate the list with the saved games.

2. Update the active game with the one the user just clicked. MainActivity updates in the background.

3. Close the LoadGameActivity.

The code works similarly to the File Browser application, and you can find the details in the online repository.

Summary

In this chapter, you saw how to add features on top of an existing application built in the reactive way. The most important takeaway here is that by keeping the chain clean and straightforward, you can add or modify the behavior even drastically without touching the unaffected code at all.

You're starting to see how reactive programming is a way to precisely structure the application to do exactly and only what it's intended to do—as well as helping with event processing chains.

Stores with lists

One topic that we quickly brushed over is stores with lists of data in them. You saw how to use a `PublishSubject` to handle updates and a cached data entry in the memory to keep the app robust.

If you're building a production app, you might want to take a look at store libraries, such as reark.io or https://github.com/NYTimes/Store. The task of making a store is a common one, so although simple ones are fine to make, more complex ones are better done with a library.

Testing reactive code | 10

In this chapter

- Testing fundamentals

- Writing tests for reactive applications

- Using tools to deal with asynchronous code

- Knowing which code to test and which not to test

Reactive architectures and testing

Like it or not, testing at least critical parts of your application is usually a good idea. Reactive applications can seem tricky to test, but the modularization they promote shows the opposite, if you write your code according to these guidelines we've been discussing:

- Make modules that have as few dependencies as possible.
- Prefer pure functions that can be composed for more complex functionality.

Testing granularity

In general, we tend to divide tests into *unit testing* and *acceptance testing*. These two test types are focused on different parts of the application and have different goals, as shown in the following lists.

Unit testing	Acceptance testing
- Fully tests small fragments of code	- Tests the way that parts of code work together
- Doesn't use framework classes (Android classes)	- Can use classes from the framework
- Ideally covers all possible execution paths (providing *code coverage*)	- Includes end-to-end testing in the extreme form, testing the full system
- Is fine-grained	- Doesn't try to cover all cases
- Usually targets pure functions, small classes	- Usually targets long chains, large classes

What about smoke testing?

Smoke testing is an extreme form of acceptance testing that covers some extremely critical use cases as a preventative measure. These could include attempts at answering questions such as, "Does the program start?" or "Is the user able to login?" You'll consider them as part of acceptance testing, though.

Test granularity

The division of these two kinds of tests, unit tests and acceptance tests, seems reasonable. But the reality is again more of a spectrum: defining a unit test and an acceptance test is always debatable. In general, the more you're dealing with pure data, the more likely you are to write a *unit test*. On the other hand, the closer you are to drawing things on screen, the more likely you are to write an *acceptance test*.

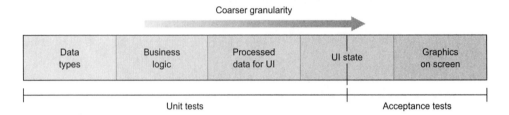

You can think about it this way: a function is straightforward to test precisely, but the way a dialog box renders on screen depends on numerous factors, some of which are out of your control.

Pure code or not?

In general, you try to maximize the amount of pure code you have. This is the code that doesn't depend on specifics of the platform (for instance, Android).

The pyramid of dependencies

In general, a reactive application at the core consists of pure functions, or at least should. These are the pieces of code you can fully control and that you can unit test.

If you draw the application modules in a pyramid, you can get an idea of the application's stability. You should have as many small modules as possible to create a solid foundation. They're then combined into bigger wholes that contain less logic and combine the smaller ones.

For the upper half of the graph you might have to set up a special testing environment. It's better to have the foundation larger.

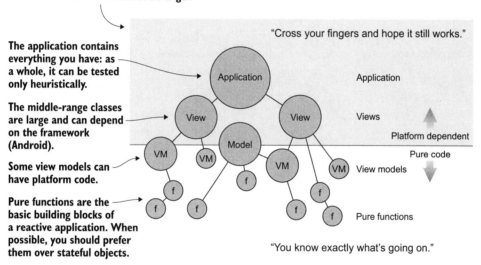

The application contains everything you have: as a whole, it can be tested only heuristically.

The middle-range classes are large and can depend on the framework (Android).

Some view models can have platform code.

Pure functions are the basic building blocks of a reactive application. When possible, you should prefer them over stateful objects.

"Cross your fingers and hope it still works."

Application

Views

Platform dependent

Pure code

View models

Pure functions

"You know exactly what's going on."

In general, the more moving pieces you have, the more that can go wrong. This is represented by the size of the program module in the pyramid.

Types of tests

If you see how to test the parts of your pyramid, you can roughly divide it into two parts: the top part is acceptance testing and possibly requires a different setup, and the bottom part is pure unit testing. If you're not familiar with the two, hang on, you'll soon get to concrete examples.

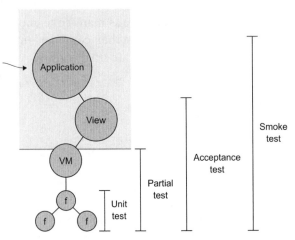

Because the code on the top of the pyramid depends on the code on the bottom, testing the top includes testing the bottom. At the top, tracing sources of specific issues.

External factors in the application

Apart from keeping an eye on the composite effect of your modules, it's good to keep in mind which parts come from external sources. Everything you didn't make should be considered potentially evil: such as APIs, platform components, third-party libraries, and that code that someone wrote a long time ago without tests.

Unit-testing basics

Acceptance testing is platform-specific and has little to do with reactive programming specifically. Here you'll focus on unit testing and how to make sure the pieces of your reactive logic work as expected.

We haven't yet covered testing reactive code or RxJava at all, so let's start from the beginning. In general, testing RxJava isn't like normal unit testing. If you aren't familiar with unit testing as a concept, don't worry, because we'll briefly cover it here before moving on.

Assemble, act, assert

With a unit test, you check that the code being tested does one thing correctly under certain circumstances.

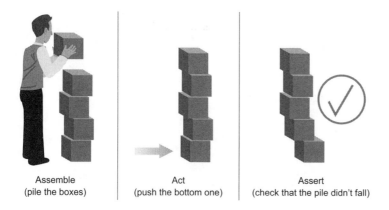

Assemble
(pile the boxes)

Act
(push the bottom one)

Assert
(check that the pile didn't fall)

The common mistake here is to mix the three steps, which results in tests that are difficult to read and maintain. *Each test should test only one thing.*

What is a test?

In terms of code, a *test* is usually a single function that performs all these steps. If the last one, assert, fails, the test is considered to fail. In this case, the entire program code is considered to be in a broken state until the test (or rather, code that it's testing) is fixed.

Code example of a unit test

Here's an example that tests a custom `sort` function for an array. It rearranges the array items in ascending order. It doesn't use RxJava yet, but the foundation will be the same whether or not the code is reactive.

You can see here the different phases of assemble, act, and assert. If even one of the asserts in the end fails, the entire test fails.

MyTest.java

First you declare the test as a public method. The test function is annotated with `@Test` so that the test runner knows it's a test:

```java
@Test
public void testMySort() {
```

The name here can be anything you want. Conventions differ depending on various factors, including the number of tests you have in the file.

Next, prepare everything for the execution of the test case:

```java
// Assemble
List<Integer> list = Arrays.asList(54, 1, 7);
```

Then, do the thing that you're testing:

```java
// Act
List<Integer> sortedList = MySort.mySort(list);
```

Finally, check that the thing produces the expected results:

```java
// Assert
assertEquals(3, sortedList.size());
assertEquals(1, sortedList.get(0));
assertEquals(7, sortedList.get(1));
assertEquals(54, sortedList.get(2));
}
```

Testing reactive chains

You can treat a reactive chain as a function: with certain inputs, it produces certain outputs.

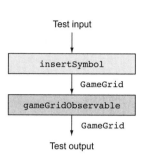

Test input

insertSymbol

GameGrid

gameGridObservable

GameGrid

Test output

You expect to get deterministic outputs when you keep the inputs the same. This is the foundation of a test case: you need to be able to predict what the output should be.

You can choose to test an arbitrary chunk of the reactive chain, or even just one step if you wish. What makes sense depends on the complexity of the custom operators—the simpler they are the more you can bundle and still get a meaningful test case.

Setting up testing for RxJava and Mockito

You have a set of techniques to use when testing RxJava, and you'll also use the Mockito library for mocking objects. In an Android project, you can include it as a Gradle dependency:

app/build.gradle

```
dependencies {
    ...
    testCompile 'org.mockito:mockito-core:2.+'
}
```

The other tools you'll use are already included in the RxJava library. They include inspectable subscribers as well as classes for testing time-dependent event chains.

On Android, you can run the tests on the command line in the project directory with this command:

```
./gradlew test
```

Testing a custom observable

Let's say instead of a traditional sort method, you have one that can potentially be executed in a background thread. You can call it with a simple list, but it'll return the sorted list in an observable when it's ready:

```
public static Observable<List<Integer>> sortList(
    List<Integer> list) {

  return Observable.create(emitter -> {
    // Sort the list and return a new instance
    emitter.onNext(sortedList);
    emitter.onComplete();
  });
}
```

You saw observables like this before. Using it is the same as without the observable, but how do you see the results?

The solution to this common problem is to use test `subscriber`. Normally you'd do something interesting in the `subscribe` function, but a `TestObserver` doesn't do anything at all. You'll be able to inspect `TestObserver` after the chain has been executed.

Introducing test subscribers

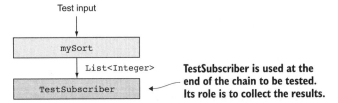

TestSubscriber is used at the end of the chain to be tested. Its role is to collect the results.

You create the observable as usual, but then you subscribe an instance of `TestObserver` to it, allowing you to check the output later.

`TestSubscriber` isn't too complex of a class, exposing only whatever it saw during the execution of the test. Let's see how it works when used in the code.

TestObservable class

One of the core tools for testing RxJava is `TestObservable`. It has useful functions that you can use to inspect what the reactive chain did. Typically, you have a couple of things you want to check. Here are the most commonly used methods of `TestObserver`.

Checking for termination

Here are the three functions you have for checking the termination of an observable:

assertComplete()

Was the observable completed in the end?

assertError(...)

For error cases, you can check for a specific error.

assertNotTerminated

If the goal is for the observable not to terminate, check that no error or completed signal was emitted.

Inspecting the values emitted

To inspect the values that an observable has emitted during the test execution, you also have three functions available:

assertValue(T)

If you expect only one value, you can use this function directly. It also checks that only one value was emitted.

assertValueCount(Integer)

If you expect more than one value, you can check that the count is correct.

getValues()

If you want to manually check the emitted values, you can get them in an ordered list. Use the JUnit standard `assert` functions to inspect them.

Testing the list sort with an observable

To get back to the example, this time you have a function that takes an input but returns an observable. You need to create a `TestObserver` to gather the results and subscribe it to the resulting observable.

BlackBoxTest.java

```java
@Test
public void testSortList() {
  // Assemble
  TestObserver<List<Integer>> testObserver =
    new TestObserver();
  List<Integer> list = Arrays.asList(54, 1, 7);

  // Act
  BlackBox.sortList(list).subscribe(testObserver);

  // Assert
  testObserver.assertValueCount(1);
  testObserver.assertComplete();

  List<Integer> sortedList =
    testObserver.values().get(0);
  assertEquals(3, sortedList.size());
  assertEquals(1, (int) sortedList.get(0));
  assertEquals(7, (int) sortedList.get(1));
  assertEquals(54, (int) sortedList.get(2));
}
```

Create a TestObserver to monitor the results of the test execution.

Subscribe the TestObserver to the observable that your function creates; this will trigger the execution of the observable.

Check the number of emitted items as well as the completion of the observable.

Retrieve the first item that the TestObserver received. And check that it is as you expect.

This test works. But wait, isn't the subscriber called *asynchronously*, and at the time of the asserts, the list would still be undefined?

Testing asynchronous code

The code here indeed *could* be run on a separate thread. You just constructed the reactive function in a way that makes it stay on the same thread.

In RxJava, *if no thread changes are declared, the reactive chains run synchronously in the same thread.* This makes testing significantly easier, and it's also the reason that you tend to avoid changing threads in view models unless absolutely necessary. Let's see what this means.

Synchronous or asynchronous

If you look back to the threading system of RxJava, you may recall that some code is pushed onto another thread, making it asynchronous. If this was the case in the test you created, it would fail.

Trying to test a badly behaving function

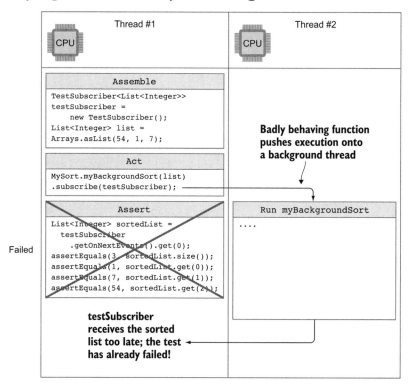

Testing a single-thread RxJava function

If the function we're testing doesn't perform any `observeOn` or `subscribeOn` calls, testing it becomes significantly easier. When the observable chain activates (at the point of creating a subscription), the observable runs on the same thread as the caller. In this case, `mySort` blocks the thread until it's ready, just like synchronous code normally would.

In this case, the FRP observable is there so you could change the thread. In a test, you have no reason to.

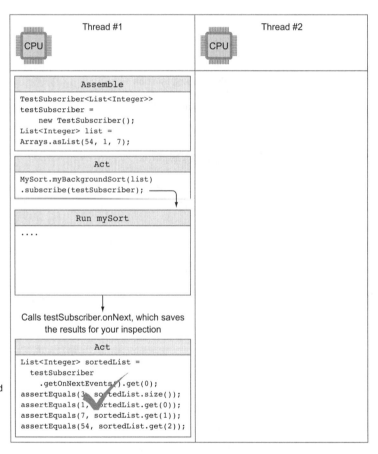

Coffee break

Try the testing functionality of the `TestObserver`.
You can open an example in the online code
repository as a starting point: in this example,
you'll be instructed to write tests for the code that's
already there.

This example doesn't follow test-driven development where you'd write
tests first, but it's good for practice. Try to catch all the relevant aspects
of the execution of the static example functions in the `BlackBox` class.

Different methods to test

In the class `BlackBox.java`, you'll find a few methods. Write tests
according to the instructions:

sortList

- Check what happens when you give `null` to the `sortList` function.
  The expected outcome is a `NullPointerException` emitted as an
  error. (If the error is unhandled in `sortList`, the test would fail.)

splitWords

The `splitWords` function splits the string you give it at the spaces
within it. The observable it returns emits the words in order. Try these
tests:

- Test with a single word.
- Test with a sentence of more than three words.
- Check that `splitWords` gives an error when given a `null` input.

openStream

The `openStream` function creates an observable that emits what you
gave it but doesn't complete. It also doesn't provide any values. This
function isn't very useful, but check that it indeed works like this.

Solutions

All of the tasks use `TestObserver` to inspect the results of the observable returned.

sortList

You can use the `assertError` function that either takes an instance of an exception or just the class that you expect to be emitted as the error. In this case, it's a `NullPointerException`:

```
// Assert
testObserver.assertError(NullPointerException.class);
testObserver.assertNoValues();
```

splitWords

You can check a single word with `assertCompleted` and `assertValue`. You don't have to check for the count separately:

```
// Assert
testObserver.assertComplete();
testObserver.assertValue("pineapple");
```

For multiple words, you can use the version of the function that takes many arguments and checks that they were the precise ones:

```
// Assert
testObserver.assertComplete();
testObserver.assertValues(
   "Once", "upon", "a", "time");
```

The error case is the same as for `sortList`.

openStream

The `openStream` function is a little special, but not too difficult to test. You check that there's no terminal event and no values:

```
// Assert
testObserver.assertNotTerminated();
testObserver.assertNoValues();
```

Writing tests for view models

You can try out some of the code you already wrote. Previously, you were focused on learning how to make it work, but you can retroactively write a couple of tests as an example. Sometimes they can be good to write before the code, and at other times they can be used to make sure the code doesn't break later because of other changes.

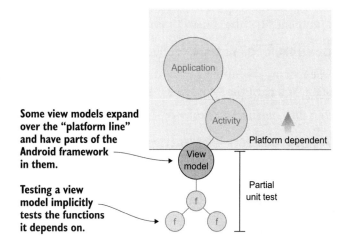

Some view models expand over the "platform line" and have parts of the Android framework in them.

Testing a view model implicitly tests the functions it depends on.

Connect Four view model

View models are around the mid level of complexity; you can write unit tests for them, but you aren't usually able to cover all execution paths. In this case, you'll check a couple of basic cases to defensively confirm that changes in other parts of the application won't break the app.

Mocking view model inputs

View models usually take inputs as constructor arguments. In tests, you can create fake ones that you can manipulate.

You slightly refactored the `GameViewModel` class, and it now has a constructor that takes three arguments:

GameViewModel.java

```
public GameViewModel(
    Observable<GameState> activeGameStateObservable,
    Action1<GameState> putActiveGameState,
    Observable<GridPosition> touchEventObservable) {
```

The roles of GameViewModel inputs

To see what's going on in the view model, you'll first review these arguments that the constructor takes.

Observable<GameState> activeGameStateObservable

The first argument is a `BehaviorObservable` that always has a last state. You trust that whatever is given us is of this nature.

Test implementation: BehaviorSubject

Action1<GameState> putActiveGameState

This is a function that allows the view model to update the state of the game based on its calculation. You assume this is reflected in the first argument, though the view model has no control over it, because there's a store to fill the role.

For tests, you need only to inspect whether this function was called: after all, it doesn't return anything. You'll get into the details in a bit, but the testing framework Mockito provides a convenient method to create a test object for you to use—the mock wrapper.

Test implementation: Mockito.mock(Action1.class)

Observable<GridPosition> touchEventObservable

Finally, you have an observable for the user's touch events on the game grid. This observable triggers whenever a touch is detected, and it emits the coordinate on the game grid that was touched.

Test implementation: PublishSubject

RxJava test implementations

In this case, you have three kinds of dependencies for the view model that you need to fulfill in your tests. They're quite common, and you can use these guidelines for all view models.

Stateful observable: `BehaviorSubject`
Event observable: `PublishSubject`
Function: *Mocked function of the same class*

Choosing what to test

You'll start with testing the initial state of your view model when an empty game is fed into it. Originally, you were getting `activeGameStage` from the model. The connection was made in `MainActivity`.

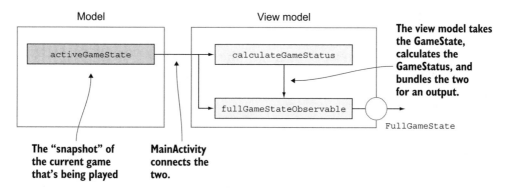

Model   View model

The view model takes the GameState, calculates the GameStatus, and bundles the two for an output.

The "snapshot" of the current game that's being played

MainActivity connects the two.

Constructing a unit test for FullGameState

How you handle all this in a unit test is by providing the view model "fake" inputs that you can manipulate, as well as attaching a `TestObserver` to the outputs to check later what came out.

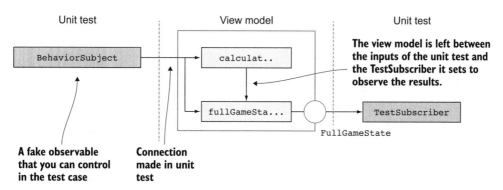

Unit test   View model   Unit test

The view model is left between the inputs of the unit test and the TestSubscriber it sets to observe the results.

A fake observable that you can control in the test case

Connection made in unit test

You still need to give the view model the other two dependencies too, but they won't be actively used in this particular test case.

Testing the GameViewModel initial state

Now you can try coding your first unit test for a view model. You'll go through it step by step.

Setting up the test cases

For convenience, you can create an `@Before` method for your test case. This will be executed before each test case in the file. This enables you to set up the view model without repeating the boilerplate code. This is a standard procedure in unit testing, but good to know in case you're not familiar with it.

GameViewModelTest.java

```java
public class GameViewModelTest {
  GameViewModel gameViewModel;
  BehaviorSubject<GameState> gameStateMock;
  Action1<GameState> putActiveGameStateMock;
  PublishSubject<GridPosition> touchEventMock;

  @Before
  public void setup() {
    gameStateMock = BehaviorSubject.create();
    putActiveGameStateMock =
        Mockito.mock(Action1.class);
    touchEventMock = PublishSubject.create();
    gameViewModel = new GameViewModel(
      gameStateMock,
      putActiveGameStateMock,
      touchEventMock
    );
  }
```

Variables usable in all test cases. The GameViewModel and all of its dependencies.

This is the way to create a mock instance of the specified class. Its type is still the same.

Create an instance of GameViewModel. If a test is needed to test the constructor, you couldn't do this here.

With these, you can go forward and write the test case. (*Test case* is just another name for a singular test function.)

The first view model test case

After the view model is set up, writing the test isn't that different from
the ones you saw before. You'll start the test by declaring the function
that defines it:

GameViewModelTest.java

```java
@Test
public void testInitialState() {
  // Assemble
  TestObserver<FullGameState>
      testObserver = new TestObserver<>();
  gameViewModel.getFullGameState()
      .subscribe(testObserver);

  // Act
  gameViewModel.subscribe();
  gameStateMock.onNext(EMPTY_GAME_STATE);
```

It's important
to remember to
subscribe the
view model just
before testing
its reactions.
Because of the
BehaviorSubject,
you could give it
the empty game
before subscribing
too, but this way,
it reads clearer.

Asserting what happens requires you to take a small step back and
think about it. The view model is already a little complex and handles
both calculating the GameStatus (is the game ended, and so forth) as
well updating the GameState based on user input.

In this test, you don't expect any updates based on user input.

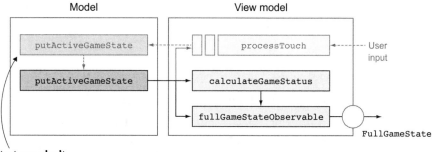

In this test, you don't
test how the user input
updates the GameState.

Verifying that the function wasn't called

In practice, what you're aiming for is that `putActiveState` should be called only when `GameState` is updated by user input. In this case, you set only the initial state, so the function should remain uncalled.

Fortunately, your Mockito mock wrapper enables you to do just this. The syntax is a little peculiar. First, remember that the `Action1` class has a method named `call`, which is used to invoke it:

```
Consumer<T> {
  apply(T value)
}
```

With Mockito, you can then verify that the `call` method was never invoked with *any* arguments. (You could specify arguments too.)

This is the syntax of the Mockito library. You call Mockito.verify (statically imported here) and then tell it that you expect that the call method has never been invoked with any parameters.

GameViewModelTest.java testInitialState (continued)

```
verify(putActiveGameStateMock, never())
    .apply(any());
```

The rest of the test is performed with techniques you've already seen:

```
    testObserver.assertValueCount(1);
    FullGameState fullGameState =
        testObserver.values().get(0);
    assertFalse(fullGameState.getGameStatus().isEnded());
    assertEquals(EMPTY_GAME_STATE,
        fullGameState.getGameState());
}
```

Just check that GameStatus is also correctly calculated as ongoing.

Could user input processing be taken out of the view model?

Your view model has ended up with many responsibilities. Indeed, user input processing could be moved into the model, for instance. You'll keep it in the view model, but on the next pages you'll extract the hard logic from the view model into a separate utility class. The view model then becomes a container for logic, but the user input logic can be tested without the view model.

Testing partial observable chains

As another example of a unit test, you'll take the input processing of the view model under scrutiny. It's the part you omitted in the preceding test. It handles the user touch processing of the Connect Four game.

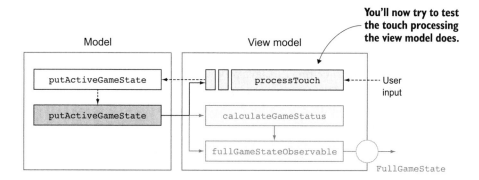

You'll now try to test the touch processing the view model does.

Extracting chains

This time, instead of testing the whole view model, you'll take out the particular bit you want to test and put it into another class as a *static function*.

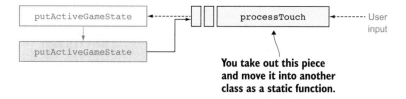

You take out this piece and move it into another class as a static function.

Static function

In Java a *static function* is also known as a *class function*. It's a function that doesn't require an instance to run, and therefore it also can't access any instance variables. These are good characteristics for extracting pieces of independent logic.

Part of a reactive chain as a static function

Static functions aren't magic, though you have to be careful to give all the dependencies they need as parameters. After all, *they can't access anything they aren't given.*

> What about accessing static variables from a static function?
>
> Apart from constants (static + final), it's not advisable to ever use static variables. Seriously, don't do it.

In this case, you can move the logic to GameUtils.java as you already have a generic utility class at hand. With static functions, the nice thing is they can be freely moved around because they don't depend on anything but potentially each other.

GameUtils.java

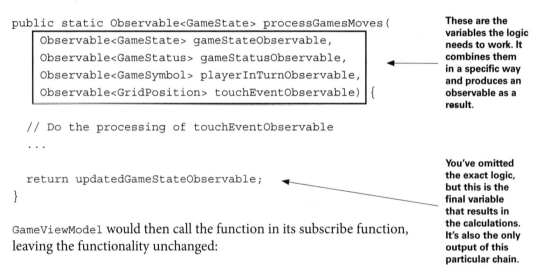

```
public static Observable<GameState> processGamesMoves(
    Observable<GameState> gameStateObservable,
    Observable<GameStatus> gameStatusObservable,
    Observable<GameSymbol> playerInTurnObservable,
    Observable<GridPosition> touchEventObservable) {

  // Do the processing of touchEventObservable
  ...

  return updatedGameStateObservable;
}
```

These are the variables the logic needs to work. It combines them in a specific way and produces an observable as a result.

You've omitted the exact logic, but this is the final variable that results in the calculations. It's also the only output of this particular chain.

`GameViewModel` would then call the function in its subscribe function, leaving the functionality unchanged:

GameViewModel.java subscribe function

```
subscriptions.add(GameUtils.processGamesMoves(
    activeGameStateObservable,
    gameStatusObservable,
    playerInTurnObservable,
    touchEventObservable
).subscribe(putActiveGameState));
```

These are now the member variables of the view model. The view model passes its member variables to the partial reactive chain.

Testing Connect Four drop logic

As a refresher, the rules dictate a drop of the marker when the user touches a grid column. You find the first empty grid tile or, if the column is full, you ignore the touch.

TestCase for a drop

For a simple test case, you'll attempt to drop the marker at (0,0), which is the top-left corner of the grid and expect it to fall to the bottom of the first row.

You can also choose the grid size, because you created the logic so that it's always passed on with GameState. For testing purposes, you'll use a grid of 3 × 3. It's easier to define the logical cases with fewer grid tiles—at this point you have to trust that 7 × 7 works.

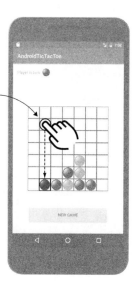

You don't allow the user to play the marker in just any empty title, but you'll simulate a drop.

processGameMoves function

The function you want to test is the one you extracted before. It has the signature of four arguments (dependencies):

```
public static Observable<GameState> processGamesMoves(
    Observable<GameState> gameStateObservable,
    Observable<GameStatus> gameStatusObservable,
    Observable<GameSymbol> playerInTurnObservable,
    Observable<GridPosition> touchEventObservable) {
```

Mocking dependencies

This time, you have four dependencies to fulfill in the unit test. The first three will be mocked with `BehaviorSubjects`, and the last with `PublishSubject`, as it's the only event observable.

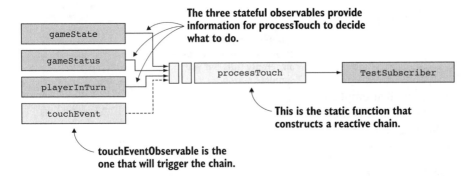

The three stateful observables provide information for processTouch to decide what to do.

This is the static function that constructs a reactive chain.

touchEventObservable is the one that will trigger the chain.

Setting up the dependencies works the same way as earlier. You can use the `@Before` function to initialize them for all tests.

Next you'll write the test for the case. You start with an empty grid and then drop one marker at (0, 0). You expect it to fall to the bottom of the 3 × 3 grid you're using for this test.

GameUtilsTest.java

```
@Test
public void processGamesMoves_testMarkerDrop() {
  // Assemble
  gameStateMock.onNext(EMPTY_GAME_STATE);
  gameStateObservable.subscribe(testObserver);

  // Act
  touchEventMock.onNext(new GridPosition(0, 0));

  // Assert
  testObserver.assertNotTerminated();
  testObserver.assertValue(
    EMPTY_GAME_STATE.setSymbolAt(
      new GridPosition(0, 2), GameSymbol.BLACK)
  );
}
```

Execute the test case by sending an instance of GridPosition to the touchEventMock

As you may remember, setSymbolAt returns a new instance of GameState. You also implemented an equal function for GameState to make this work.

Summary

This was a tech-heavy chapter with a lot of details about RxJava. Sometimes you need to see how it really works to get an understanding of the benefits gained.

You saw techniques for successfully testing a view model as well as plain reactive chains as static functions. You can test the model in a similar way, though sometimes you have to choose what to mock and what not to. Think first about why you want to test, and then what exactly. After that, knowing the right approach is easier.

Reactive programming and TDD

You can write tests before the code, in the fashion of test-driven development. But with reactive programming, the compiler is your friend, and after you've figured out a solution that compiles, it often works. I leave it up to you how you use tests in your development, though.

Testing asynchronous operations

This isn't a book about RxJava testing, so I left out some parts. In particular, this chapter didn't cover how to test operations that are time-dependent. In RxJava, you can move time freely in the unit tests if you use `TestScheduler`.

We didn't cover `TestSchedulers` because they're not commonly needed—usually the use case would be time-outs relating to searching, or perhaps animations. But for architectural purposes, these kinds of input processing functions are more of a detail.

The end of part 2

You should now have a good idea of the kind of architectural components that can be used in reactive applications. In the third, and last, part of the book, you'll go deeper into some areas, such as networking and animations.

You can always return to part 2 as a reference to common parts of architectures.

Advanced RxJava architectures | part 3

In this part

In this last part of the book, you'll take a deep dive into complex example apps built with RxJava and the architectures you've learned.

Chapters 11 and 12 show how to create a real-time chat application using the WebSocket Protocol (usually called just WebSockets). You'll learn about a suitable place to attach handlers for incoming messages as well as how to keep the state of the app up-to-date.

Chapter 13 focuses on a special case of containing animation state in the view model and transitioning between different incoming values.

Finally, chapter 14 explains the internal workings of a fully functioning maps client. You'll see how to model complex view outputs into a reactive system.

 Problems are not stop signs; they are guidelines.

—Robert H. Schuller

Advanced architectures | **11**
Chat client 1

In this chapter

- Setting up a chat client that uses a WebSocket

- Wrapping listeners as observables

- Accumulating values from an observable

- Managing the view model lifecycle

Chat client with WebSockets

You'll use the example of an instant messaging chat client to explore common elements of applications that don't fit stores or view models. The example spans two chapters, with the more complex parts in chapter 12.

While exploring this example, you'll also learn about more advanced techniques of dealing with lifecycles and view bindings.

Chat client UI

You're going to keep it nice and simple for now. You'll show only a list of messages (including sent messages) and a text field accompanied by a Send button.

The chat room will also be anonymous to start with, though this could later be changed.

Because the UI is basic, you'll start by tackling the part that seems the trickiest: sending and receiving messages over the internet.

First you'll take a little detour to learn how to make the basic app in a nonreactive way. Then you'll refactor it to incorporate new features.

How to transfer messages

The chat messages need to be transferred somehow. Assuming you have the server already, when you transfer data on the internet, you use HTTP.

Sending data with traditional HTTP

As you've seen already, what happens on the web is that the client sends an HTTP request, and the server responds to it with the newest data. The HTTP connection is closed after the exchange.

Between the HTTP requests, no data is transferred and no active connection is open. Sending a message could work in this fashion, but how about receiving?

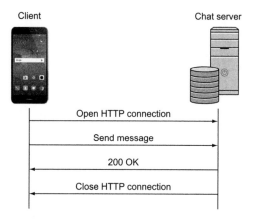

Client   Chat server

Open HTTP connection

Send message

200 OK

Close HTTP connection

> ### Does the HTTP connection always have to be closed?
>
> The underlying network layer performs optimizations to minimize new connections. Usually, the connection is kept open in case new requests come in. But the point here is that the client always has to ask for new information, even if the connection is still open.

WebSockets

The problem with the client sending requests to the server is that only the server is able to respond. Traditional HTTP provides no way for the server to initiate the exchange—for instance as in our case when a new message is available.

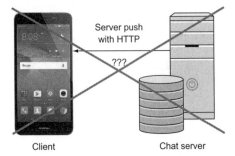

Client   Chat server

Solution

This is where WebSockets come in. Conceptually, you open a solid connection between the client and the server. While the connection is open, both the client and the server can send messages to each other, and they're processed instantly.

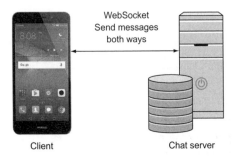

Client   Chat server

In this way, you can not only send messages, but also receive them in real time. How exactly WebSockets are implemented is a topic for another book, but for us the necessary information is that you can use WebSockets for sending and receiving data.

WebSockets as broadcasters

Let's start with the most obvious, which is creating a connection to test that the WebSocket itself works. This is done to get the building blocks ready before you start with the UI.

The backend with WebSockets

For this example, you'll use a custom backend. It receives a message from one client and publishes it to all clients, *including the one that sent it.*

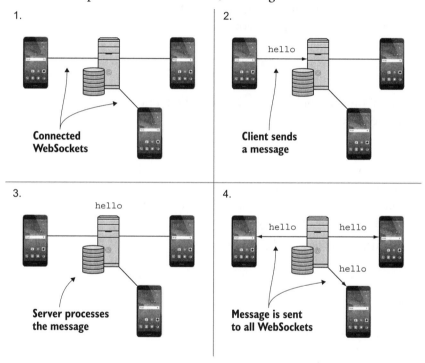

1. **Connected WebSockets**
2. **Client sends a message**
3. **Server processes the message**
4. **Message is sent to all WebSockets**

Are WebSockets reactive?

What you see here looks a lot like a publish subject. Indeed, the server is conceptually a publish-subscribe link to all the clients.

The difference with RxJava comes from the fact that the connection isn't guaranteed and can fail unexpectedly. Normally, when executed within the same machine, you know that as long as your program is running, the subscriptions work as expected.

WebSockets do indeed match well with RxJava, though, as you'll see!

Connecting to the server

How does the connecting work in terms of code? You've created a simple test backend in Node.js that you can find in the online examples. But you need to create your own instance of the server. This doesn't require previous knowledge, though; just follow the instructions online.

WebSockets Android library

Although it could be fun, you don't want to invent the wheel again, so you'll use a library to make the connection to your backend. You can include the library by adding the dependency to your gradle file:

```
compile 'com.github.nkzawa:socket.io-client:0.3.0'
```

This dependency is a fork of the Android part of a library called *socket .io*. It does what it's supposed to do: WebSockets.

First connection

Using socket.io isn't too complicated; you need to create a socket and open a connection. After that, you can send and receive messages. The `END_POINT_URL` is the server URL I mentioned earlier, just put into a constant. You'll log the connect event to see it works.

After you're finished, you also have to close the connection:

MainActivity:onCreate

```
socket = IO.socket(END_POINT_URL);
socket.on("connect", args ->
  Log.d(TAG, "Socket connected"));
socket.connect();
```

MainActivity:onDestroy

```
socket.disconnect();
```

Sending and receiving messages

After WebSockets is open, you can start sending and receiving. You already saw the mechanism to receive messages: you can declare a handler that's called whenever a message arrives from the socket.

Sending is done through the emit API, which takes the type of the message as well as the message itself. Both of these are strings.

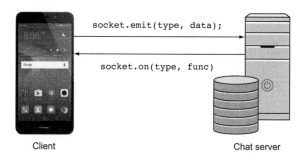

```
socket.emit(type, data);

socket.on(type, func)
```

Client   Chat server

For your message, you'll use the server-defined type chat message. To test the sending, you can first add a listener for messages of this type:

```
socket.on("chat message", args ->
  Log.d(TAG, "chat message: " + args[0].toString()));
```

After this, you'll see the log whenever you (or another client) sends a message. Remember that sent messages are received by all clients connected to the WebSocket.

```
socket.emit("chat message", chatMessageJsonString));
```

Because you can send only strings, the message needs to be serialized. Next you'll see how to create the serialized JSON string.

ChatMessage structure

You already saw the data type used for a chat message, and this is something you've defined yourself.

Your chat message has three things: message ID, timestamp, and the message itself. Here's the outline in pseudo code:

```
class ChatMessage {
    String id
    long timestamp
    String message
}
```

You're keeping things simple for now and won't even save who sent the message. These fields can be added later.

You'll generate the ID on the client side; this is to track messages later. If many clients send the same message, you'll know which one was yours.

The timestamp is also created on the client side whenever the message is created. The constructor looks like this:

```
public ChatMessage(String message) {
    this.id = UUID.randomUUID().toString();
    this.timestamp = new Date().getTime();
    this.message = message;
}
```

Converting the object into JSON

One more thing you need to do is serialize the `ChatMessage` into a JSON that looks something like this:

```
{
    "id": "aa4cdec6-5069-4055-8770-e28be9499ef3",
    "timestamp": 1484143186210,
    "message": "Hello World!"
}
```

For purposes of the example, you're omitting the time zone. In real-life applications, it would be necessary.

Gson parser

You'd perform the serialization and parsing with a library called Gson. In this case, it takes an object and returns a JSON-formatted string representation of it. It also works the other way around, parsing JSON strings.

Gson uses some black magic and reflection to figure out what the class contains, and uses that to do the parsing. There are configurations you can define for it, but at this time you won't need them.

Using Gson

You need to create an instance of Gson first and then use the instance to do its job. For efficiency, you'd normally keep the created Gson instance and use it again the next time.

```
ChatMessage chatMessage =
  new ChatMessage("Hello World!");


Gson gson = new Gson();
String chatMessageJsonString = gson.toJson(chatMessage);
```

The string you have at the end is the string representation of the `ChatMessage` instance. You'll use this to send your data through the socket to the server; the server then does the reverse, reading the string into an object again.

Including a Gson dependency

Gson isn't part of the default Android tool set so you need to import it explicitly. In the app gradle file, you add a line to tell the compiler that Gson is required:

build.gradle (app)

```
dependencies {
  ...
  // Gson serializer
  compile 'com.google.code.gson:gson:2.4'
```

Sending ChatMessages

You now have a way to convert the messages into strings that you can send through the socket. What's left is actually sending them:

```
String chatMessageJsonString = gson.toJson(chatMessage);
socket.emit("chat message", chatMessageJsonString);
```

The last line finally sends the message to the socket—to be published to all the sockets connected to the server.

Message data flow

Notice that in your application you emit only the created `ChatMessage` to the socket. You deliberately don't save it anywhere locally. This way, you know that everything that shows in each of the connected chat clients is the same: they show only instances of ChatMessage received through the socket.

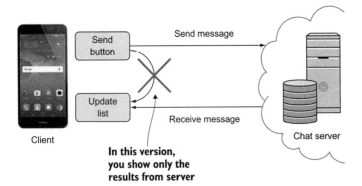

Why do you limit message flow like this? Why not directly put the listed messages at least on the device that's sending them?

Showing the messages that haven't yet been sent would require additional logic to handle the error case. The ideal solution might be some kind of a pending state.

For now, though, depending on the use case of the application, it's fairer to the user to not give a potentially false impression of having sent the message.

Errors in sending ChatMessages

In this implementation, you'll ignore any errors. If a message sending fails, the message is lost. After sending, you lose the reference to the message altogether.

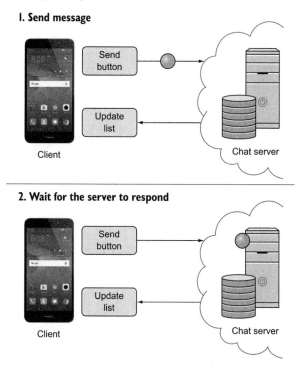

1. Send message

Send button — Update list — Client — Chat server

2. Wait for the server to respond

Send button — Update list — Client — Chat server

In the next chapter, you'll make the app handle error situations better. Our chosen approach guarantees that every client sees the same, but if the internet connection drops, you'll be in trouble.

Running the app

All of the code you wrote can go to `onCreate`. The application now will only open a connection, attach a listener, and send a message (to be received in the listener).

Do you need to wait for a connection before emitting?

The library you use for WebSockets is smart, and you can send messages even before the connection is open. The socket.io library will queue them automatically.

Wrapping listeners into observables

Using `socket.on` for listeners requires you to also release the listener with `socket.off`.

This would mean a matching call in the `onDestroy` activity.

MainActivity:onDestroy

```
socket.off("chat message", listener);
socket.disconnect();
```

Simple enough, though you'd need to have ahold of the listener function. But because you'll want to process the message further with RxJava, let's make it behave more like what you'd expect.

Listeners with Observable.create

Making just a listener is something you saw already with the file browser example: you define it in the `subscribe` function and channel all the received values to the emitter:

```
Observable<String> createListener(Socket socket) {
  return Observable.create(emitter -> {
    socket.on("chat message", args ->
      emitter.onNext());
  }
}
```

You can use this instead of creating a listener. Here's the listener declaration as it was:

```
socket.on("chat message", args ->
  Log.d(TAG, "chat message: " + args[0].toString()));
```

It thus becomes simpler:

```
createListener(socket).subscribe(chatMessage ->
  Log.d(TAG, "chat message: " chatMessage));
```

Releasing the listener on unsubscribe

You need to somehow call the respective `socket.off` function when you're finished with the listener.

In RxJava, you're finished when the subscription that was created is released; you need to save the `Disposable` and dispose of it just before disconnecting the socket:

MainActivity:onCreate

```
messageSubscription =
  createListener(socket).subscribe(...);
```

MainActivity:onDestroy

```
messageSubscription.dispose();
```

Now the question is, how can you execute the cleanup code when the subscription is released?

Subscription cleanup code

Fortunately, this isn't an atypical problem, and RxJava has a solution. You can add arbitrary code to the subscriber that will be executed when unsubscribing.

You do this by technically adding a new subscription to the subscriber—and the code that it contains is triggered at the point of unsubscribing.

If this sounds a little complicated, the code at least is relatively short. You have to keep a reference to the listener and call `socket.off`:

```
Observable.create(emitter -> {
  final Emitter.Listener listener =
    args -> emitter.onNext(args[0].toString());
  socket.on("chat message", listener);
  emitter.setDisposable(Disposables.fromAction(
    () -> {
      socket.off("chat message", listener);
    }
  ));
});
```

BooleanSubscription is just a utility to create code that executes when the subcription is released.

Coffee break

Many RxJava wrappers can be found in the RxBinding library from Jake Wharton. But sometimes you need to make your own, or to have the ability to do the cleanup code for other reasons.

Let's try the cleanup mechanism you already saw; you can take the previous code as a starting point.

1. Make an observable wrapper for the item click events of a ListView.

The function should have the following signature:

```
Observable<View> itemClicks(ListView view)
```

The `View` emitted is the clicked item view.

At the point of unsubscribing, you expect the custom observable to release the listener.

2. Make an Integer observable that keeps track of the number of its subscribers and emits this number as the first value to new subscribers.

This is just an observable, so it doesn't depend on any input (such as a view):

```
Observable<Integer> createCountingObservable()
```

Here you'd return only the create observable, nothing else.

Remember that the `subscribe` function is created only once for each observable, so all subscribers share it. This time, by not using the lambda notation for the `subscribe` function, you can create member variables that are shared by all subsequent subscribers. Remember, the lambda notation is a shorthand for an anonymous class.

You can ignore any possible threading issues in this exercise.

Solution

Here are the solutions to the two exercises of this coffee break:

1. Item click listener

You have a couple of things to do here: to set up the listener and to make sure the listener is still the same when cleaning up:

```
Observable.create(emitter -> {
    AdapterView.OnItemClickListener listener =
      (adapterView, view, i, l) ->
        subscriber.onNext(view);
    listView.setOnItemClickListener(listener);
    emitter.setDisposable(Disposables.fromAction(
        () -> {
          if (listView.getOnItemClickListener()
            == listener) {
          listView.setOnItemClickListener(null);
        }
      })
    );
});
```

2. Counting observable

After the lambda is expanded, the task of counting becomes easier:

```
Observable.create(
  new ObservableOnSubscribe<Integer>() {
    int count = 0;

    @Override
    public void subscribe(
        ObservableEmitter<Integer> emitter) {
      emitter.onNext(count++);
      emitter.setDisposable(Disposables.fromAction(
        () -> count--
      ));
    }
  }
);
```

Basic UI

You now have a way to send and to receive hardcoded messages. Let's create the simple UI you saw before and see a list of messages as well as a possibility to send them.

Let's look at the design again to remind ourselves how it should look.

Nothing too fancy here. You just need to create components in the XML. You'll use a traditional `ListView` since it's less code than a `RecyclerView`. You're welcome to use the upgraded version yourself, though.

We won't go through all of the UI XML here; you can find it in the online repository. The only special thing is that you use `stackFromBottom="true"` for the `ListView`. This way, it behaves as you'd expect an instant messenger to do.

Send button

Because you can already see the sent messages in the logs, you can start the UI with the implementation of the Send button.

Because you already have a way of sending messages, you can add a listener and do the sending there. On Android, the listeners always execute on the UI thread, so you don't even have worry about that.

MainActivity:onCreate

```
EditText editText =
  (EditText) findViewById(R.id.edit_text);

findViewById(R.id.send_button)
  .setOnClickListener(event -> {
    String message = editText.getText().toString();
    ChatMessage chatMessage = new ChatMessage(message);
    socket.emit("chat message", gson.toJson(chatMessage));
  });
```

This will now emit a message to the socket, and if the connection is working, you'll immediately see the server push the same message back to you. Even if there's no way to show the message in the UI yet, you can see the logs.

Showing messages

You'll aim to show a list of all received messages during the running of the application on the `ListView` you created. The way to show them is an `ArrayAdapter`. You'll create one of the default Android layouts for the items.

For now, you'll continue to stack everything into `MainActivity`. After the logic becomes more involved, you'll start gradually introducing the reactive architecture to address the growing complexity.

Drafting the view model and the view

In our case, the only view that renders data is the `ListView`, because the `EditText` and `Button` are only for sending. Later you could, for instance, disable the Send button based on internet connection, but until something like that comes up, you can leave it alone.

In our reactive way, you want to think about the full data set the view needs in order to draw itself. It's a list of items, so it'd seem like a list of strings is sufficient information to draw all of it.

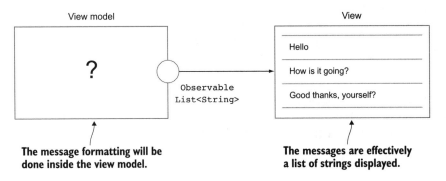

The message formatting will be done inside the view model.

The messages are effectively a list of strings displayed.

The reason you spend time thinking about something that seems simple is that the intuitive way of creating the connection is wrong. Sometimes when doing reactive programming, it's better to take a step back first and analyze the situation from the beginning.

So bear with me for a few pages as we go through the steps needed to finally connect the dots and make the connection work.

Creating an ArrayAdapter

MainActivity:onCreate

```
ArrayAdapter<String> arrayAdapter =
  new ArrayAdapter<>(
    this, android.R.layout.simple_list_item_1);
```

The adapter doesn't support multiple parts in the layout or formatting, but for our purposes, it's fine. A custom adapter and a layout would allow for greater flexibility in rendering.

Because the `ArrayAdapter` is used for rendering only, you'll semantically group it together with `ListView`. The whole structure will look like this:

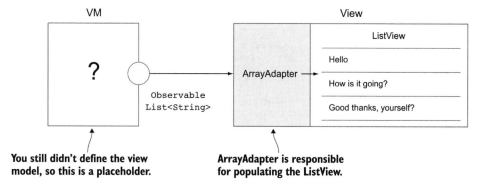

You still didn't define the view model, so this is a placeholder.

ArrayAdapter is responsible for populating the ListView.

Using the ArrayAdapter

The interface of the `ArrayAdapter` is that of normal arrays. What you want is a way to redraw the whole list based on the new set of data you received. You're missing a couple of pieces, but the updating code is as follows:

```
items -> {
  arrayAdapter.clear();
  arrayAdapter.addAll(items);
}
```

Couldn't you just call .add on the adapter when new messages arrive?

`ArrayAdapter` indeed has a method for adding singular items. At this stage, it would be possible to add the messages one by one. But you'll see later why this solution doesn't scale—it would put the burden of keeping track of the items on the adapter, which is directly tied to the view.

The view model

We started with the view to get an idea of what kind of data you need to produce in the view model. In the end, what you want is a list of messages.

You already wrapped the event listener into an observable before, so you can use that as an input to the view model. Notice, though, that it gives the messages one by one. You need to find a way to aggregate them into a single list. This is also why the arrow looks a little different in the picture: it doesn't represent state, but events.

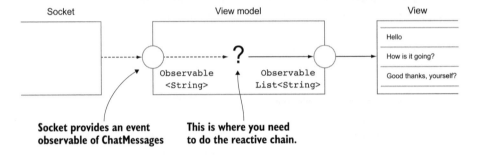

Socket provides an event observable of ChatMessages

This is where you need to do the reactive chain.

Setting up

You'll create a placeholder for the view model and then fill in the logic:

```
class ChatViewModel {
  BehaviorSubject<List<String>> messageListSubject;

  public ChatViewModel(Observable<String>
    chatMessageObservable) {
    ...
  }

  public Observable<List<String>> getMessageList() {
    return messageListSubject.hide();
  }
}
```

Initial implementation

For now, you can move the logging logic of incoming messages to the view model and forget about the unsubscribing and disconnecting; you'll get back to that in a bit.

You can put the logic in the constructor of the `ChatViewModel` where the dots are in the first draft:

```
public ChatViewModel(
  Observable<String> chatMessageObservable) {
  chatMessageObservable.subscribe(chatMessage ->
    Log.d(TAG, "chat message: " chatMessage));
}
```

This again logs the incoming messages.

Parsing and accumulating

In our view model, you have an input of message JSON and an output of a list of formatted strings for displaying in the `ListView`. You need to do two things: get the actual message from the JSON and accumulate the incoming messages.

Currently what comes through the socket is, for example, as follows:

```
{
  "id": "aa4cdec6-5069-4055-8770-e28be9499ef3",
  "timestamp": 1484143186210,
  "message": "Hello World!"
}
```

To parse it, you'll go back to your Gson library and use the reverse of `toJSON`. It takes the JSON string and the class into which you want to parse it:

```
ChatMessage chatMessage =
Gson.fromJSON(json, ChatMessage.class);
```

You'll put all of the processing steps together in a bit.

Accumulating ChatMessages

What you have is an observable that always gives the latest message as it arrives. What you need is an accumulated list of the last item and everything you received before it.

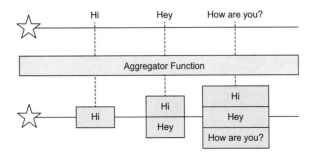

Notice that in this case it isn't necessary for the observable to end at all. You don't know when the socket might close, but on the other hand, nothing special is happening in terms of displaying the messages when it does.

Marble diagram

To make your graphs more concise, you can use the marble format again. Here's the same conversation abstracted into marbles.

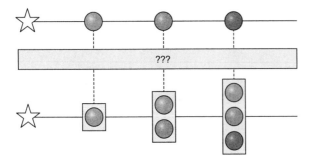

RxJava operator scan

This time, there's unfortunately nothing off the shelf you can directly use. What you can do, though, is use the higher-level operator scan and set it up with your requirements. It's a powerful operator when you need to do any kind of accumulation.

The scan allows you to define a function that accumulates the values with a certain way of combining. In pseudocode, the operator works like this:

```
scan(
  initialValue,
  (accumulatedValue, newValue) -> {
    ... Calculate newAccumulatedValue
    return newAccumulatedValue;
  }
)
```

Let's break it down. What you have here is, first, the `initialValue`. It's like the seed of the accumulation. In our case, this is an empty list—in the beginning, you don't have messages at all.

Marbles with scan

If you draw another picture with the scan, you'll have to add the initial value as an empty list. This is emitted immediately before any other values. The accumulator function is defined in the middle. It adds the marble to the list of previous marbles.

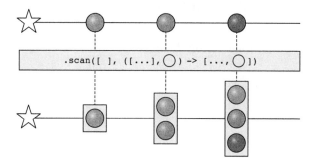

Putting together message processing

You saw the marble diagram for the scan accumulation. Notice that the function receives two parameters: the previously accumulated values (in our case, an array) and the new one that just arrived. The types of these two don't need to be the same.

What you want to do is to receive an array of the previous messages and return a new array with the new message added to it.

arrayAccumulatorFunction

```
([...], ◯) -> [..., ◯])
```

If you rename the function parameters, the usage of the function becomes clearer:

```
static List<ChatMessage> arrayAccumulatorFunction(
    List<ChatMessage> previousMessagesList,
    ChatMessage newMessage) {

  List<ChatMessage> newMessagesList =
    new ArrayList<>(previousMessagesList);
  newMessagesList.add(newMessage);
  return newMessagesList;
}
```

This is the function you saw inside the scan before. It starts with an empty list and adds each marble it received at the end of the list, producing a new list.

You'll see how it's used when you put all the pieces together on the next page.

ChatViewModel Constructor

For now, you'll put everything in the constructor of the ChatViewModel.

The last thing is to convert the ChatMessage types to strings. You can do this with a flatMap that opens the list and "loops" through all the items, converting them with the toString function. It uses the toList function you've already seen to collect the transformed ChatMessages back into a list.

```
public ChatViewModel(
    Observable<String> chatMessageObservable) {
  Gson gson = new Gson();
  chatMessageObservable
          .map(json ->
                  gson.fromJson(json, ChatMessage.class))
          .scan(new ArrayList<>(),
                  ChatViewModel::arrayAccumulatorFunction)
          .flatMap(list ->
                  Observable.from(list)
                          .map(ChatMessage::toString)
                          .toList())
          .subscribe(messageList::onNext);
}
```

If you look back to the original picture, you can now replace the question marks with the preceding implementation.

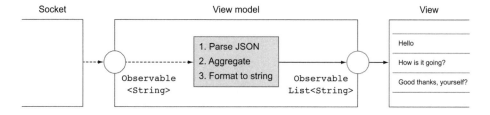

These are now the responsibilities of the view model. Later you'll see that some of them might be shifted to other modules of the application, but what's important is that as long as the view stays the same, the output of the view model doesn't need to change.

Consuming values from the view model

You've already seen how the owner, or the container of the view model, manages the connection between the data and the view. The view model is intentionally kept separate from the view to promote modularity and testability.

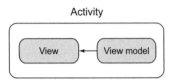

The view and the view model are equal parts of the activity (or fragment) and aren't directly aware of each other.

How you establish the connection is by subscribing to the outputs of the view model and updating the view in the subscriber function:

MainActivity:onCreate

```
viewSubscriptions.add(
  chatViewModel.getMessageList()
    .observeOn(AndroidSchedulers.mainThread())
    .subscribe(list -> {
      arrayAdapter.clear();
      arrayAdapter.addAll(list);
    })
);
```

MainActivity:onDestroy

```
viewSubscriptions.clear();
```

View model lifecycle

You still have one thing that you left out of your view model implementation: how to release the subscription you made to the `chatMessageObservable`. After all, you added the `socket.off` code to be executed when unsubscribing, but with the current implementation, it'll never be unsubscribed.

What you did so far was release the connection between the view model and the view, but here you need to handle the subscription between the model and the view model.

What you had before you started with the view model were `subscribe` and `unsubscribe` tied to the Android `Activity` lifecycle.

Let's save the created subscription and release it appropriately:

MainActivity:onCreate

```
messageSubscription =
  createListener(socket).subscribe(...);
```

MainActivity:onDestroy

```
messageSubscription.dispose();
```

What you can do with the view model is something similar. You'll move the subscription code away from the constructor of the view model and make another function that saves the subscription so that it can be released later.

The preceding code will thus change to call functions on the view model instance instead:

MainActivity:onCreate

```
viewModel.subscribe();
```

MainActivity:onDestroy

```
viewModel.unsubscribe();
```

Making the view model lifecycle

In general, everything that makes subscriptions to something outside of itself needs to have a lifecycle. In this case the view model subscribes to the observable given to it, which is tied to the socket. The view model itself doesn't know this, though, but in principle all subscriptions to outside observables should be released.

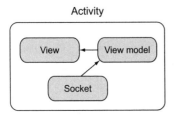

Making the view model aware of its subscriptions

The problem is that everything is in the constructor and you essentially throw away the subscription that the subscribe method returns:

```
public ChatViewModel(
    Observable<String> chatMessageObservable) {
  Gson gson = new Gson();
  chatMessageObservable
          .map(json ->
                  gson.fromJson(json, ChatMessage.class))
          .scan(new ArrayList<>(),
                  ChatViewModel::arrayAccumulatorFunction)
          .flatMap(list ->
              Observable.from(list)
                          .map(ChatMessage::toString)
                          .toList())
          .subscribe(messageList::onNext);
}
```

Subscribe and unsubscribe methods

The goal is to move the subscription creation to a `subscribe` method of the view model and collect the subscriptions in a `CompositeDisposable`. This `CompositeDisposable` will then be released when calling `unsubscribe`.

You're effectively matching the lifecycle `onCreate` and `onDestroy` methods of the activity (or fragment) to those of the view model (`subscribe` and `unsubscribe`).

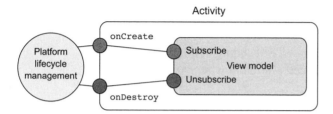

When the view model is created, you'll save the `chatMessageObservable` until it's needed:

```
public ChatViewModel(
    Observable<String> chatMessageObservable) {
  this.chatMessageObservable = chatMessageObservable;
}
```

Then in the `subscribe` function, you'll use it and save the subscription. It's the same chain you had in the constructor before:

```
public void subscribe() {
  subscriptions.add(chatMessageObservable.map(json ->
    ... the chain that used to be in constructor
  );
}
```

In `unsubscribe`, you simply release this saved subscription:

```
public void unsubscribe() {
  subscriptions.clear();
}
```

You can find the entire view model code in the online code repository.

Summary

This chapter might resemble some earlier ones, but you nevertheless learned new techniques and got more comfortable with view models. Each application is slightly different and requires adjusting the approach to take. View models are a good starting point for building your architecture. And if the view models of your application start growing too big, you can start growing parts of the code into other components, such as the model.

Cleaning up when unsubscribing

One special thing you saw how to do is clean up observables after unsubscribing. This isn't something you need often, but when you do, there's no going around it.

Attaching these additional "cleanup" subscriptions is a powerful tool when you need to be on top of what's happening—and it can also be used for debugging when you aren't sure why an observable is being unsubscribed.

View model and architectures

You didn't see new components to the architecture and you didn't even implement a store. I kept it simple for now to get the technical details out of the way so they wouldn't obstruct the bigger points I'll make in the following chapter.

Here the important takeaway is how view models can be tied to a lifecycle of another container. This is the basis for making hierarchies of modules in the architectures, and you'll use this strategy in the following chapter.

Advanced architectures
Chat client 2 | 12

In this chapter

- Pending messages status for chat client

- Stores with multiple inputs

- Initializing a store from a REST API

- Model layer as a container for business logic

View models, stores, and the model

We touched on the topic of a store in an earlier chapter. It's a powerful tool for isolating state in a place that can be easily identified and maintained.

In this chapter, you'll expand the working chat client to use a store for greater flexibility. In the preceding chapter, you put everything into one big view model, and although this worked, it doesn't scale too far.

In addition to a store, you'll create a layer around the store that can handle business logic universal to the application. Normally, this layer is called the *model*, but you'll get to that later.

Recap of the chat client

To quickly remind yourself of what is in the chat client, let's look at the UI so far. It has a list of messages, a text input, and a button to send a message (to be received by other connected clients).

It's not a complicated piece of software as a whole, and for our purposes that's a good thing. Seeing patterns is usually easier when you have less code to distract from the core functionality of the application.

Chat client architecture

Currently, you have a basic reactive architecture with a view model and a view. The view model connects to a WebSocket, creating a two-way pipeline for the data. For a refresher of how WebSockets work, refer to the beginning of chapter 11—the details aren't important now.

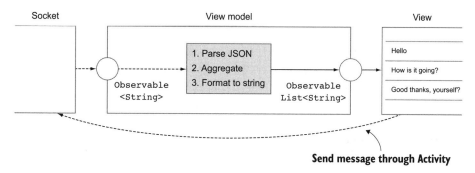

Send message through Activity

In this case, you chose to send the message not through the view model but directly from the button click handler. This is registered in the `onCreate` main activity block.

Code structure

You've separated only the view model as an independent module. All the other code is in the Android mother class called `MainActivity`. The initialization of the view as well as connecting the view to the view model are there.

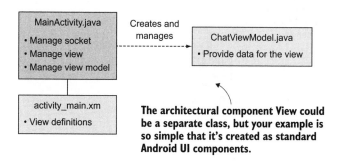

The architectural component View could be a separate class, but your example is so simple that it's created as standard Android UI components.

All in all, it's tidy as it is, and would be fine if the features stayed as they are. Next you'll add more features.

Message pending state

The first major improvement you'll implement is a pending state for outgoing messages. The messages will show in a different visual style before they've been successfully confirmed by the server.

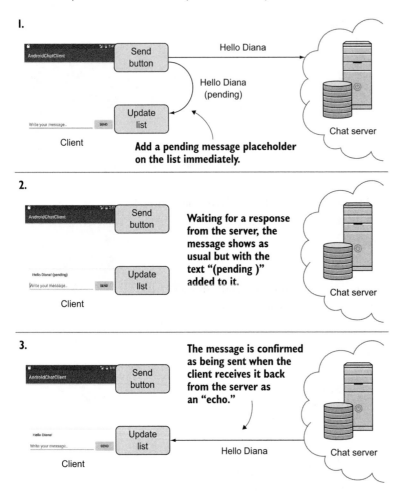

Handling state updates

Our current way of handling incoming messages is with an aggregator function that takes the new messages and appends them to the end of the list. You may remember this graph from before.

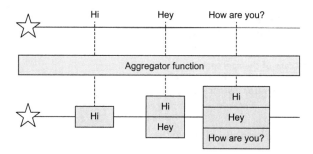

This is still valid, but now you face a problem: where initially the message is pending, it needs to be *updated* when its delivery has been confirmed. The aggregator function would append it at the end, causing a duplicate.

This is how it would behave if you tried to use it.

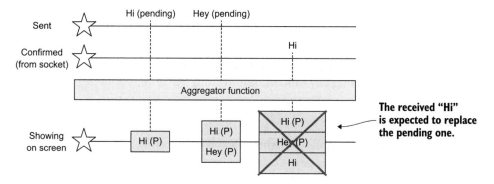

The received "Hi" is expected to replace the pending one.

Store as an aggregator

To understand how to solve the problem, let's look at the aggregator function itself. It's wrapped with an RxJava `.scan` operator that holds state inside—the list of messages that have already been received.

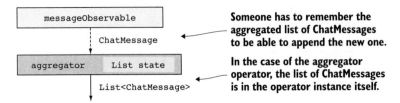

If you take a step back and see what the store looked like, this particular aggregator looks a lot like a store.

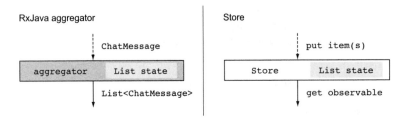

The difference, as compared to the stores you saw before, is that you had a way to get a stream of *items with the same ID* from the store. But nothing prevents you from exposing any kind of output from the store.

Is the aggregator a store?

This is where the code gets more complex semantically. Many reactive operators hold state, such as `.distinctUntilChanged`, which filters repeating values from the observable. *To filter based on the last value, this operator needs to know the previous value.*

The aggregator is a kind of store with state in it, but the state has limited access, which is a good thing. You know that the aggregator gets its values only from the source observable and nowhere else.

Switching the aggregator into a store

Now that the state logic is getting more complex, it's better to forget about a separate aggregator function and switch to using a store. The benefits here are as follows:

- A store can be shared between different parts of the application.
- It's clearer where complex state is stored.
- You can easily make the store persist itself.

Here's how the `ChatClient` looked with the aggregator in it. Notice everything is bundled in the view model. This isn't necessarily bad, but as the program grows more complex, it's good to keep the view models reasonably lean.

Previous data flow with the aggregator

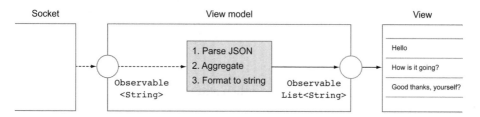

What you want to do is take the accumulation part away from the view model and extract it into a store. But it's not prudent to have the store do its own parsing, so you'll add another box for that operation. You'll see soon where it'll fit in terms of code.

Data flow with a store

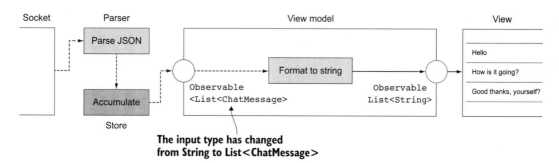

The code for the store

If you feel a little confused about how this will look in the written code, don't worry. You'll now see what goes where and then proceed to make an initial implementation of the store.

Notice that at this point you aren't yet solving the original problem of confirming the pending messages. Hold tight.

Files and classes of different parts of the old flow

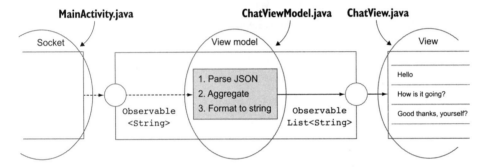

This is pretty straightforward—three classes. You'll then add the new one, which is the store.

Files and classes of different parts of the revised flow

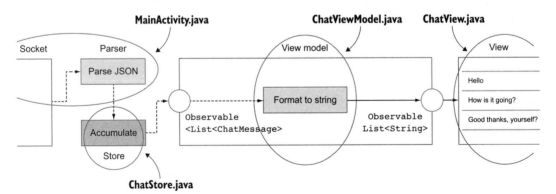

In the new flow, you have one new class: the `ChatStore`. But the parser code has been moved to the activity! Isn't this a bad practice?

The story of the parser

To be fair, the parsing code is just one line in addition to creating the Gson instance. It's thus quite safe to put this code line in the activity. The main problem with these kinds of little pieces of code is they'll start to accumulate eventually. Even if it isn't dangerous now, you'll see a little later where to put the parser in a more scalable architecture.

Initial store implementation

OK, enough talking. At this point, the code for the store isn't big—and this is exactly what you want. If possible, it's better to make architectural refactoring before making the functional changes that it enables. This requires having a plan, but as you do more reactive programming, you'll start to see patterns and modules that make sense to extract.

In the first store you won't go crazy but will simply replicate the behavior of the aggregator. Notice that the store always appends the new value to the end of the list and emits the full list to all subscribers:

Initial Store implementation

```
public class ChatStore {
    private List<ChatMessage> cache =
            new ArrayList<>();
    private PublishSubject<List<ChatMessage>> subject =
            PublishSubject.create();

    public void put(ChatMessage value) {
        cache.add(value);
        subject.onNext(cache);
    }

    public Observable<List<ChatMessage>> getAll() {
        return subject.hide();
    }
}
```

The updated view model

The view model with its reduced responsibilities becomes simple.

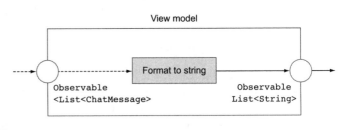

You might even ask whether it's worth it anymore, but it's better to leave it there. A view model is useful to have because there's almost always UI-related code that can't go into stores.

Reduced view model code

```
public ChatViewModel(Observable<List<ChatMessage>>
    chatMessageObservable) {
  this.chatMessageObservable = chatMessageObservable;
}

public void subscribe() {
  subscriptions.add(chatMessageObservable
    .flatMap(list -> Observable.fromIterable(list)
      .map(ChatMessage::toString).toList())
      .subscribe(messageList::onNext)
  );
}
```

The output of the view model. You didn't include the code, but it's a BehaviorSubject exposed to the view.

In this listing you could give the view model the full store instead of just the observable of chat messages. This is largely a question of need—usually it's better that the modules of code know as little of each other as possible. In this case, the view model won't insert chat messages into the store but only consume them.

> Is it a good idea to insert items into a store in the view model?
>
> This is a good question, and there are different opinions. We'll discuss some of them a little later, but in short it's cleaner not to put items into the store in the view model. This enables each module to handle only either incoming or outgoing data.
>
> But if there aren't too many lines of code involved, it might be more convenient to do everything in the view model.

The updated activity code

The main activity of the app is getting an increased number of responsibilities, but for now you're letting it grow.

First you need an instance of the store in the activity. This way, you can keep it around in case you need it in some other part of the activity.

MainActivity declaration

```
public class MainActivity extends AppCompatActivity {
    private Socket socket;
    private ChatStore chatStore;
    private ChatViewModel chatViewModel;
    private CompositeDisposable viewSubscriptions =
            new CompositeDisposable();
```

The initialization code is starting to grow, but don't worry about it yet. Notice also that you're creating a new subscription from the socket to the store.

MainActivity onCreate

```
chatStore = new ChatStore();
viewSubscriptions.add(
    createListener(socket)
            .map(json ->
                    gson.fromJson(json, ChatMessage.class))
            .subscribe(chatStore::put)
);
```

You need to save the new subscription and to release it when the activity is destroyed. Previously, that was done through the view model lifecycle, but because the view model is no longer responsible for aggregating the messages, you'll add it to the `viewSubscriptions` for now so it's released at the correct time.

Coffee break

Add a search to the client that allows the user to filter the messages based on an arbitrary string in the string field.

Exercise

You're looking at a filter that matches the word written in the search field to the contents of the messages on the list. You won't trigger a search against the backend or anything like that.

You can find the starting point for the exercise online: it has the search input already in place. You job is to expand the app in a way that allows the user to filter their messages.

Tips

Where should you put this code? Although you could put it in the `MainActivity`, the code has more to do with connections between specific view components. The view model is usually the correct place for all kinds of UI logic.

What you need to do is make sure you have all the information you need and then apply the filtering in the `subscribe` function. There are many ways to filter it, but try to do it with as much RxJava as possible.

Solution

It's good you already have the view model, because adding the logic there fits well. To see your expanded view model, you can draw a little picture.

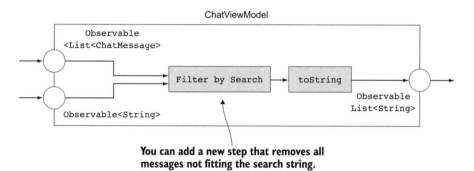

You can add a new step that removes all messages not fitting the search string.

Notice that you want to update the list if *either* of the inputs changes— if the user changes the search string or if you get new messages (new messages not fitting the search wouldn't show).

The code bits

You can use tools you already learned. You want to filter based on the search string, so you need to make a `combineLatest`. You could implement a function for the `combineLatest` operator, and manually loop through the items, but you can also do it in the RxJava way.

Both ways work, but for the exercise's sake, here's the RxJava version:

```
Observable<List<ChatMessage>> filteredChatMessages =
  Observable.combineLatest(
      chatMessageObservable, searchTextObservable,
      Pair::new)
    .switchMap(pair -> Observable.from(pair.first)
      .filter(chatMessage ->
          chatMessage.getMessage()
            .contains(pair.second))
      .toList()
    );
```

Implementing pending messages

To start with the pending messages, you first need a way to tell if a message is pending. It's either pending or it isn't, so a Boolean would seem to be sufficient. You'll add this flag in the `ChatMessage` type.

```
class ChatMessage {
  String id
  long timestamp
  String message
  bool isPending = true
}
```

You'll set it `true` by default, because the ones you'd create are pending to begin with.

Rendering the pending state

With the default value of `true`, all of your messages are now pending by default. But how to display them to the user?

This is why you have the view model lying around; its only job is to decide how the messages are formatted. You can use it to add a (pending) text at the end of each message that hasn't been confirmed as sent.

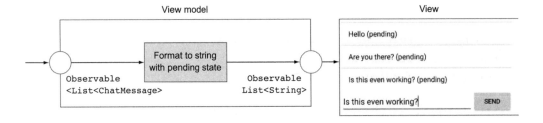

On the right side. you can see how it'll look. Before you have a way of confirming the arrival, it'll all be pending forever. You'll fix that soon enough.

Chat message formatting function

To add the extra text for pending messages, you'll create a new function in the view model. This logic could be moved into the view, but for now you'll keep it in the view model.

ChatViewModel member method

```
private static String formatMessage(
      ChatMessage chatMessage) {
   StringBuilder builder = new StringBuilder();
   builder.append(chatMessage.getMessage());
   if (chatMessage.isPending()) {
       builder.append(" (pending)");
   }
   return builder.toString();
}
```

The preceding code uses a `StringBuilder` for a slight optimization, though in this case it's hardly necessary. You can use the function in the processing of the messages instead of the `ChatMessage::toString` you had there before. It loops through all the messages it receives, formatting them into strings.

Partial ChatViewModel subscribe function

```
chatMessageObservable
  .flatMap(list ->
    Observable.fromIterable(list)
       .map(this::formatMessage)
       .toList())
```

> ### You loop all the messages every time. Isn't that a performance problem?
>
> With the small number of messages you have, the effect of formatting is minimal. But with larger lists, performance could become a problem.
>
> To optimize message formatting, a caching strategy could be created. It's possible to create a unique hash for each message and save the results of the formatting. In some cases, the code might need to be moved to the view in order to process only the messages currently displayed.

Replacing pending messages with confirmed ones

Now you're at a point where you have a store for the messages and a way to indicate to the user whether they're pending. It's not beautiful, but you're free to make it prettier during the next coffee break if you want to.

To see what you want to accomplish, let's look at where the aggregator is now replaced with a store.

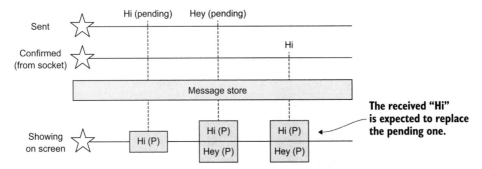

The intended behavior is that the new confirmed message *replaces* the one that was pending. The full list then goes to the view model that in turn updates the information in the view. The message that has arrived through the socket is no longer pending.

You can also draw the same picture with your arrows: the store has two inputs and one output.

Message ID

With a store, you just need to know whether a message that you receive is the same that you sent. How do you do this?

Fortunately, you already did, although secretly. Early on, you added an ID property to each created message, which is unique:

```
class ChatMessage {
  String id
  ...
```

In general, it's good to distinguish data objects based on an ID because they might change over time. Much like an orange rots, but it's still the same orange—only its properties have changed over time.

Message update flow

You'll need to add a way to mark all incoming messages as confirmed. Some of them are sent by your users; some come from others. In terms of your store, you don't need to distinguish; you just need two channels to treat them a little differently.

In reality, our class structure is a little less sophisticated, and you already have a pending state upon creation. The point here is that you have a layer before the store that makes sure the messages are in their correct state, depending on where they arrive.

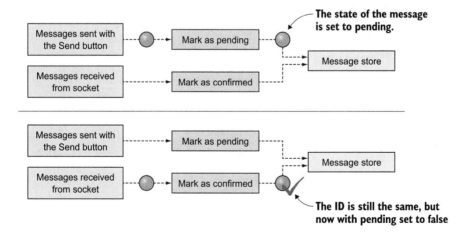

Updated store code

You might have wondered about your latest implementation of the store. It's a plain one in which the new items are added to a list.

```
public void put(ChatMessage value) {
    cache.add(value);
    subject.onNext(cache);
}
```

This doesn't take into consideration the ID of the message at all: there might be duplicates. The quotation marks are there because you haven't defined in the store what a *duplicate* means—from its point of view, it has only objects of type `ChatMessage` in a list.

Using a map to keep duplicates away

The store you had was fine for what it was doing, but you need to change it if you want to have only the latest message for each ID. This may sound complicated, but what it means is that the pending status might change while the ID stays the same.

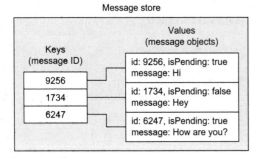

Message store

When you set a value, you use the ID to replace the old one if it exists.

Coding the map

We won't go into too much more detail here, but this particular store accepts messages and sends the (possibly) updated list to all subscribers:

```
public class ChatStore {
  private Map<String, ChatMessage> cache =
    new HashMap<>();
  private PublishSubject<Collection<ChatMessage>>
    subject = PublishSubject.create();

  public void put(ChatMessage value) {
    cache.put(value.getId(), value);
    subject.onNext(cache.values());
  }

  public Observable
    <Collection<ChatMessage>> getStream() {
    return subject.hide();
  }
}
```

The change doesn't add any lines but is significant in terms of functionality.

Side effect: message order

You might have noticed already that the output of the store changed into a collection of ChatMessages. A *collection* is an unordered list, and the reason it happened is the map doesn't rely on the order in which items are inserted. You could say the messages were in the right order because of luck.

You obviously need to sort the messages, but you need to decide: does the store guarantee messages sorted by the timestamp or will you do it in the view model?

In your case you'll choose the view model, since the order is required only because of how it's displayed in the UI. You can check the code online to see how it works—it adds one step to the processing.

Pending state handling code

The last thing to do before you'll have a working pending state is separating the two paths from which you can add items into the store. Let's look at the flow from the beginning of the chapter.

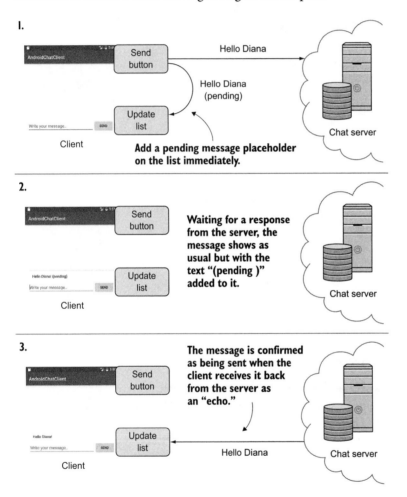

Adding the code

You'll put this code into `MainActivity` for now to see that it works. But `MainActivity` is starting to grow alarmingly, and this is logic you should be unit testing. Therefore, after writing the initial proof of concept, you'll move the logic into a separate class.

Message confirmation logic

You first put the message in the store as a pending message. It will thus appear immediately on the user's message list.

The first entry point is at the click handler of the Send button. Notice `isPending` is set to `true` by default.

```
sendButton
  .setOnClickListener(event -> {
    ChatMessage chatMessage =
      new ChatMessage(editText.getText().toString());
    chatStore.put(chatMessage);
    socket.emit("chat message",
      gson.toJson(chatMessage));
});
```

The other point is when you receive messages from the socket. You want to mark them as not pending before adding them to the store. You add a functional style setter to `ChatMessage` that creates a new object. Modifying an object in reactive programming isn't a good idea.

```
createListener(socket)
  .map(json -> gson.fromJson(json, ChatMessage.class))
  .map(chatMessage -> chatMessage.setIsPending(false))
  .subscribe(chatStore::put)
```

Coffee break

Now you have a refactored chat client that uses a store instead of an aggregator operator.

It might seem like a lot of hassle for not much, but to see some of the benefits, you'll now implement the loading of the chat history from the server when the app starts.

The HTTP API

It turns out you have an API for retrieving the full message history from the server. The history doesn't date too far back, though, so don't worry about loading times.

A branch on the online code repository has the API boilerplate code. You'll use a Retrofit HTTP interface declaration that returns the message history as far as the server has it.

```
public interface ChatMessageApi {
    @GET("/messages")
    Observable<List<String>> messages();
}
```

Your task is to use this API when the app starts and prepopulates the store with the history.

Could you make a more sophisticated aggregator?

If you've been wondering about the necessity of the store, you could make a complex aggregator that fulfills the new requirements, but it would become a pseudo-store without admitting it. In these cases, when there starts to be a lot of state inside the chain, it's better to cut it and create a store.

Also, inserting contents into the aggregator would be tricky—with store, it's straightforward.

Coffee break solution

With the HTTP API set up and running, the task of loading messages isn't too tricky. The only question here is, should you block the app until the history has been loaded? If the user interacts with the UI before the history is loaded, it might inadvertently overwrite some of their messages.

This kind of a loading state could be done with a loading spinner to replace the list while loading, but here you'll consider the potential risk of delayed message history loading reasonably small. You can call the API when the activity is created and put the results in the store.

MainActivity onCreate

```
/// Create APIs and Store
chatMessageApi = ...
chatStore = ...

loadOldMessages();
```

MainActivity loadMessages

```
private void loadOldMessages() {
  chatMessageApi.messages()
    .subscribeOn(Schedulers.io())
    .observeOn(AndroidSchedulers.mainThread())
    .subscribe(messages -> {
      for (String messageJson : messages) {
        ChatMessage chatMessage =
          gson.fromJson(messageJson, ChatMessage.class);
        chatStore.put(
          new ChatMessage(chatMessage)
            .setIsPending(false));
      }
    });
}
```

The model

You'll refactor the message logic and move it into a new class. This class will be called the *model*, though it's sometimes also known as the *data layer* or something similar.

The model is additional code around the store that you don't want to put into the store itself. Currently, all of this is dumped into `MainActivity`, which isn't a great place for it. You'll see soon why this is, apart from the obvious accumulation of unrelated code in one file.

Data layer as a container

You'll attempt to define the model as all of the logic except for the view model and the view. Here you left out some smaller bits, such as the parsing, but you can see the details in the online code.

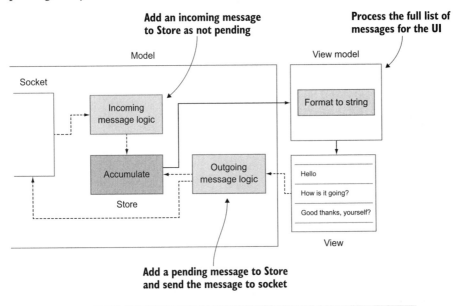

Is it better to start with diagrams or code?

The code dictates what the diagrams can represent. Here you took the connection points and dependencies and defined the model with a reasonably small interface. Sometimes, though, when you start implementation, you may notice that you overlooked something and have to adjust the plan accordingly.

Simplified high-level architecture

Fortunately, you followed good architectural practices and kept the connections between the parts of the application small. In the end, you can draw the high-level graph as a typical model-view-viewmodel diagram. Notice that what's atypical here are the reactive principles by which the modules have been built.

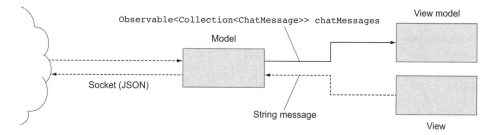

The model on the spectrum

If you have a look at the spectrum, you'll get a better understanding of where the model stands. It's responsible for *application-wide* state management and connectivity.

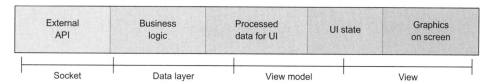

Usually, you'd further split the model internally, because it quickly becomes a big chunk of functionality. This is also your case, and you have the store that provides the local state management for your app.

It should also be noted that because of the large responsibilities, the model can be reasonably covered by unit tests.

The code for the model

Now you'll see what the model contains. You take the modules that
were in `MainActivity` as well as the connecting code. You'll also need
to keep the subscriptions you create and you'll store them again in a
`CompositeDisposable`.

The new ChatModel class

```
public class ChatModel {
  private Gson gson = new Gson();
  private Socket socket;
  private ChatStore chatStore = new ChatStore();
  private CompositeDisposable subscriptions =
    new CompositeDisposable();

    . . .
```

You won't go through all of the model as it has the code you already
wrote. But you'll go through the connection points to the outside world
because those are the most critical ones. There are also a couple of
changes there.

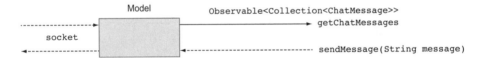

Aren't there too many CompositeDisposables?

If you're wondering about the number of `CompositeDisposables`
you keep creating, unfortunately it's inevitable. Each module that
independently creates subscriptions needs to be able to release them
as well. If you look at it from the other point of view, when you have
a stateful module, such as one with a store or a socket connection, it's
hard to avoid creating subscriptions as a setup.

Connections code

The code that handles messages from the socket stays the same; you just move it to an onCreate function of the ChatModel:

Partial ChatModel onCreate function

```
subscriptions.add(
  createListener(socket)
      .map(json ->
        gson.fromJson(json, ChatMessage.class))
      .map(chatMessage ->
        chatMessage.setIsPending(false))
      .subscribe(chatStore::put)
);
```

The outgoing one has changed a little. It's now a function that takes only the string that should be sent. The sender doesn't need to know anything about timestamps and pending states.

ChatModel member function

```
public void sendMessage(String message) {
  ChatMessage chatMessage = new ChatMessage(message);
  chatStore.put(chatMessage);
  socket.emit("chat message", gson.toJson(chatMessage));
}
```

You'll also add a couple more methods to give the owner of the model flexibility for establishing a socket connection. In addition you'll have an onDestroy method for releasing the CompositeDisposable.

Model lifecycle

The model needs to be created and destroyed, and it thus has a lifecycle. This means that "someone" needs to create and destroy it.

The model here is a stateful module, just as the view model is. They're independent, though, in that their lifecycles don't need to match. For starters, however, you'll put both in `MainActivity`.

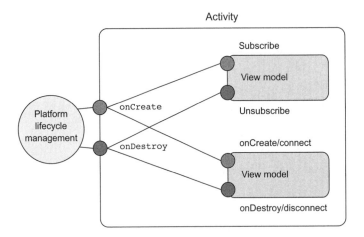

Here the activity is the platform container that has a specific lifecycle. In Android, `Activity` is created for performing a specific task (activity) and is destroyed after it's completed.

In any case, the lines you draw in the diagrams indicate where the lifecycle methods are called. Here we have everything in the `onCreate` and `onDestroy` main activities.

What about the onStart, onStop, onResume, and onPause activities?

The Android lifecycle of an activity is a little more complex than just creating and destroying. Here you've taken shortcuts that might lead to undesirable behavior. You might want to, for instance, close the socket if the activity is paused or to disable view updates. This is Android-specific, though, and you can see examples of various options in the samples of the reark.io project online.

Simplified MainActivity onCreate

```
// Create ChatModel
chatModel = new ChatModel();
chatModel.onCreate();
chatModel.connect();

// Create ChatViewModel
chatViewModel = new ChatViewModel(
  chatModel.getChatMessages());
chatViewModel.subscribe();

// Initialize the View etc.
```

If you wonder about subscribing the view model to the model before connecting the view to the view model, remember that we use behavior observables. The new subscribers (for example, the view) get the latest values immediately.

The teardown is usually the reverse of the creation.

MainActivity onDestroy

```
chatViewModel.unsubscribe();
chatModel.disconnect();
chatModel.onDestroy();
```

Switching lifecycle containers

On Android, an application can consist of many activities, even if yours has only one. What if they all need access to the store and thus the model that contains it?

You can take the model out of the activity and assign it to a higher-level container. As the last topic in this chapter, you'll see next how this can be done.

Singleton modules

Though you won't use the possibility in our example, you'll look at how the model can be moved into another lifecycle and still keep the connection to the view model.

The situation you face on Android and many other platforms is you have short-lived modules that all share data and logic. In the solution, you take the model out of the activity and create it in the application instead.

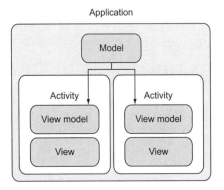

The creation of the model becomes tied to the application. `Application` is a little special, though, in that you can't control when it's closed. If you choose to keep the socket open for the entire life of the app, you need to accept that you can't explicitly close it.

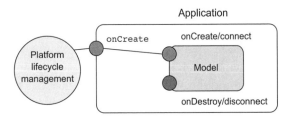

```
public class ChatApplication extends Application {
  private ChatModel chatModel;

  @Override
  public void onCreate() {
    super.onCreate();
    chatModel = new ChatModel();
    chatModel.onCreate();
  }

  public ChatModel getChatModel() {
    return chatModel;
  }
}
```

Getting ahold of the model

You've now moved the model to the application super scope, but how do you get it from there to use in the view model? What you can do in this case is get a reference to the application from the activity that owns the view model. This is Android-specific, but on every platform there are different ways of fulfilling dependencies.

MainActivity onCreate

```
ChatModel chatModel =
  ((ChatApplication) getApplication()).getChatModel();
```

You don't need to take care of the lifecycle of the model in the view model anymore. This is done in the application. You need only to take care of the lifecycle of the modules that you create.

Can you use Dagger for managing dependencies?

Absolutely! Dagger is a library made for dependency injection. It's a good match for reactive architectures and is a powerful tool for managing scopes. Dagger is a topic for another book, though, so we won't dive into it here.

Android tools for production use

You've been consciously avoiding too many libraries in this book to keep the focus on Rx. But several libraries and tools are available to use for serious development.

Dagger

http://square.github.io/dagger/

If you've used Dagger, you might have already been wondering why you're doing the dependency management with it. The answer is simply because Dagger is a beast of its own.

Dagger allows you to declare which module goes where: for instance, the model could be automatically injected to everywhere it's needed. The key is that the user of the module doesn't need to know where it came from.

I recommend using Dagger for larger production setups.

Subjects

Subjects are a little tricky in production use. In RxJava 1.x, they're prone to `MissingBackpressureException`, which indicates there's too much data to handle. You should be conscious of the data you receive from the server and implement back-pressure handling in places where needed (see the ReactiveX docs for more information).

RxJava 2.x has workarounds for that, and the updated `Observable` doesn't in fact have it.

For view model outputs, you can also try `RxProxy`, which solves some issues in traditional subjects.

https://github.com/upday/RxProxy

Unexpectedly terminating observables

Another problem sometimes faced is, in case of an unexpected error, you lose the whole subject/observable as it terminates. For these cases, you can either try to implement error handling or convert the observable into notifications with `materialize`. That's another topic, though, but have a look at what it does if you're faced with the problem.

Declaring error handlers

Error handling is always a bit of a challenge, mostly because of the difficult question, "What should happen in case of an error?" The very least you have to do, though, is always declare an error handler:

```
.subscribe(subscriber, errorHandler);
```

If you don't declare an error handler and an error comes, *the default implementation crashes your app.* If you're not sure what to do, or it doesn't matter, you can log it.

Logging and threads

If threads are giving you a headache, you can easily augment the `Log` function to also print the thread name. You can get the name with `Thread.currentThread().getName()`.

Stores

The heart of the application is the store, or several of them. Typically, you'll create one for each kind of data. The store is also known as the *repository*, which you may encounter in other resources.

Most stores hold lists of data objects, similar to database tables. In production software, you'll probably want to move into using a library, such as reark.io or a newer https://github.com/NYTimes/Store. You can also consider commercial solutions, such as Realm, or go lean with SqlBrite.

Reark.io

The stores in reark.io can use a traditional SQLite `ContentProvider` behind the scenes, enabling you to get updates in all processes of the Android application. This is particularly useful if you have background processes or widgets.

You can start with a simple store and minimal set up, though, and later upgrade into SQLite.

Summary

This was a long chapter that brought together many concepts you saw earlier. The following are a few tips on where to go from here.

View models

View models are a fancy name for containers of reactive logic. They do have a role, though, which is to create a layer between the logic and the view.

- The bindings from view models to the view layer can be changed to use another library.

- You learned that view models contain both inputs and data going back to the model—in some reactive frameworks, these are separated.

Model

The model has no clear best form. It can be constructed as a layered wrapper around a store or even as a separate data processing layer. Often testability gives good guidance for choices.

Presenters

On Android, the presenter is a popular part of the architecture nowadays. But it isn't such a critical part of a reactive application and hence you didn't see it in action.

As far as architectures with RxJava go, a presenter is best used for complex views as a way to extract the rendering logic from the view. Therefore, it'd fall somewhere between the view and the view model.

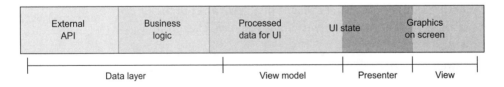

The goal should still be to keep the view shallow, but sometimes the sheer number of subcomponents creates a need for a presenter.

Transitions with Rx | 13

In this chapter

- Creating animated UIs with Rx and view models

- Creating parametrized transitions

- Understanding where the line should be between the view and the view model

Transitioning between states

This chapter shows some rather technical possibilities of reactive programming. It has a reasonable amount of mathematics, but it's all explained, so hang tight.

In UIs, you often have in-between states, in which, for example, a drop-down isn't quite open, but "opening." You animate it from close to open.

The user clicks the button, and the drop-down starts to open with an animation.

In this case, a scroll indicator appears when the drop-down is fully open.

There are a few approaches to animations, and you'll take a short tour before you start.

The fire-and-forget strategy

In the simple case of an animation being relatively fast (less than 300 ms), you can start an animation and let it finish no matter what the user does. We call this *fire and forget*. It's easy and indeed the typical way of animating UIs.

The fire-and-forget approach has limitations, and they become more pronounced the longer the animations become.

The most obvious problem appears when you think of a user who impatiently clicks rapidly many times. If the user clicks before the animation has finished, what should happen?

The glitch

Forgetting the animation state after it's started works for short animations. For slightly longer ones, it makes the UI perform a glitch if the user is too fast—or if the application state changes because of external reasons, such as an incoming notification.

In general, the problem is always the same: you need to start a new animation before the old one is finished. Your only choice is to reset the animation.

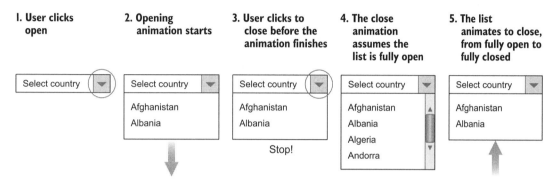

What went wrong?

In reality, steps 3 and 4 are right next to each other, so it's a little difficult to follow what's going on. Let's break down the progress by drawing a graph:

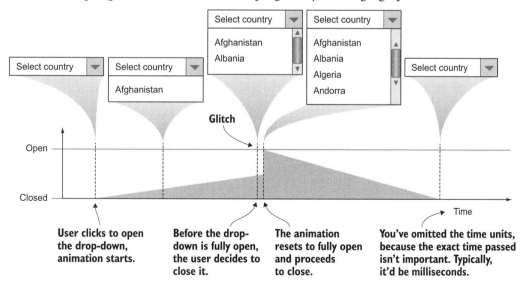

The sharp jump in the "openness" of the drop-down is what the user sees as a glitch. The drop-down suddenly jumps from half open to fully open.

How it should have been

How you want the animation to work seems straightforward: you want to continue it where it left off. In our example, the drop-down never fully opens because the user is fast and clicks Close while it's opening.

In this scenario, the drop-down has to start to close in the middle of its opening.

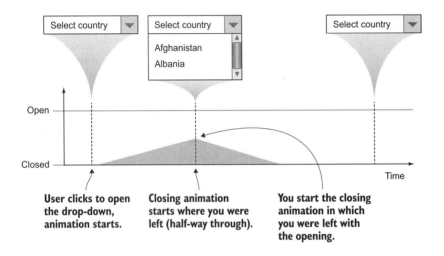

User clicks to open the drop-down, animation starts.

Closing animation starts where you were left (half-way through).

You start the closing animation in which you were left with the opening.

What about queuing transitions?

In addition to fire and forget and continuing where you left off, there's a third way to deal with animations and transitions. You can perform every animation in full before starting a new one. This is how CSS transitions work, for instance.

We won't be discussing queuing animations in this book, because Android has no inherent support for them and queuing is the expected behavior in only a few cases, from the user's point of view.

As a user, why would you want to see the drop-down fully opening before closing again—when you just explicitly told it to close? The only excuse for queuing is that it'd better than fire and forget, but if you need to spend some effort on it, you might we as well do it the right way!

More complex scenarios

You can also have more complex sequences, because nothing prevents the user from opening the drop-down again while it's closing. Of course, in the case of a drop-down, that's highly unlikely, but this could pertain to a sliding menu or something that takes longer to transition.

Quality of details

In general, UIs that work reliably when they're much slower are perceived to be of higher quality. Often the users also "test" the UI by making rapid or unexpected interactions. The solution you'll create will be robust and able to handle all the cases.

Back and forth

If the user is acting unpredictably—or just changing their mind—you might get an "openness" graph that goes back and forth between open and closed.

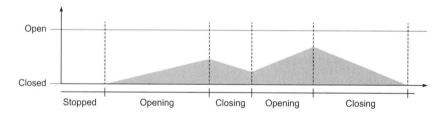

UI states aren't true or false

You have two main takeaways here. First, the animation state, and thus the UI state, can't be represented with simple true and false values. Second, you need to keep track of the animation state and always continue from where you left off. Think about what this paragraph would look like with fire and forget!

You may say that this is an exaggeration as a potential example, but in reality it's not. The user often tries to break your UI *deliberately*. They might just see how it behaves when rapidly clicking or notice a glitch and try to reproduce it. Your job isn't to create features that can be broken—it's often better not to animate if it becomes too long and it can't be done properly.

Fortunately, we'll now learn how to make it work. You'll introduce a state between 1.0 and 0.0 instead of true and false.

Animation progress using one number

Let's do a little more research before you dive into the reactive part of
this chapter—you first have to get a solid understanding of the problem
before going forward with a solution. If you're already familiar with the
way of describing the animation progress with a float from 0.0 to 1.0,
you can skip this section. Otherwise, it's time for a bit of mathematics.

Percentage of openness

The first concept you introduce is the percentage of how much the
drop-down is open.

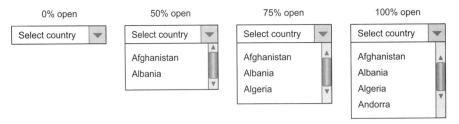

You can see that the percentage is always from 0% to 100%, and
anything else wouldn't make sense.

Ratio

To make things easier, you'll convert the percentages into floating-point
numbers so that 0% is 0.0, and 100% is 1.0. This way, if you want to take
50% of a number, you can multiply it by 0.5.

Here are some examples with the Java notation:

0% = 0.0   100% = 1.0   84.5% = .845

In programming, you usually call numbers such as these ratios.
Sometimes they're denoted with only the letter r.

If you use this knowledge with your graphs, you can change the vertical
axis to be from 0.0 to 1.0. It's still the same "openness" graph.

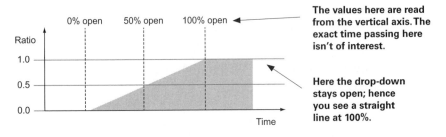

Reactive parametrization

After our little side tour, we're back to reactive programming. Parametrization of animations and transition is interesting to us because they work well with our reactive paradigms as well as view models.

You're operating close to the view, and you're already pushing the line between the view model and the view. Animation logic is surprisingly complex. If you're doing anything nontrivial, extracting that logic from the view might be better.

You're pushing the boundary of the reactive chain toward the view, extracting the animation logic out of it.

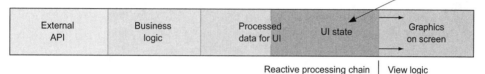

| External API | Business logic | Processed data for UI | UI state | Graphics on screen |

Reactive processing chain | View logic

The idea is to have one observable that holds the state for the transition status—the ratio of where you are from 0.0 to 1.0. You'll put this observable into the view model. The associated view, on the other hand, knows how to draw itself in a specific state depending on the ratio it receives. Notice, though, *that the view doesn't even realize it's being animated*. It just receives a new value on each *animation frame*.

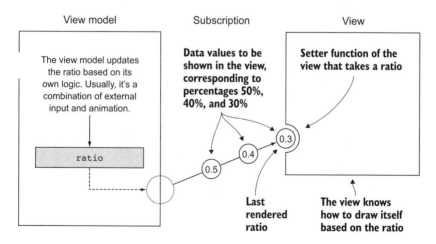

View model | Subscription | View

The view model updates the ratio based on its own logic. Usually, it's a combination of external input and animation.

ratio

Data values to be shown in the view, corresponding to percentages 50%, 40%, and 30%

0.5 0.4 0.3

Last rendered ratio

Setter function of the view that takes a ratio

The view knows how to draw itself based on the ratio

Example: The fan widget

A drop-down perhaps isn't the best example because good implementations of it are available on most platforms—and the animation is reasonably fast and isolated.

The situation changes, though, when you make custom components. As an example you'll create a fan widget that spreads the options it contains when clicking.

The original fan, coined years ago by Markus Berg from Futurice, reacted to the hovering mouse cursor. But on mobile devices, you usually don't have a hovering trigger so you'll use a click instead. You'll see that the source of the trigger is easy to change if so desired.

Drawing the fan open

As always, you have several approaches to choose from. Personally, I prefer to get something showing on screen as soon as possible, so I tend to start with the view that's responsible for the presentation.

You already saw the closed and open states of the fan as pictures, but let's break down the more complex of the two: open.

For simplicity's sake, you'll define each fan item to open 20 degrees clockwise from the last. This won't scale nicely to many items, but in a specialized case, the number could be smartly adjusted.

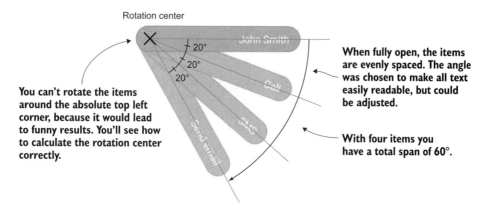

Notice again that at this point what you're doing is drawing logic that will work together with the reactive outputs. The geometry and mathematics are the same, no matter which platform you're using, but when you get to the details, you'll use Android as an example.

If you haven't made UI components of this complexity before, it's a perfect time to start. You'll go through everything necessary step-by-step.

Sounds like complicated mathematics—is it necessary?

You won't often need to delve into this kind of math, but here we make an exception and go a bit deeper. If you aren't interested in the details, you can download the parts of the code that cover the math, and use them as they are.

Setting the transformations for the child views

You assume that you have the subviews, or children of the view, in place. These are the individual items that together make the fan.

On Android, you have a possibility for a `ViewGroup` (a container) to override the transformation of all of its children one by one. You have a function that takes the desired angle of the view as well as the rotation center. If you aren't fully familiar with rotations that's not critical—you'll cover the necessary details here.

The total rotation angle of each child

You're still drawing the fan fully open, so for each of the fan items, the rotation angle increases by 20 degrees. The header stays without any rotation.

The rotation for the second item (after the header) will be $2 \times 20° = 40°$.

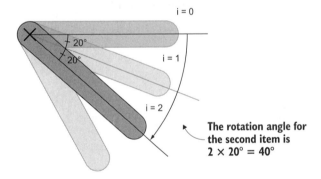

The multiplier is therefore the index of the child. The angle can be calculated as follows:

```
int rotationAngleDegrees = index × 20
```

The magic number 20 is for degrees.

Here the index starts from 0, meaning the first item would be positioned at 0 degrees (horizontal). The second would be 20 degrees, and so on.

Setting up the rotation center

Rotation center may sound fancy, but it just means the point where everything is attached. It's like an axis around which the items revolve.

Think of a little stick around which the individual "leaves" rotate. This is the rotation center.

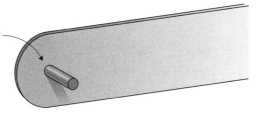

You can try removing the rotation center from the code and see what happens. In this particular case, the rotation center is important to set correctly.

Offset of the rotation center

In your list design, the left side is a semicircle. The center of this circle is the center around which you want to rotate. You can calculate the center of rotation from the height of the child. The center is at half of the height, if you consider the top-left corner as the zero point.

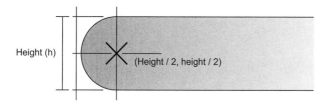

Height (h)

(Height / 2, height / 2)

```
int rotationCenterX = child.getHeight() / 2
int rotationCenterY = child.getHeight() / 2
```

This is the *offset* of the rotation center, and you'll use it to make the views behave in a coordinated manner.

How is the rotation center used in detail?

We won't go into the exact mathematics, but in general you can perform operations in steps. First you move the view so that the desired rotation center is at (0, 0). Then you apply the rotation around (0, 0). Finally, you transform the view back to where it was.

The Android way of setting child transformations

On many platforms, there's an easier way to define rotations, but on Android you have to use a bit of a special trick.

First you create your custom `ViewGroup` class. You can call it `FanViewGroup`.

In this class you'll override the function `getChildSaticTransformation` that receives as parameters the child `View` and a `Transformation`. The given transformation is what you're expected to modify, and this is the place where you apply your rotation. You also have to return `true` to indicate you indeed did apply a transformation.

The syntax here isn't the prettiest possible, but what matters is the part where you rotate. You place this code in your custom `ViewGroup` class:

```
@Override
protected boolean getChildStaticTransformation(
    View child, Transformation t) {

  final float childIndex = indexOfChild(child);
  final float childHeight = child.getHeight();

  final int rotation = childIndex * 20;
  final int rotationCenter = childHeight / 2;

  Matrix matrix = t.getMatrix();
  matrix.setRotate(rotation,
    rotationCenter, rotationCenter);

  return true;
}
```

You end up with something that looks like this:

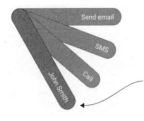

The header should stay still while the items move from underneath it. You'll have to reverse the index calculation.

Reversing the child order

The only thing left to do is make sure the header stays on top. The way to do this is by changing the index calculation to be the reverse:

```
index = getChildCount() - indexOfChild(child) - 1
```

The `getChildCount()` function returns the total number of children in your `ViewGroup`. You also have to deduct 1 because arrays are zero-based.

After the index change, the items should be correctly ordered. In general, when developing, you can play around for a bit and see what works for each scenario. In this case, the design was decided up front, so you'll stick to that.

You end up with a fan that's as you wanted but *permanently* open. After a coffee break, you'll finally see how to attach it to the reactive part of the application logic!

What's a matrix?

A *matrix* is a mathematical structure that can hold all transformations of a view. This includes moving it (translation) as well as rotation and scaling.

While matrices are extremely useful for creating cool effects, for our purposes you don't need to understand what they do. You can think of the matrix as a type that contains everything you need to know about where and how the child view is drawn on the screen.

Coffee break

Before diving deep into the reactive part of the chapter, play around with the view transformations and see what kind of effects you can produce.

The advantage of learning how to calculate different kinds of transformations is that you'll soon see how to animate all of them.

Although you shouldn't go crazy calculating everything manually, often you can create a wow effect with a reasonable amount of well-placed effort:

1. Create a transformation that shows the children underneath each other. See if you can create a "list" by setting the transformations one by one.

> **TIP** The `Matrix` class has a function for this, called `setTranslation`.

You can call as many functions on the matrix as you want.

2. Try combining two kinds of transformations. If you call any of the set methods, it resets everything else, and you should do this when you start.

With the pre and post methods, you can either "pre-pend" or add transformations on top of the ones you already defined. You can, for instance, first rotate as before and then scale with the `postScale` method.

> **TIP** The scale methods use the same kind of ratios we were discussing before. If you give a number 1.0, nothing will happen—0.5 is 50% and 2.0 is 200% (double size).

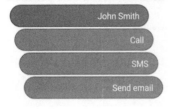

Here's an example of a "list" where you apply a translation both horizontally and vertically. The vertical translation is larger to make sure the items don't overlap.

Animating with RxJava and Android

Hopefully, you enjoyed your little detour of crafting a view for your reactive logic. Although this isn't a book about how to draw view components, the way to construct them for reactive purposes is slightly different and therefore you'll spend some time with them.

The key to writing all view components in reactive programming is that they must contain as little internal logic as possible. In this case, you know that you're planning to animate the fan, but the view you just made has no concept of animation. You'll add the animation later without modifying this view.

Parametrized fan view

You now have a static view that stays open. The next step is to add support for the *openness ratio*. In practical terms, you'll add a possibility to give the view a floating-point number between 0 and 1, expecting the view to redraw itself in a way that represents that state of openness.

You'll still refrain from animating, but you'll prime the view to be able to display any openness from 0 to 1. You'll do this through adding a setter function to your custom `ViewGroup`.

```
public void setOpenRatio(float r)
```

You can test the resulting view with different numbers to ensure that it will work when ready:

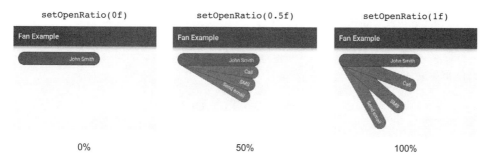

You'll make the program logic so that you can also give any number in between these. This kind of a view is called a *parametrized* view. You give it a number, a parameter, to represent how open it should draw itself, and the view knows how to do just that.

Code changes to FanView

When the animator calls the `setOpenRatio` with a new value you want to (1) save the value that was given to you and (2) trigger a recalculation of all the transforms of the children. *Notice that this will happens 30 times a second when the animation is ongoing.*

Saving openRatio

The first step is simple: you add a field to the `FanView`:

```
private float openRatio;
```

and save the value in a setter function you create:

```
public void setOpenRatio(float r) {
  this.openRatio = r;
  . . .
```

Next, you trigger a redraw, or invalidate the transformations of all the children. On Android, you have a loop through all children to tell the platform that the transformations have been invalidated:

```
public void setOpenRatio(float r) {
  // Save the latest openRatio
  this.openRatio = r;

  // Invalidate the children
  final int childCount = getChildCount();
  for (int i = 0; i < childCount; i++) {
    View view = getChildAt(i);
    view.invalidate();
  }
  invalidate();
}
```

Applying the ratio

The code where you want to add your ratio is in the `setChildStaticTransformation`. Here are the calculations you already came up with before the coffee break:

```
final float childIndex = indexOfChild(child);
final float childHeight = child.getHeight();

final float rotation = childIndex * 20;
final float rotationCenter = childHeight / 2;
```

The values `rotation` and `rotationCenter` are the ones you use when finally applying the rotation transform. This code always draws the fan fully open.

When doing parameterizations, you need to think carefully about the value that you want to animate. In this case, the answer is the `rotation` itself, while the `rotationCenter` stays the same.

In this case, the operation is relatively simple: you take the rotation angle and multiply it by `openRatio`. This impacts all of the children individually, as the function is called for each one separately. The `rotationCenter` stays the same.

```
final float rotation = childIndex * 20;
final float adjustedRotation = openRatio * rotation;
```

You'll then use the `adjustedRotation` instead of the original one:

```
matrix.setRotate(adjustedRotation,
    rotationCenter, rotationCenter);
```

Isn't saving variables in views bad?

Usually, you try to minimize the number of values the `View` class saves in itself, but in these cases it's inevitable. Because the Android platform calls `setChildStaticTransformation` later, at some point after functions that invalidate have been called, you have to save `openRatio` somewhere meanwhile.

But you shouldn't expose the `openRatio` of the view as a getter. The view should stay as only a consumer of the reactive chain, as you'll see soon.

The view model

That was a lot of work to finally get to the important bits. More often than not, though, the core of the logic isn't that complex after the surrounding code has been structured correctly.

Connecting the view model and the view

Let's look at where you are in the big picture that you started with at the beginning of the chapter.

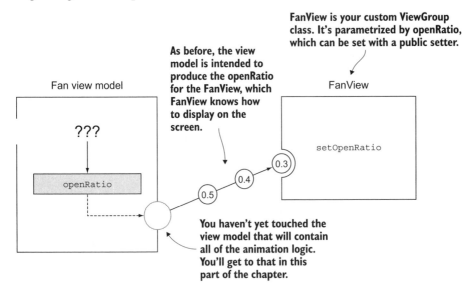

You've completed the right side of this diagram, creating an endpoint for openRatio. You'll move on to the view model now, and see how you can make it output the desired openRatio states.

What if you open FanView more than 1.0?

For the FanView to be fully open you'd set its openRatio value to 1.0. This is equivalent to false in the traditional sense. On the other hand, 0.0 means FanView is closed.

Semantically, 2.0 doesn't make sense: trying to set the openRatio value to 2.0 should never be allowed to happen. But, in this case an openRatio of 2.0 would simply expand the fan beyond the values you set for it. If you want to open the fan wider, change the maximum angles instead.

View model inputs and outputs

You want to make the fan expand when the users click it. You'll thus give the view model an event observable of user clicks.

The output of the view model at this point is just the ratio, which is of type float. The view you constructed before knows how to show itself based on openRatio.

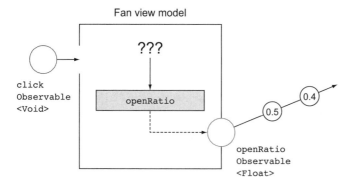

View model creation code

You'll create the view model and then connect it to the view. The way you construct the view model is similar to before. The only unusual thing here is you connect the two only through the openRatio number—the view never gets a Boolean value at all.

If the view needs to know it's fully open or fully closed, it can check the openRatio for exactly 1.0 and 0.0, respectively.

MainActivity.java onCreate

```
FanViewModel fanViewModel
    = new FanViewModel(clickObservable);

// Make binding for the actual fan
fanViewModel
  .getOpenRatio()
  .observeOn(AndroidSchedulers.mainThread())
  .subscribe(fanView::setOpenRatio);
```

View model logic

In the first iteration, you'll take `clickObservable` events to toggle the fan open or closed (depending on its current state). No animation occurs yet, though, but bear with me as we're building toward it.

True or false

Internally, the view model still needs to know whether the fan is supposed to be open or closed—it needs a Boolean value. But in this case, you won't expose the Boolean at all, because the view you just made *renders ratios*.

Semantically, what this means is that the fan view doesn't need to "know" anything else but `openRatio`. The Boolean value from its point of view is already contained in this number (0 is closed, 1 is open).

Nevertheless, as mentioned, you'll have the Boolean inside the view model and you'll toggle it based on the clicks. The Boolean is then converted into either 0 or 1, for `false` and `true`, respectively.

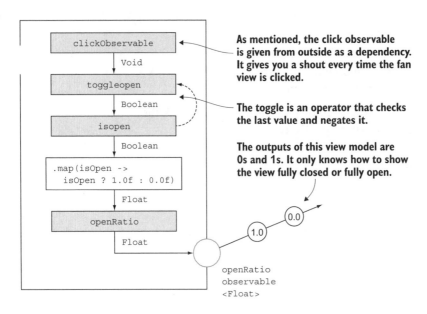

As mentioned, the click observable is given from outside as a dependency. It gives you a shout every time the fan view is clicked.

The toggle is an operator that checks the last value and negates it.

The outputs of this view model are 0s and 1s. It only knows how to show the view fully closed or fully open.

View model processing flow in the simple case

If you look at the true/false implementation of our view model, you can see that the view model changes its `openRatio` from 0% to 100% immediately when toggling. What you've achieved so far is opening possibilities to add the in-between states, which you'll do next.

View model emits initial value (closed)

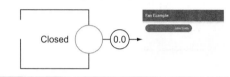

User clicks the view

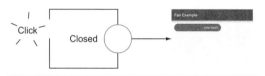

View model logic is executed to determine new state

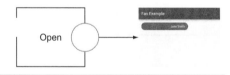

View model emits updated value (open)

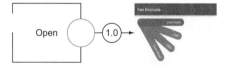

Animating parametrized values in view models

Finally here! You have everything set up to smoothly transition from 0% to 100% open—from 0.0 to 1.0. Currently, as soon as you request the fan to open, the openRatio changes immediately to 1.0. Similarly, when you request to close it, the openRatio goes to 0.0 instantaneously.

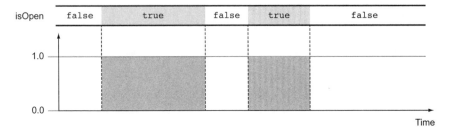

You want this transition to be smooth.

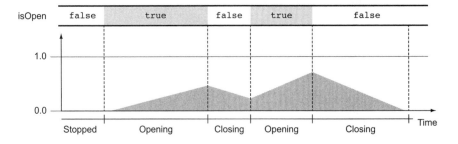

You can see a couple of boundary conditions here:

- When the isOpen Boolean changes, start animation to either 0.0 or 1.0, for closed and open, respectively.

- Always use the *current* ratio as a starting point for the animation. This is how you avoid the glitch.

- If animation is ongoing, cancel it before starting a new one. You don't want to queue animations, though you could if you really wanted to.

Opening the fan with animated openRatio

When you look at the opening sequence of the fan with the animation, you have two things: is the Boolean `isOpen` `true` or `false` and what is the `openRatio` of the fan?

`isOpen` becomes the target state of the fan toward which the animation progresses.

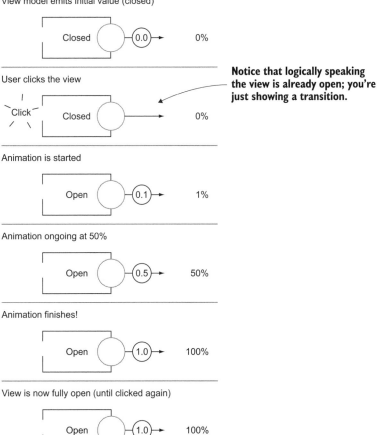

View model emits initial value (closed)

Closed — 0.0 → 0%

User clicks the view

Notice that logically speaking the view is already open; you're just showing a transition.

Click — Closed — → 0%

Animation is started

Open — 0.1 → 1%

Animation ongoing at 50%

Open — 0.5 → 50%

Animation finishes!

Open — 1.0 → 100%

View is now fully open (until clicked again)

Open — 1.0 → 100%

animateTo operator

On more abstract terms, what you need is a way to have a "delayed" observable that reluctantly changes from one value to another over time. The process is like squeezing the water hose so it takes longer for the water to flow through. This is how it looks when reduced to an operator:

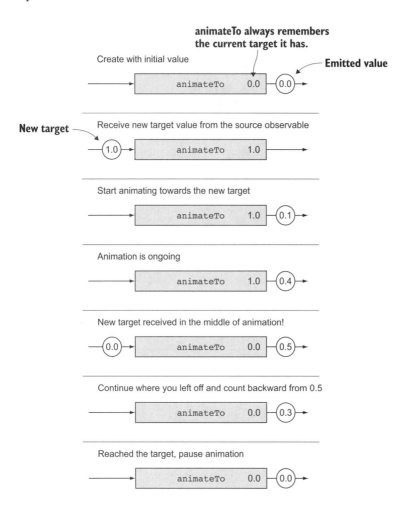

View model logic with animateTo

Going back to our view model, you can add this operator to create a transition instead of directly emitting the target value.

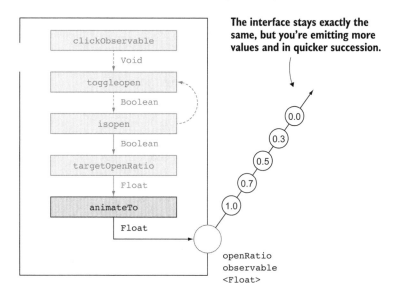

Notice how the view doesn't need to be changed at all to accommodate this change: it simply receives more values and has to be efficient enough to able to draw them on time.

The target `openRatio` here is the trigger for the animation.

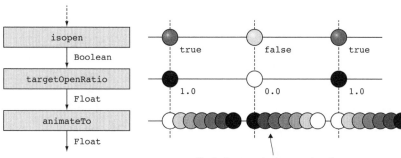

animateTo operator on Android

Ah, great, you're done! But there's just one more thing: there's no such thing as an `animateTo` operator.

The good news is, this operator isn't too difficult to make. In the examples online, I've implemented a generic `AnimateToOperator`. It always uses the last value from its source as its animation target. Whenever this operator gets a new value, it stops what it was doing, and starts an animation towards that value.

You use the platform component `ValueAnimator` for the animation itself. It takes a start and an end and proceeds to animate between those. It also synchronizes with the natural updating frequency of the platform animations, so it's safe to use.

I won't show the full code here, but the heart of it is a handler for incoming values:

```
// Reset any existing ValueAnimator.
if (valueAnimator != null) {
  valueAnimator.end();
  valueAnimator = null;
}

// Create a new animator from last value to the new target
valueAnimator =
  ValueAnimator.ofFloat(
    (Float) lastValue, (Float) targetValue
  );

// Track updates and inform the subscribers
valueAnimator.addUpdateListener(...);

// Start the animation!
valueAnimator.start();
```

Using animateTo in the view model

You've left the code of the view model until very late, but only because the code becomes simple to write. Almost so simple that it's confusing to show it before a proper explanation. Here it is, though, the full view model:

```
public class FanViewModel {

  private final BehaviorSubject<Boolean> isOpen =
    BehaviorSubject.createDefault(false);

  private final BehaviorSubject<Boolean> openRatio =
    BehaviorSubject.create();

  public FanViewModel(
    Observable<Void> clickObservable) {

    clickObservable
      .subscribe(
        click -> isOpen.onNext(!isOpen.getValue()));

    Observable<Float> targetOpenRatioObservable =
      isOpen.map(value -> value ? 1f : 0f);

    Obsevable<Float> animatedOpenRatioObservable =
      AnimateToOperator.animate(
      targetOpenRatioObservable, ANIMATION_DURATION_MS
    );

    animatedOpenRatioObservable
      .subscribe(openRatio::onNext);
  }

  public Observable<Float> getOpenRatio() {
    return openRatio;
  }
}
```

You're saving the target state as a Boolean indicating whether it's open.

The openRatio percentage to be displayed in the view.

The only outside input you need is the click observable for toggling between open and closed.

Toggle between open and closed.

Calculate the animation target values and apply the animateTo operator.

Mirror the calculated observable to the exposed view model output. With this, you get the BehaviorSubject functionality.

Expose an output observable from this view model. Ths is the value the view will render.

Adding a dimmed background

Next you'll add a little extra feature that dims the background when the fan is opened. This is akin to a modal dialog box—though because this is an example, you aren't concerned about the user experience here.

You also add a static maps background to give a feeling of where the fan could be used in a real app.

The background is gradually dimmed as the fan opens. In the end, there's a layer of 25% black on top of it.

The view is constructed from three parts that are on top of each other:

FanView   DimmerView   Background

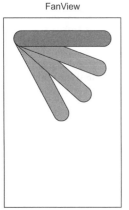

You'll next animate the opacity of this dimmer view as the fan opens and closes.

Coding the dimmer

You could choose from a few approaches to code the dimmer, but you'll use a simple solution here and directly use the openRatio exposed from the view model. You have to make a little adjustment to it because the setAlpha function takes an integer between 0 and 255.

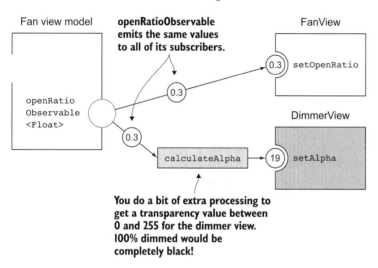

In terms of the code, here's the onCreate activity that sets up everything. See the rest of it in the online code examples.

```
// Retrieve the views we want to use
FanView fanView = (FanView) findViewById(R.id.fan_view);
View dimmerView = findViewById(R.id.dimmer);


// Make binding for the actual fan
fanViewModel
    .getOpenRatio()
    .observeOn(AndroidSchedulers.mainThread())
    .subscribe(fanView::setOpenRatio);


// Make binding for the dimmer
fanViewModel
    .getOpenRatio()
    .map(ratio -> (int) (64f * ratio))
    .observeOn(AndroidSchedulers.mainThread())
    .subscribe(dimmerView.getBackground()::setAlpha);
```

This is what you saw before: the fan view setOpenRatio.

You use the same getOpenRatio as the basis for the dimmer.

Apply a little adjustment to match what setAlpha expects.

Attach the observable to the background alpha.

Summary

To be fair, this chapter was more about advanced UI development than reactive programming. But you can see how observables make sense when dealing with changing states in your UIs.

Animation and view models

Although it isn't always advisable to put all animation logic in view models, at least you should consider doing so when it's either long or affects many places of the UI at the same time: such as the dimmer view in our example. Any state handling that is in the view is always more precarious and harder to test.

You could take the example further and move the creation of the fan items to an adapter that reads the view model, or even animate each item individually. By doing so, you'd increase the testability of the code as well as its flexibility—with this solution all of the items are forced to move at the same time. Usually it's better not to overdo view models, rather keep the animations simple.

What next?

Parametrization of transitions is a powerful technique to control the state of the UI. As long as you make your view accept values from 0.0 to 1.0, you can use the `animateTo` operator for virtually anything: the view model for the drop-down example would have looked strikingly similar.

If you're interested in tweaking your UI transitions further, you can look up parametrization and easing functions.

The next and the last chapter doesn't use animations, but you'll see other interesting techniques used in reactive programming.

Making
a maps client | **14**

In this chapter

- Exploring a real-life example of a reactive app

- Handling dragging state in Rx event streams

- Expanding Rx chains as the app grows

437

Maps example

Maps have become more and more prominent in modern applications. Although it's uncommon to have to write your own, you'll go through building a simple maps client as an exercise. After completing the chapter, you'll understand more of the internal workings of any maps application—or have a basis to fulfill you own custom maps use case.

If you aren't familiar with the way maps work, don't worry; on the way you'll learn everything necessary. A bit of mathematics is involved, but as before, the more complex functions will be given to you as utility tools. If you're interested in the more involved parts you can find additional information about map calculations online.

Why maps?

Maps might seem like an unusual thing to build, but you'll see that many parts in a map can be made with Rx. You'll take an approach that uses as much Rx as possible in this example, yielding perhaps slightly surprising results. The maps will still work as normal maps would, but in the process you'll see how to truly separate the data and how much you can stretch the line between the data and the rendering—on the spectrum toward the left.

Basics of map rendering

For our purposes, the world is a square. This is the so-called *Mercator projection*: you imagine the map of the world to be stretched so that it fits a square perfectly.

As you know from Google Maps, though, the map can be zoomed in. This is accomplished by increasing the zoom level, which can be understood as the number of tiles the whole world is divided in to.

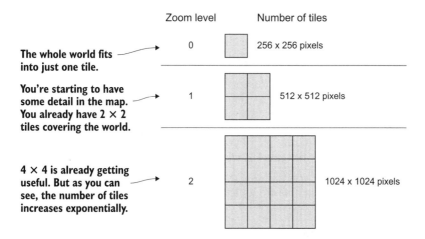

If you consider the tiles to be little square images of constant size (usually 256×256 pixels), on zoom level 0 the whole world is a single tile. On zoom level 1, you have a total of 2×2 tiles. The levels are powers of two, and usually go up to 18—which would result in 2^{18} times 2^{18} tiles, or $262{,}144 \times 262{,}144$ tiles. Depending on your map tile provider, you may have access to different levels of detail.

0, 0	1, 0	2, 0	3, 0
0, 1	1, 1	2, 1	3, 1
0, 2	1, 2	2, 2	3, 2

Indexing tiles

The tiles are indexed from the top-left corner, in a way that the first one is (0, 0), the next one to the right is (1, 0), and so on.

Getting started with map tiles

As you often do, you start with the nonreactive part and see what the resulting view should look like when still—you'll add the logic to make it work afterward. You don't know yet what kind of streams are required, but you can recognize a map when you see one!

A window to the world

For instance, on zoom level 18, which is one of the most detailed ones, you have a gigantic number of tiles that cover the world. No mobile device could hold them in memory at the same time, so you have to limit what you download and display.

On one hand, you have the potentially huge bitmap that's split into pieces—and on the other hand, the size of the UI component that the user sees on their screen.

For our illustrations, you'll for now use zoom level 2, which yields a square of $2^2 = 4$. The tiles are usually 256 × 256 px, so you'll stick to that. The entire world at zoom level 2 thus fits into a bitmap of total size of 1024 × 1024 px.

Imagine now that in your UI you have a map of size 700 × 700 px. The whole world doesn't fit into the map at this zoom level.

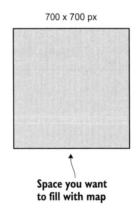

Space you want
to fill with map

Combing the grid and the window

When you overlay these two, you can see that only some of the tiles fit on the screen.

0, 0	1, 0	2, 0	3, 0
0, 1	1, 1	2, 1	3, 1
0, 2	1, 2	2, 2	2, 2
1, 2	1, 2	2, 2	2, 2

← **The extra tiles are hidden from the view, and you don't need to draw them.**

For now you aren't concerned with the maps that will be drawn on the tiles. Let's just create a view that can draw *empty tiles*. How much responsibility you give to the view is again a choice you have to make, but in this exercise you'll see what's the bare minimum.

Do you need to understand how map tiles work in detail?

You go through the domain more as a curiosity than a prerequisite. The key is to know what's roughly in there to later see where it fits in the reactive logic. So no, it's fine if some of the tile logic escapes you!

What data is needed to draw empty tiles?

You want to draw empty tiles with a number on them, and in your flow of processing data and then drawing it you'll start with the interface between the view model and the view.

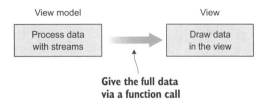

As you may remember, when you switch from the reactive logic to the imperative one, you usually make a subscription to the view model output and connect that to the view. The view will have an interface for setting the tiles, which triggers a redraw:

```
class TileView extends View {
  void setTileData(...)
}
```

The single parameter here contains *all information* the view needs to draw what I described before. The question you might be asking is, what is the "..." in the setTitleData function?

0, 0	1, 0	2, 0	3, 0
0, 1	1, 1	2, 1	3, 1
0, 2	1, 2	2, 2	2, 2
1, 2	1, 2	2, 2	2, 2

Before moving forward, try to think about what would be the plainest data structure to represent the kind of grid on the left. When you say *plain*, we mean a data format that gives the view *the least information* about what it's drawing, while still being able to draw it. For now, you forget you're drawing maps, so you just want to draw exactly what I described before.

Data format for drawing tiles

In addition to forgetting we're drawing maps, let's even forget you're dealing with a grid of tiles—let's draw only one tile.

When drawing, a tile has an xy-position, width, height, and in our case the two integers that represent its index on the big grid.

You can draft a tile class to hold this information in pseudocode:

```
class Tile {
  int screenX, screenY
  int width, height
  int i, n
}
```

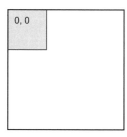

You have take-off! You can now draw your first tile. (You'll go through the details of the drawing code later; in our case you'll draw directly on canvas, but separate view instances would also be possible.)

OK, so you have one tile, but how about the others? That's simple, right? You'll just send the view a two-dimensional array of tiles to represent the grid.

This is where your brain can sometimes betray you, and you reach for a bigger hammer than you need. The goal is to have the view know as *little as possible* while still achieving the desired outcome. The view doesn't need to know that the tiles represent a grid. You can send an iterable collection of tiles, which, from the view's point of view, "coincidentally" makes up a grid.

The final interface for now becomes the following:

```
class TileView {
  void setTileData(Collection<Tile> tiles)
}
```

Making an initial view model

Now that you've figured out an interface between the view model and the view, you can create classes for both. It's good to put in place the "containers" as soon as you have an idea what they might be—this way, the code doesn't start to pile up in one class and you can better decouple it before it becomes a mess.

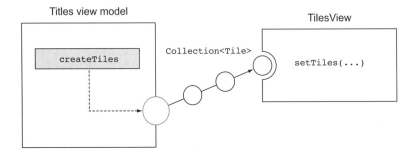

You can test your configuration by providing a set of hardcoded tiles from the view model. The view doesn't know they are hardcoded; the next time you need to change the view is only when you start showing the real map images.

Trying out a view model with fixed output

```
class TilesViewModel {
  private static final TEST_TILES = Arrays.asList(
    ...
  );

  private BehaviorSubject<Collection<Tile>> tiles =
    BehaviorSubject.createDefault(TEST_TILES);

  public Observable<Collection<Tile>> getTiles() {
    return tiles.hide();
  }
}
```

Create a few hard-coded instances of tiles. They don't even need to form a grid.

Initialize the behavior output with the hard-coded tiles. You can later use the same for updating them.

Connecting the view model to the view

In the host of our reactive logic—on Android, typically an activity—
you create an instance of the view model and connect to the view,
which was already created:

```
TilesView view = ...;
TilesViewModel viewModel = new TilesViewModel();
viewModel.getTiles()
  .observeOn(AndroidSchedulers.mainThread())
  .subscribe(view::setTiles);
```

These few lines fully define how the view model relates to the view: the
type of the data transferred from the view model to the view is defined
by the signatures of the functions.

Here's what happens when the application launches:

1 The app is started.

2 Views are created.

3 The Rx initialization code starts executing.

  - The view model is created with fixed values.

  - The view model is bound to the view with a subscription.

  - The view model's behavior observable output immediately sends
    the hardcoded data value.

4 The app has been started and waits for input. Because the view
   model doesn't have updating logic, no further data is sent to the
   view.

Normally, after the last steps, the app would react to input coming from
the user or the network, but in the case of our little prototype, nothing
will happen. But the good thing is that because the connection between
the view model and the view has been set up, you can add that reactive
bit later.

Calculating tiles based on zoom level

After putting in hardcoded values for the list of tiles, you can start putting in the logic to create them dynamically.

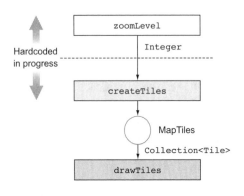

First is the zoom level, which you've already introduced as a concept. You can again start by creating a zoom level observable with a hardcoded value and add the step immediately after it—you can later figure out how to change the zoom level. This will probably be done through controls in the UI, but for the time being, it's not important.

Calculating tiles

What you want is a function that takes a zoom level and gives you all the tiles on that particular zoom level. You might need to modify this later, as we already know you'll have other parameters too, but it's a starting point. If we try to keep the functions pure and concise in their functionality, it's likely you can reuse them even if you later realize you missed something.

When is it good to use coded values in development?

In reactive programming, you often start with the view and expand the logic step by step away from it. By using observables that produce fixed values—either with `Observable.just` or `Observable.from`—we can "mock" the beginning of the chain while keeping the application compiling and running.

The decoupled operations and steps in reactive programming allow you to construct the chain in a way that allows you to (1) run the application after each addition and (2) protect you from changes to the working code as soon as it's ready.

Calculating all tiles of a zoom level

As you saw earlier, the dimensions of a full grid of tiles are defined by the selected zoom level. In the example you had, the zoom level was 2, yielding a 4 × 4 grid. What you want now is the flexibility to be able to generate the tiles for any zoom level.

0, 0	1, 0	2, 0	3, 0
0, 1	1, 1	2, 1	3, 1
0, 2	1, 2	2, 2	3, 2
0, 3	1, 3	2, 3	3, 3

Number of
tiles per side =
$2^{zoom\ level}$

In this example:
$2^2 = 2 \times 2 = 4$

Tile pixel size

If you look at the information in the tile again, you have one property missing: how to calculate the screen coordinates?

```
class Tile {
  int screenX, screenY
  int width, height
  int i, n
}
```

You need to know the pixel size of the grid tile on the screen. In this case, you could hardcode another observable, but in reality in the maps application, the tile size is always 256 × 256 px. Although you could be purists and make it possible to change, in this case you can take a shortcut and use a constant:

```
Collection<Tile> calculateTiles(int zoomLevel) {
  Collection<Tile> tiles = new ArrayList();
  int size = Math.pow(2, zoomLevel);

  // Loop through horizontal tiles 0..size
    // Loop through vertical tiles 0..size
      // Create and add the tile

  return tiles;
}
```

Moving map tiles

To get the dragging events, you'll use a bit of a different approach from before. You'll plug directly into the view's `setOnTouchListener` and use a little utility class to make an observable that fits your needs out of the touch events. You can see the implementation online.

What is of interest here is that you'll get an observable that emits an xy-value for each change of the position. Notice that the value is indeed just the change—it might be (–5 px, 20 px), which translates as 5 px left and 20 px down.

```
Observable<Point> xyMovementEvent
```

What you still need, though, is some way to update the tiles you have to represent the "moved" state of the map.

Cropped tiles

Because the tiles already have an xy-position (the view doesn't know about the grid), you can move all of the tiles *at the same time*. You also want to crop the world map and show only the parts that overlap with the "window"—the component visible in the UI.

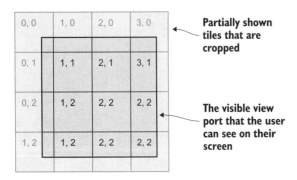

Partially shown tiles that are cropped

The visible view port that the user can see on their screen

Map offset

Next you'll add in the view model this xy-value that indicates how much the tiles have moved from the origin.

You already have the zoom level, which tells you the number of tiles the entire map image consists of, but you also need to know the offset between the map and the "window," or the view, in which you're showing it. We'll call this the *offset*.

The offset answers the question, "How many pixels is the origin of the top-left map tile from the origin of the view?" The *origin* in this case means the top-left corner of any given rectangle—or the point (0, 0) in its own coordinates.

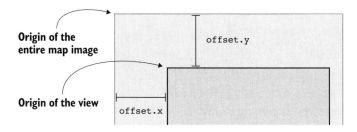

Using the offset to move tiles

You could expand the function calculateTiles, but you can also make a new one that takes the tiles from the step you already created.

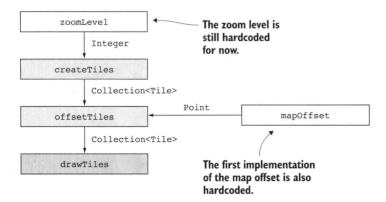

The zoom level is still hardcoded for now.

The first implementation of the map offset is also hardcoded.

Notice that the calculateTiles function remains unchanged for now, and you'll just add another processing step. In pseudo RxJava code, this looks like this:

```
zoomLevel = Observable.just(2);
mapOffset = Observable.just(new Point(10f, -5f));


// The function that uses these
Observable<Collection<Tile>> getTiles(
    zoomLevel, mapOffset) {
  return Observable.combineLatest(
    zoomLevel.map(this::calculateTiles),
    mapOffset,
    Pair:new
  )
  .flatMap(pair ->
    Observable::from(pair.first)
      .map(tile -> this.offsetTile(tile, pair.second)
      .toList()
  );
}
```

Hardcoded zoomLevel value as well at the mapOffset. You can later replace these with functioning observables.

This is the function that will be called to create the observable for tiles.

Calculate the initial tiles based on the zoom level only.

Process each tile separately and collect results back into a single collection with .toList().

The offset function

You can see on the previous page that you're trying to come up with a function that takes a collection of tiles and an xy, and returns a new collection of tiles in which the tiles are all moved.

There are many ways of doing this, but you'll keep it simple and not try to do too much premature optimization.

Notice that because you aren't dealing with a grid specifically, but a collection of tiles, you can simplify the processing functions. Here's the offsetTiles function in Java (no Rx needed):

```
Collection<Tile> offsetTile (
    Collection<Tile> tiles, Point offset) {
  return new Tile.Builder(tile)
        .screenX(tile.screenX + offset.x)
        .screenY(tile.screenY + offset.y)
        .build();
}
```

Create a new tile based on the old one. Only screenX and screenY are affected.

As you saw in the code, when you use the function, you first have to expand the collection into an observable, process, and then turn it back into a list:

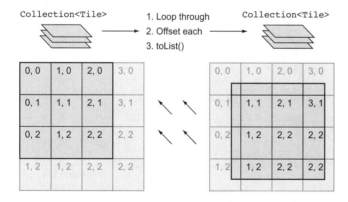

Dragging the map

Before the coffee break, you left the app in a condition where it was initialized with static data and left dead in the water. This is a viable approach when starting a reactive programming application—first you define the basic set and then plan the details of the act.

What you do next is determine the external inputs your app has to respond to. Here the answer comes from the user, or how the map will be used. The user will be able to drag the map to see a different part of it.

You still don't have the map images or any concept of the tiles being a map, but trust me, you'll get there. With reactive programming techniques, you can make the "skeleton" of the logic first and gradually add the functionality—just as you did with Connect Four in the earlier chapters. So for now you'll be moving about the simple tiles you've drawn.

Dragging and reactive

Conceptually, dragging consists of two aspects: the state of whether the mouse button or finger is down and of the xy-movement while doing so.

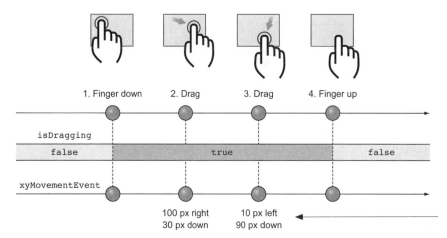

These number values are a little exaggerated. Typically, you'd get an event on every frame, which yields just a few pixels offset per event.

This information can be expressed as observables: one of type `Observable<Boolean>` and another one of `Observable<Point>`. You can use the concept of a *point* a little liberally here, because it represents a vector, but what you really want is just numbers corresponding to the x and y movements.

Notice that you'll continue receiving drag events as long as the user is doing the drag. You might get one, three, or two hundred of them.

In this observable, you're not interested in the *dragging state*. In other words, the observable doesn't contain information of whether the finger is pressed—it gives the drag events only if and when they happen. It doesn't complete and isn't interrupted at any point.

It might in reality look like this:

When the dragging stops, this event observable doesn't give us any notice. The events simply stop coming for a while.

How about calculating movement from the starting point of the dragging?

There are two ways to do drag events: what you did or always calculating the drag *from the drag start*. The drag start approach is useful if you want to be able to cancel the drag and revert to the original position.

Here you're opting for individual events that tell every time how much the user dragged *since the last drag event*. If you don't need the offset from the drag start, this keeps the observable simpler, as you don't need to distinguish between the drags.

Updating the offset with the xyMovementEvents

You now have an observable that tells you how much to increment the offset. You've had similar cases before, in which you need the last value of the value you're updating. You'll have to create an operator that uses the last value of the mapOffset observable as well as the incoming xyMovementEvents.

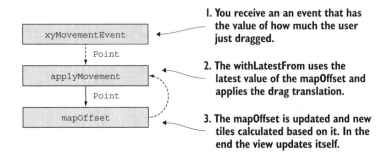

I. You receive an an event that has the value of how much the user just dragged.

2. The withLatestFrom uses the latest value of the mapOffset and applies the drag translation.

3. The mapOffset is updated and new tiles calculated based on it. In the end the view updates itself.

The idea is to accumulate the events into a behavior observable mapOffset, which indicates the "permanent" offset as opposed to the individual move events.

The code for the conversion can be something along the following lines of code. You use a subject here to make it possible to use mapOffset in the calculation of itself. The initial value is given to the subject.

```
Observable<PointD> calculateUpdates(
    Observable<PointD> mapOffset,
    Observable<PointD> xyMovementEvents) {
  xyMovementEvent
    .withLatestFrom(mapOffset, Pair::new)
    .map(pair ->
      new Point(
        pair.first.x + pair.second.x,
        pair.first.y + pair.second.y
      )
    );
}
```

The code so far

If you put everything together, you now have a simple draggable tile canvas (without the ability to change zoom). Here's the view model:

```
class TilesViewModel {
  public TilesViewModel(
      Observable<PointD> xyMovementEvents) {

    // Create the dragging subject
    mapOffset = BehaviorSubject
      .createDefault(new Point(0f, 0f));

    // Initialize dragging updates to the offset
    calculateUpdates(mapOffset, xyMovementEvents)
      .subscribe(mapOffset::onNext);

    zoomLevel = BehaviorSubject
      .createDefault(DEFAULT_ZOOM);
    tiles = getTiles(zoomLevel, mapOffset);
  }

  public Observable<Collection<Tile>> getTiles() {
    return tiles;
  }
}
```

Here's the binding code in the onCreate function of Activity:

```
tilesViewModel =
  new TilesViewModel(xyMovementEvents);
tilesViewModel.getTiles
  .subscribe(tilesView::setTiles);
```

You can change the zoom level manually by changing the constant DEFAULT_ZOOM. Notice that at this point it won't work well with high zoom levels because the algorithm you wrote creates all of the tiles on the entire map layer. For zoom levels above 10, this is thousands or hundreds of thousands of tiles.

Viewport and hiding tiles

Now comes the slightly tricky part. Before you can start drawing tiles, you need to somehow find out which ones are currently in the view port. You need to have a way to calculate the range indexes you cover horizontally and vertically.

Here you can see only a part of the tiles. The visible range is tiles of indexes from 43 to 46 horizontally and from 21 to 24 vertically. You can use a rectangle data structure to represent this.

```
Rect {
   int left, top, right, bottom
}
```

In the example, you would create a Rect with the values for left, right, top, and bottom, respectively:

```
new Rect(43, 21, 46, 24)
```

Calculating the rectangle of visible tiles

To calculate visible tiles, you need at least the map offset relative to the whole map layer and the tile size. With these two values, you can already get the top-left corner of the tiles.

Top-left corner of visible tiles

The mathematics here are more of a detail, so we won't dwell on them. The left index is calculated with the following:

```
left = Math.floor(-mapOffset.x / tileSize)
top = Math.floor(-mapOffset.y / tileSize)
```

The minus sign is there because the offset is the movement of the map layer compared to the view port, so it's usually negative. To have a negative index, on the other hand, doesn't even make sense.

That was relatively simple, but how do you get the bottom-right corner?

Using the view port size

The size of the UI component on the screen is decided ultimately by the operating system layout engine—in this case, Android. At the time of creation you don't know the size: it depends on the screen size and could even change because of rotation.

A value that can change over time and multiple times? Sounds like a behavior observable. You can add it as a placeholder and create a new piece of chain that can calculate the rectangle of visible tile indexes.

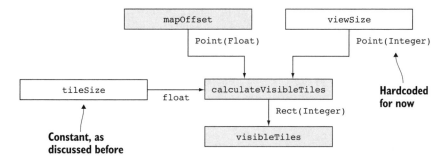

With this, you have a place for a function that can calculate not only the left and top, but also right and bottom:

```
right = Math.ceil(viewSize.x - mapOffset.x / tileSize)
bottom = Math.ceil(viewSize.y - mapOffset.y / tileSize)
```

Plugging in the visible tiles

So you now have the range of tiles that you want to show. It could be something like "vertically from index 308 to 312 and horizontally from index 3 to 6." This gives the exact tiles that are needed to cover the visible view.

You can revise your previous graph that produces the tiles and replace it with your new, reduced, tiles. You can discard the zoom level here, because it isn't necessary after all. The zoom level would indicate the maximum number of tiles, but at this point it isn't relevant for us.

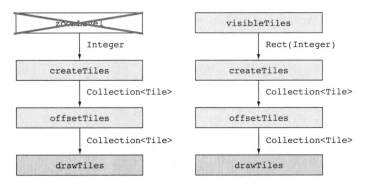

Notice, though, that `offsetTiles` is still here. Now `visibleTiles` and `offsetTiles` use the same `mapOffset`, but this is fine. Conceptually, you're still on solid ground: the map tile hiding optimization isn't "beautiful" but it's hidden in the `visibleTiles` observable so that the rest of the chain doesn't have to worry about it—you smartly predict which tiles will be shown and create only those.

What happens to the zoom level?

Later you'll use the zoom level to calculate map coordinates and to make sure you show map only times that are valid.

Loading map tiles

You're going quite fast now, but it is easier to stay on track when you keep in mind the different parts of the app already there:

1 The view still takes a collection of tiles to render.

2 The zoom level is hardcoded, but it isn't actively used.

3 The dragging affects the map offset, which you use to position the tiles and to discard ones that aren't visible.

43, 21	44, 21	45, 21	46, 21
43, 22	44, 22	45, 22	46, 22
43, 23	44, 23	45, 23	46, 23
43, 24	44, 24	45, 24	46, 24

Currently you have a draggable UI that shows multiple tiles with their numbers on them.

Each tile represents a map tile picture, and you only create the ones that are visible. You're finally at a point where you can start loading images from the internet!

Map tile APIs

Where do you get the tiles then? A few sources are available, but OpenStreetMaps is the easiest to use because it's open data. To try it out. you can put it in your browser and replace the numbers in the URL with the respective values:

https://b.tile.openstreetmap.org/**<zoom level>**/**<x>**/**<y>**.png

For instance, with 10/3/4, you'd get a tile at the zoom level 10 that is fourth from the top left and fifth from the top (the numbers start from zero).

All of the maps sources work in a similar way. You just need to know the zoom level and the horizontal and vertical indexes to retrieve tiles.

Downloading map images

What you have now is a system in which the view model processes your input and produces a list of tiles that your view knows how to show.

You now want to switch the view to render images instead of blank tiles: but should the view model load the images and give them to the view, or should the view do it independently?

Here the questions are more of a pragmatic nature. Images aren't really "pure" data and in general it's not necessary to process them with RxJava. But the view model has a lifecycle whereas the view usually doesn't, so it's easier to release resources from the view model.

In this case, you'll put the retrieval logic to the view and create an additional component that handles the downloads and caching. There is no need to inform the view model about whether the image was loaded; it's simply there to calculate which tiles should be visible.

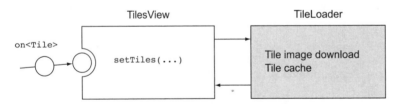

If the view model employed logic that depended on the image load state, it would be good to uncouple the view from the image loader. But as long as the connection is one-way, you don't have a conceptual problem.

Map tile loader

You still have to answer one question before you can download tiles in the view: how does the view know the zoom level? Currently, you're only pushing a list of tiles to the view.

You could expose the zoom level directly from the view model, but in this case you gain more flexibility by expanding the `Tile` type instead: you can just add the zoom level to each tile. Theoretically, this enables you to draw tiles of different zoom levels inside one view—probably not useful in reality.

But by having each tile as an independent rendering "unit," you do avoid the hypothetical error scenario in which the zoom level is changed and you still have the tiles from the previous zoom level visible.

In the end, the view might need to know the selected zoom level, but for now it doesn't seem necessary.

```
class Tile {
    int screenX, screenY
    int width, height
    int i, n
    int zoomLevel
}
```

The `TileLoader` interacts with `TilesView` in this sequence:

1 `TilesView` `setTiles` is called, and new tiles are drawn.

2 `TilesView` informs `TileLoader` of the new required tiles.

3 `TilesView` draws each tile.

   - Draws the actual tile if the image is in `TileLoader`.

   - Draws a placeholder if the image download is in progress.

4 `TileLoader` refreshes the `TilesView` when downloads are finished, triggering a redraw of step 3.

The implementation of the `TileLoader` is standard network retrieval and cache. You can see the details of it in the online code samples.

Adding zoom-level controls

You'll add the zoom-level controls to allow the user to change the granularity of the map. This will finally replace the hardcoded value you've been using until now.

You can see the zoom level plus and minus buttons in the original designs. You'll attach an event listener to each and change the zoom level accordingly.

The graph

What you have is relatively simple, though if you describe it properly in a graph, you end up with two paths that can both update the zoom level.

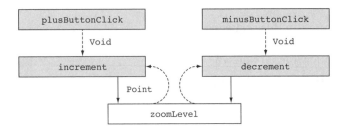

You can again use the RxBindings library to get the click event observables. With those, you always need the last value of the zoom level in order to either increment or decrement it.

The code

With the observables defined, you can finally write the code that creates and connects them. The result is the zoomLevel subject that you'll later use as an observable.

```
BehaviorSubject<Integer> zoomLevel =
  BehaviorSubject
    .createDefault(DEFAULT_ZOOM_LEVEL);

Observable<Void> plusButtonClick =
  RxView.clicks(plusButtonView);

Observable<Integer> increment =
  plusButtonClick.withLatestFrom(
    zoomLevel, (event, lastZoomLevel) ->
      lastZoomLevel + 1
  );

Observable<Void> minusButtonClick =
  RxView.clicks(minusButtonView);

Observable<Integer> decrement =
  minusButtonClick.withLatestFrom(
    zoomLevel, (event, lastZoomLevel) ->
      lastZoomLevel - 1
  );

Observable.merge(increment, decrement)
  .subscribe(zoomLevel::onNext);
```

The zoom level map offset restriction

If you now use the zoomLevel observable instead of the hardcoded one, you can see the map zoom in and out. The tile provider always has a limitation on the preciseness of their maps, and you zooming away from 0 doesn't make much sense. These are details for the user experience, though.

One problem is that because the map offset stays the same, the map zooms from the top-left corner of the view. This isn't intuitive, because as a user you'd want to see the middle of the view stay still.

The other limitation is you have no concept of latitude or longitude, so you can't show specific locations on the map. But you'll address both of these concerns next.

Adding support for map coordinates

So now you have a map that shows map tiles, and that one can drag and zoom. Almost there!

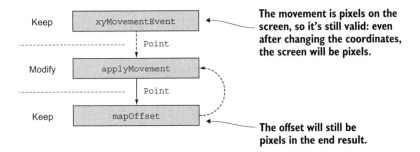

Let's recap what you have in terms of positioning the map on the screen. The map offset is ultimately what decides the position.

What you'd like to do is to make the center of the view a specific map coordinate defined as latitude and longitude. This way, when we zoom in and out, the map stays still.

What you aim to accomplish is to have a way to define the map center as coordinated and derive the mapOffset from these coordinates.

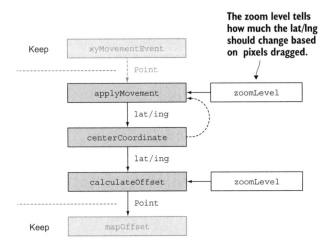

The mathematics

It might seem complex to add support for lat/lng coordinates, but again you can find resources online. You'll cut corners here a bit and assume a few functions that are useful.

To get a pixel location on the map plane based on a lat/lng coordinate:

```
public PointD fromLatLngToPoint(
    double lat, double lng, int zoom, int tileSize);
```

To get a lat/lng location of a pixel coordinate on the map plane:

```
public PointD fromPointToLatLng(
    double lat, double lng, int zoom, int tileSize);
```

I. Map still

2. User drags

Find new center in pixels.

3. New center calculated

New center lat/lng

4. New center set

Building the code for lat/lng map center

How do you change the code to implement the new chain? First you
have to identify the "roots" of the calculations and work up from there.
You already have the pixel movement observable, and that's one of
your starting points. This time, however, you'll use map coordinates to
update the center lat/lng instead of the offset directly. Let's thus start
with the center lat/lng. You'll create a custom structure to hold the
coordinates:

```
class LatLng {
  double lat, lng
}
```

With this, you can create a behavior observable that will always contain
the latest coordinate for the center of the view (such as coordinates
of New York). Because you know you'll need to update the center, for
starters you'll make it a subject. The value given will be the location at
which the map opens.

```
BehaviorSubject<LatLng> centerCoordinate =
  BehaviorSubject.createDefault(DEFAULT_LATLNG);
```

Calculating mapOffset based on lat/lng center

You can already do the calculation of the offset and think about the
movement later. In this case, you have one hardcoded latlng positon
and fix the top-left corner of the map on that.

```
Observable<PointD> topLeftOffset =
  Observable.combineLatest(
    centerCoordinate, zoomLevel,
    (latlng, zoomLevelValue) ->
      fromLatLngToPoint(
        latlng, zoomLevelValue, TILE_SIZE
      )
  );
```

This code would show the selected DEFAULT_LATLNG in the top-left corner of the map. You want to show it in the center, so you'll again apply a transition based on the view dimensions.

```
Observable<PointD> mapOffset =
  topLeftOffset
    .withLatestFrom(
      viewSize,
      (lastViewSize, topLeftOffsetValue) ->
        new PointD(
          topLeftOffsetValue.x + lastViewSize.x / 2,
          topLeftOffsetValue.y + lastViewSize.y / 2
        )
      )
    );
```

Drag processing with lat/lng center

Now you have a system that can process the lat/lng positions into proper offsets. You replace the old mapOffset in the chain with this one and feed it into the view that can render it.

Now the only thing left to do is to make the update for the centerCoordinate based on the drag event values. Notice that mapOffset is now a closed observable and can't be changed from the outside: centerCoordinate is the only way mapOffset can be updated.

```
xyMovementEvent
  .map(event -> {
    int lastZoomLevel = zoomLevel.getValue();
    PointD pixelCenter = fromLatLngToPoint(
      centerCoordinate, lastZoomLevel, TILE_SIZE);
    PointD newPixelCenter = new PointD(
      pixelCenter.x + event.x, pixelCenter.y + event.y
    );
    return fromPixelToLatLng(
      newPixelCenter, lastZoomLevel, TILE_SIZE
    ),
  })
  .subscribe(centerCoordinate::onNext);
```

Summary

Ironically, in this final chapter, you used perhaps the least architectural components. Much could be refactored, but the number of lines in each file isn't alarming, and thus you could get away with plain Rx code.

Complexity of maps clients

It might seem like you made some extra effort before reaching the final implementation, but in the end maps applications aren't easy to make. One advantage of the reactive approach is you usually don't need to throw away code but rather write more "modules." In this maps application, you still have the map offset value even after all of the changes.

> ### Is it more efficient to do all calculations in one big function?
>
> You're creating many small steps to create something seemingly simple. The reason for this is you keep a better track of what's going on and you need to touch already working (and tested) parts less often.
>
> In functional programming, there are strategies to reduce the memory footprint of your application in terms of making copies of arrays and other immutability restrictions. You can later even choose to merge some steps if and when performance becomes a problem. Merging is always easier than un-merging!

This grid-based tile approach could be used for something else, such as a high-res photo viewer. Imagine a picture of the moon in incredible detail, so much that the data can't fit into the memory of the client device. If you have this huge image tiled either in a local repository of images or a server API, you can use the exact same code to show it—instead of lat/lng, you would need another way to navigate through the tiles. To change this in your reactive approach is easy, though you need to change just the one operation after the drag and before calculating the offset.

Tutorial for developing on Android | appendix

In this appendix

- Installing the Android development environment

- Understanding the basics of Android development

Developing on Android

Android is one of the traditional native platforms for mobile. It's at its core Java and XML, deployed and distributed in .apk files. The IDE used to be Eclipse-based, but nowadays it's Android Studio, based on IntelliJ IDEA.

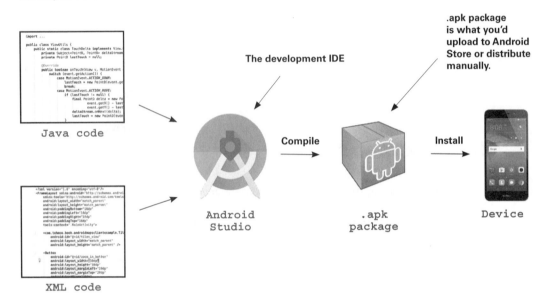

Gradle for Compiling

The Android compilation is carried out by a tool called Gradle (https://gradle.org/), which has its own configuration files.

Our sample projects are configured, though, so you usually don't need to worry about this. The Android SDK is the shared component that does the hard work.

Android development environment

Android is available for both Windows and Mac. We'll go through the basic installation here to get you started—we'll use screenshots from Mac, but the steps are the same for Windows as well.

If you already have Android Studio installed and running, you might still want to read the later parts of this appendix for an overview of Android development.

Installing Android Studio

Although command-line tools for Android do exist, Android Studio is by far the most popular choice for an IDE. It's free and available both for Windows and Mac. Go to https://developer.android.com/studio/ to download the installer.

The installer is a standard one, and after downloading, follow the steps to get it set up.

Which version of Android Studio do you need?

At the time of writing, the latest Android Studio version was 2.3.2, but newer ones don't generally cause problems. If you encounter older Android Studio projects, they might need to be migrated, which is done automatically.

Installing SDK components

Android Studio brings together all the arts that you need to develop Android apps. Some of the parts, however, are *systemwide*: they'll be available as libraries to any apps installed on your system.

Google has made a separate SDK manager for keeping this bit up-to-date. It has support for different versions of Android as well as different tools you might need.

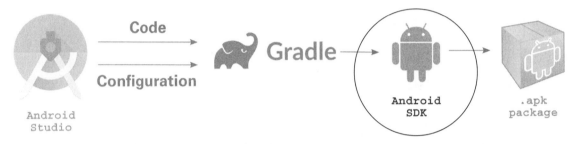

During the installation process of Android Studio, or at the latest when opening it, you'll be asked to install Android SDK components. The defaults work for us.

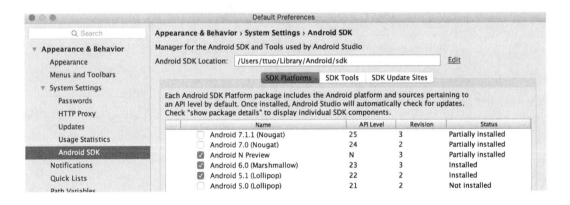

Which versions of Android do you need?

After Android 4, the APIs have become quite stable, and there's no big difference among versions. If you want some newer features, you may have to increase the minimum version, but normally your app will run on anything 4 and above.

Downloading example projects

You can find the code examples on GitHub at https://github.com/ tehmou/Grokking-Reactive-User-Interfaces. You can find downloads for all the projects based on the chapter.

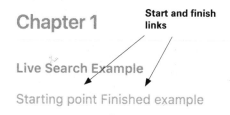

Typically, you'd see a link to the starting point of the project as well as the finished example. You can use the latter to compare your progress with the reference implementation.

Git tags as downloads

In the example, we use *git tags* to mark the start and end of the project. Fortunately, to be able to download the project, you don't need to know the details, just that it's a way to "tag" a specific time in the history of the project.

Using Git to check out projects

You won't learn to use Git here, but it's a powerful version control tool. If you aren't familiar with it, you can stick with the downloads. You'll briefly see how to get started with Git next.

Git clone

With Git, checking out is called *cloning*. You clone the repository to have a local copy for yourself. For this, you need to navigate on the front page of the project and find the Clone or Download button. The button reveals the clone URL.

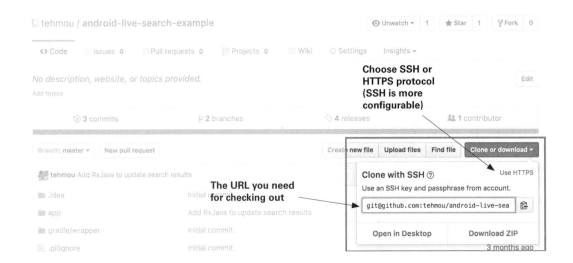

Cloning the repository with the clone URL

After you've found the URL, you can use the Git commands to clone it. You shouldn't need to log in because the repository is public. On UNIX systems, the checkout process is along the lines of the following:

```
cd <directory>
git clone <clone url>
```

If you're running Windows 10, you can install the Ubuntu shell to get the UNIX commands.

Running the project

After you've downloaded or checked out a project, you can open it in Android Studio. It might ask whether you want to update the Gradle version or other parts of it, but you can decline and first see whether it runs as is. To run the project, click the Play button after opening the project.

After opening the project, you can run it by clicking the Play button.

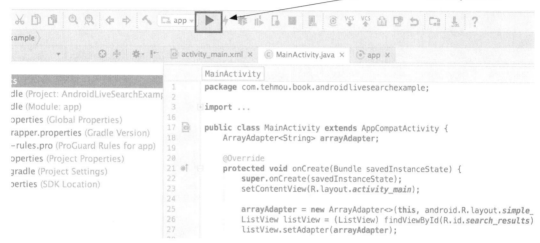

Creating an emulator instance

Unless you have a development device connected, you'll be presented with an empty screen prompting you to choose the target. Because you don't have any targets yet, click the Create New Virtual Device button.

Start creating a new virtual device.

> **What are virtual devices?**
>
> *Virtual devices* are emulators that are stored on your computer. They have a virtual disk and memory, much like a real device.

Configuring virtual devices with AVD Manager

The tool used to configure virtual devices is the *AVD Manager*. The list presented looks a little scary, but the available virtual devices mostly differ in terms of screen size. Some might have special qualities, but you can go with a default one. Here you can see Google's Nexus 5X selected. You choose it and click Next to continue.

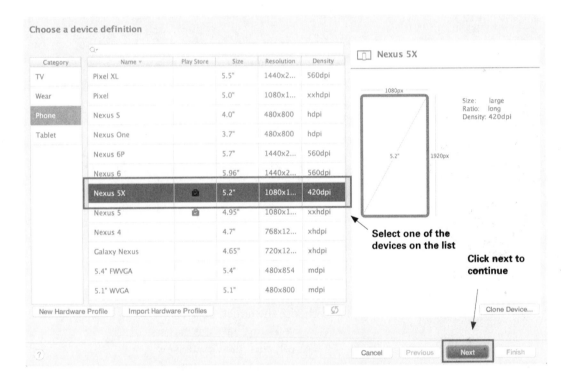

Finishing the configuration

To finish the configuration and installation of the virtual device, you need to jump through a few hoops of potentially downloading extra components or clicking Next on default values.

There are no hard choices there, though, so just comply with the AVD Manager until you have the emulator running.

Running apps in the virtual device

Applications are internally deployed with a tool called *ADB*, for *Android Device Bridge*. It detects all emulators, as well as physical devices connected to the computer, and allows you to deploy on them.

Android emulator

The Android virtual device looks like a normal phone and runs the same software found in vanilla Android phones. Most manufacturers make adjustments to the basic Android operating system.

Additional control buttons

On the right side, you have a few buttons for actions such as simulating a rotation of the device. They're useful when testing the way your app reacts to different situations.

What if your device isn't showing?

Sometimes you might encounter a problem: ADB doesn't find your device, even though you know it's connected. In these cases, you can try to kill the ADB process on your system and deploy again. This will restart the ADB daemon that runs in the background.

Android project structure

Let's go through the interesting bits of an Android project in terms of the filesystem.

Source folder

The actual code files are by default in the src folder.

/app/src/main/java

In Java projects, the files are arranged by the package. Usually, the starting point is named along the lines of MainActivity.java, and you'll see in the next section what this means.

Resources folder

On Android, you have a few kinds of resources that an app typically uses. They're located in the res folder:

/app/src/main/res

The resources you can put in this folder include the following:

- XML layout files
- Picture files
- String and color definitions

Gradle config

The project has two build files: one for the project and one for an app. A project can contain many apps, but in our cases it's always just one. You'll usually use the build file of the app, if necessary at all.

Project build config

/build/build.gradle

App build config

/app/build.gradle

Android manifest

The last file to list is the main definition for the app. It's again
app-specific, because a project might contain more than one app.

/app/src/main/AndroidManifest.xml

Because this is an important file, let's look at one and what it contains:

```xml
<?xml version="1.0" encoding="utf-8"?>
<manifest
  xmlns:android="http://schemas.android.com/apk/res/android"
  package="com.tehmou.book.androidchatclient">

  <uses-permission
    android:name="android.permission.INTERNET" />

  <application
    android:allowBackup="true"
    android:icon="@mipmap/ic_launcher"
    android:label="@string/app_name"
    android:supportsRtl="true"
    android:theme="@style/AppTheme">

    <activity android:name=".MainActivity">
      <intent-filter>

        <action android:name="android.intent.action.MAIN" />
        <category android:name="android.intent.category.LAUNCHER" />

      </intent-filter>
    </activity>

  </application>

</manifest>
```

Permissions indicating what your app is allowed to do. The user will be asked to allow these permissions when installing.

Definitions for the resource of the app icon, name, and so forth.

Defines an activity that will be the starting point of the application

This section just tells the system the activity to be used at launch.

What are activities?

You'll next see the building blocks of Android applications, which include activities. For now, it's enough to think of an activity as a specific screen that's shown to the user. The `MainActivity` activity is typically the one that's displayed first.

Android platform components

In terms of the UI, Android is structured in layers. You'll start with the lower-level layer and explore them one step at a time.

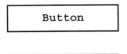

View

The smallest functional UI elements on Android are called *views*. All visible components extend the `View` class—these include buttons, text inputs, and images.

A view can consist of several nested views. A button might have a background as one view and text as another.

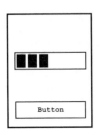

Activity

An application consists of distinct tasks the user performs. These could, for instance, be choosing a contact to whom to send a message or searching for a location on a map.

An *activity* makes it possible to access the network, disk, and so forth through its *context*.

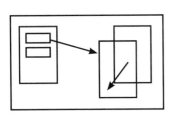

Application

The first class that gets instantiated when running the app is a descendant of `Application`. It's more a container than anything else: it manages one or more activities, though the activities are able to independently invoke other activities. The `Application` class itself is normally quite small, because the logic goes into the activities.

What about fragments?

One or more platform components sit between views and activities. The *fragment* is a special independent module that's like a view with a context. Using a fragment isn't required, though, so I don't cover them much in this book.

Summary

In this appendix, you saw how to set up the Android development environment and how to explore the example projects. What you have here is but a quick look into the Android platform from the developer's point of view. For basic Android programming, a host of other books and resources is available.

How much of the Android platform do you need to know?

The chapters of this book cover most of the necessary information for you to be able to follow along even if you aren't deep into Android programming. It is, however, useful to at least have Android Studio running to be able to check the examples.

index